BEWARE OF LIMBO DANCERS

Beware of
Limbo Dancers

A Correspondent's Adventures
with the *New York Times*

ROY REED

The University of Arkansas Press
Fayetteville
2012

Copyright © 2012 by The University of Arkansas Press

ISBN-10: 1-55728-988-3
ISBN-13: 978-1-55728-988-9

16 15 14 13 12 5 4 3 2 1

Designed by Liz Lester

☉ The paper used in this publication meets the minimum
requirements of the American National Standard for Permanence
of Paper for Printed Library Materials Z39.48-1984.

LIBRARY OF CONGRESS CATALOGING-IN-PUBLICATION DATA

Reed, Roy, 1930–
 Beware of limbo dancers : a correspondent's adventures with
the New York Times / Roy Reed.
 p. cm.
 Includes index.
 1. Reed, Roy, 1930– 2. Journalists—United States—Biography. I. Title.
 PN4874.R3585A3 2012
 070.92—dc23
 [B]
 2012024928

Dedicated to all honest reporters.

"You from the press?" Without waiting for anyone's answer, he said, "The minute somebody tells you move, you move!"

"No one's asked us to move yet, Officer," Reed of the Times, *who traverses the South forever, as a man seeking lost and holy visions, a wandering nomad of the Arab tribe of Sulzberger, said, with some dignity.*

—WILLIE MORRIS, *Yazoo* (1971), reporting on the racial desegregation of the schools of Yazoo City, Mississippi, in the winter of 1970

CONTENTS

ACKNOWLEDGMENTS

My thanks to Arthur Ochs Sulzberger, who is known as Punch to older readers of the *New York Times*. Punch was the publisher during my tenure. He was generous not merely with the company's money but also with his encouragement of new and bolder methods of reporting and writing. In the history of the paper, he will be remembered for keeping the *Times* in the upper ranks of the world's great newspapers, often at considerable cost in money and headaches.

I regret that it's too late to thank personally a number of others who were important to my life and career. I'm thinking of four editors at the *Arkansas Gazette:* Harry S. Ashmore, the executive editor; A. R. Nelson, the managing editor; Bill Shelton, the city editor; and Bob Douglas, who became managing editor and later my colleague in the Journalism Department at the University of Arkansas. They taught me to respect good newspapers and the craft of reporting.

Turner Catledge, executive editor of the *New York Times*, and Clifton Daniel, the managing editor, hired me and kept me on the payroll in spite of repeated derelictions. Irv Horowitz, for many years the assistant national editor of the *Times,* deserves my thanks for his unshakable patience as he tracked me and the other national reporters across the map. All those men are dead now.

There was another *Times* person who, while having no discernible connection to this book, remains warm in my memory. Dixon Preston, the manager of the Atlanta bureau for many years, earned the devotion and gratitude of a generation of the paper's Southern correspondents. She was good to me, and I think of her often when I remember traveling to some inhospitable little old town and needing a clipping or a phone number or just a shoulder to cry on by long distance. She, too, is dead.

Among other friends from the *Times*, I am grateful to Claude Sitton, my predecessor on the Southern beat. He got me hired when he became national editor. He had more to lose than anyone else if I

went wrong, and he made sure that I didn't. Gene Roberts, another national editor, rescued me from the swamps of Washington and sent me to the swamps of New Orleans, which I recognized at once as my natural habitat. Dave Jones, his successor as national editor, kept me moving when news was sparse and when my inclination was to stop and rest. I also thank Punch Sulzberger's son Arthur, now the *Times* publisher, who pulled strings and got me a club membership in London when he was a competing reporter with the Associated Press. The club was a Fleet Street dive, and we were not deluded that we were gentlemen.

Larry Malley, the director of the University of Arkansas Press, and his staff of editors, marketers, and designers have my gratitude for their helpfulness and patience.

Two members of my family work as copy editors, those shadowed caryatids without whose support the world of letters would fall down in a heap of hyphens, commas, and runaway sentences. Very special and heartfelt thanks to my daughter Cindy Buck, an editor with years of experience, and my grandson Bernard Reed, a talented beginner with bright prospects, for their careful scrutiny of this book. They have reduced its wind content and made it better. Once again, and never often enough, I thank my wife, Norma Pendleton Reed, for her patience and support.

WHO, WHAT, WHERE, WHEN, WHY

I am old and full of days. They push me toward the ground like the summer sun. But I have work yet to do. My line is storytelling, and I have one more to tell before the days outnumber me and put me out of business.

I joined the United States in 1930. On February 14 of that year, I became a citizen. I have never regretted it. Both my country and my home state of Arkansas have embarrassed me from time to time, but year in and year out they have mainly stuck by me. That is no small matter.

I was barely old enough for small chores like gathering the eggs when I overheard my grandmother talking about me to my mother. She said, "That's the slowest mortal that ever lived." I have tried to maintain that steady pace throughout my career. I have never deliberately busted a deadline, but I looked on them during my newspaper days as suggestions, like stop signs in Italy. I'm sure that my casual outlook grieved my editors. But I take the view now, as I did then, that dealing with reporters like me was the reason they were paid the big bucks.

My grandmother said "slow," but she meant "lazy." She was onto me. I have picked up most of what I know by standing to one side watching others do the work. Exertion does not agree with me. I did not burn the midnight oil to become a political liberal, for example, or a racial integrationist or a religious skeptic. I was just minding my own business; there were no blinding revelations; there was no hard work.

I made no strenuous study of politics. My editors routinely assigned me to cover politicians and government because it came my turn. I found the liberals more to my liking. They were generally better storytellers and more likely to make me laugh. A leftist inclination came in handy in a more serious way when I began to write about the race issue. It might also have caused a problem. Few of us reporters

had any use for the organized and often hate-filled segregationists. I have sometimes wondered whether we gave the sons of bitches a fair shake.

The same liberal inclination led me away from the Republican Party. It distresses me to say that because I was born a Republican. That is, my father was a Republican, as were his father and his grandfather. It is not a mere figure of speech to say that my great-grandfather was a Lincoln Republican. He was a soldier in Lincoln's army. (For those who still care, I had people on the other side, too.)

My family were all hill people, some from Tennessee, some from Alabama, a few from faraway Indiana, but always hill people in geography and sentiment. They remained hill people when they got to Arkansas. In the nineteenth century, that meant you were a Republican. You were an outsider if you were anything else. I leaned toward Democratic candidates as a youth because my father did by then. But as late as 1952, as I looked toward my first vote for president, I was a Taft Republican. I underwent some awakening that I cannot remember and ended up casting my first vote for Adlai Stevenson. I have voted for his heirs ever since.

I watched the Republican Party become more and more reactionary during the rest of the twentieth century. Now, in the second decade of the twenty-first, it has become something more than the party of selfishness; it has revealed its soaring contempt for anyone less privileged than its moneyed leaders.

I am not talking about the ordinary members of the party. Those tend to be decent citizens. They support the church, the Scouts, and the libraries. An ordinary Republican would not dream of forging a check on his neighbor's bank account or knee-capping a Democrat. But their betters in the party, those who run it, bankroll it, and trumpet its message on the air, seem bent on grabbing more, more, more, and still more of the national treasure, and they don't care what they have to do to get it. The kindest thing I can say about those leaders is that they resemble the robber barons of the nineteenth century. It might be more truthful to compare them to the chieftains of the Mafia. In fairness, they do not engage in gang warfare, and their shakedowns are almost always within the law. Don't get me started on vote stealing.

I don't recall any serious cerebration on the question of religion.

In my early years, I had a shallow belief in God, and with each passing year it grew shallower, easily uprooted by every passing squall. I was a faithful churchgoer, and I look back with gratitude at much of what I learned from the preachers and the Sunday-school teachers. After high school, I was sent to Ouachita Baptist College, where my parents assumed that I would learn to become a proper Baptist. Instead of improving my religious belief, my year there eroded it further. I was sitting in the pew of some church somewhere one Sunday, after hundreds of such Sundays, and as I listened to the preacher that day I said to myself, "Naw, I don't think so."

I don't call myself an unbeliever because I might one day find myself called to account. If that should happen, I would not like to be embarrassed by having to plagiarize H. L. Mencken, who was once caught practicing the speech he would deliver if he woke up in front of the Pearly Gates. It began, "Gentlemen, I was mistaken." I have given serious thought to the question of atheism versus faith, and I have come to this conclusion: I don't give a rat's ass one way or the other.

So here I am, running late. The only thing old men are good for is telling stories, and I am finally ready after years of procrastination to tell this one. Southerners have always understood that an event is not finished until it is told. What's the point of freezing all day on a deer stand in December, straining to keep quiet, if not for the pleasure of sharing the day's adventures that night?

The story at hand is about a life unremarkable except for its stunning good luck. The hero was a child of the Great Depression, and the story might have been one of unrelieved despair. But he was sheltered by people who refused to surrender to circumstance. Those people in turn were lucky in being planted not a thousand miles to the east in the grit of a gloomed city but rather in the protective hills of Arkansas, a place ignorantly condemned to squalor in the national mind. The hills were not lowland lush, but they offered survival and promise. The boy grew up not just with hope but with expectation as part of his inheritance.

Had he ever thought of it, he would have said that hopeful expectation was a just and lawful right. He never knew until he was well into manhood that hope was for the few during those times. Much later, as he encountered suffering in Asia and injustice in Africa and smoldering

oppression in his own American South, he learned the value of pessimism. But he always understood that pessimism for him and his kind was a luxury, a conceit that could be worn when it suited him and thrown off when he tired of it, like a tight-fitting pair of shoes. This is a story of a happy life. If you do not like happy stories, find another book.

I recommend Job's. There was a man with a lot on his mind. You won't know what I'm talking about if you haven't read the Old Testament. You may object that you are an unbeliever and don't have time for such. That's your business. But I have to tell you that I contemn you and your ignorance. I have no more use for an unlettered infidel than I have for a fundamentalist bigot who has never read anything *but* the Bible. Most Americans grow up with the Bible. Its creation story, its teachings, its strictures, horrors, outrages, even its glorification of genocide and crimes against humanity, all of it is part of our mythology. An American who does not know the main stories of the Bible and a few verses of Scripture is as poorly educated as one who does not know anything about George Washington, the Battle of Vicksburg, or the civil rights movement.

Of all the lurching, twisting, and stretching that constituted my growing up, nothing changed me so much as becoming a newspaper reporter. It was in a succession of newsrooms that I experienced the cultural shocks that forced me to see the world in all its many realities. Wrenching as it was, I had to change my attitude and my opinions over and over. The newsroom of the Joplin, Missouri, *Globe* gave me a glimpse of a race prejudice that I had never before heard of—against American Indians, who lived a few miles away in Oklahoma. The newsroom of the *Arkansas Gazette*, where I held my next reporting job, gave me a full view of the race prejudice against African Americans that I had only recently acknowledged fully. The newsroom of the *New York Times* forced me to change my opinion of New Yorkers, a race I had grown up disliking from afar. Before my experience at the *Times* was finished, I had become extremely fond of more than a few New Yorkers. I even learned to love a handful of Pennsylvanians and Ohioans. All those people that Southerners dismissively called Northerners, those who for so long had scorned my people and whom we had scorned in return, began to look better after I spent time among them.

And so my education continued as I moved from Little Rock to Atlanta, from Washington to London, from the nightclubs of New Orleans to the billy clubs of Selma, from the bombs of Birmingham to the bombs of Belfast, from the nightriders of the Mississippi Klan to the Paki-bashing yobs of Great Britain, from the bayous and rivers of the American South to the loughs of Ireland and the lochs of Scotland, from the drawls of Georgia to the mystifying growls of Ulster and Yorkshire, from the people of my beloved Arkansas hills to the strangers in worlds I had only heard of.

It began with the South. The nation's bad boy. Half a century ago there was still another earnest attempt to straighten the kid out and make a Christian out of him. That story has been told many times, but a lot of people have forgotten or never bothered to learn it. So I am going to tell it one more time the way I saw it happen with my own eyes.

But first, a swift sketch of another boy I used to know.

BEWARE OF LIMBO DANCERS

CHAPTER 1

Learning to Fear Geese and Believe in Bears

He was at a neighbor's house. His parents had gone inside, and they were all talking in a way that was not the way people usually talked. He had seen their faces. Something had happened, and they spoke in low voices. They were talking about someone who was not there.

They had put the boy on the porch with someone bigger than he was but not as big as the people inside. The other person was different from him. The person's voice was more like his mother's than his father's. When the person spoke, he thought something might happen, something that had nothing to do with the other thing that had happened, and that this person on the porch would make it happen. He was early in his third year.

Time passed. His grandparents and his aunt and uncle lived nearby, past where the geese blocked the road and hissed at him and made him cry. He went with his uncle Ernest Graves to the corn field one day and lagged behind. He fell full length into a muddy puddle. The uncle carried him home and his aunt Lola made him presentable.

A long time afterward, he would learn about the time before his memory ran. His aunt Lola said, "You were the squallingest baby that ever was. I spent many an hour rocking you in an old straight chair. A rocking chair wouldn't do. You wanted to be rocked in that old straight chair. Every time it rocked, it would thump hard against the floor." His uncle Rubin Reed, one of his father's many brothers, teased the hero all his life. "One day when you were a little over a year old, I was taking a nap on the front porch and you came running out without a diaper on. You jumped up on my chest and peed all over me."

Time races. The boy is four. They are all in the storm cellar. The boy is not afraid; he is intensely interested. When they leave the cellar, they see that their house has been moved off its foundation. They learn that Mr. and Mrs. Hill's house, down a path through the woods, has been blown away. "Mr. Hill," she had said to him, "don't you think we'd better get to a safer place?" "Yes, Mrs. Hill, I think we'd better," he had replied. Respectable married people of their generation did not call their mates by their first names. The Hills went out and lay in a ditch and watched as their house splintered and swept over them.

The boy is five years old in the fading photograph. He is wearing a white shirt, a necktie, and wool knickers and is seated with his legs crossed. His eyes are narrowed and fixed on the near distance. His mouth is shut fiercely, and he seems to harbor a strong opinion.

The boy is five in another picture, one printed only in an old man's memory. He has been put in the backyard to tend his baby sister. She toddles into hot coals in the trash pile and is taken to the doctor. He is ashamed.

The boy is seven. His friend is a girl a year older. They are walking on a woods trail to a neighbor's house. The girl stops and points through the trees. The boy sees a distant stump. What is that? she says. He does not know. It is a bear, she says. The boy agrees.

He is learning to swim. He edges into the swift current of the Ouachita River, and the water takes him away. His uncle Ernest pulls him out, rescuing him a second time. Later that year, on a stormy spring night, he is spending the night at the uncle's when the grown-ups decide it is time to go to the storm cellar under the house. They rouse the boy from a deep sleep and send him ahead while they gather coats and a kerosene lamp. They get to the cellar and the boy is not there. Worried voices, frantic shouts. Then they find him. Having missed the cellar door, he has wandered on through the darkness and fallen back asleep on the dry ground under the wooden floor of the house.

The family is riding in a car. His little sister opens the forward-slung rear door. The wind seizes it. She is pulled out of the seat and sucked toward the pavement. The mother whirls from the front seat and grabs the disappearing dress tail and holds on until the father stops the car.

The boy is ten. The preacher is telling about Hell. Some of the

older children are saved and are baptized in Glazie Peaux (Pole, we all called it) Creek. The preacher, his uncle Jesse Reed, comes to the boy's house and prays over him. The boy is saved, and the preacher baptizes him in the same hole of water.

The Hanging Rock. Not a place for executing criminals but a ledge overhanging the road that runs beside the Ouachita River. The boy imagines that cars wedge there when the river rises and floods the road. Later, the rock and the road sit at the bottom of Lake Ouachita.

A summer of malaria on the Poole Farm, which his family rents. The farm sits in rich bottomland in a bend of the Ouachita River. His mother drives the Model A Ford to Hot Springs, thirty miles away, to buy medicine. She is accompanied by a neighbor, Luther Sharp. Is the medicine for the boy's father, who is sick in bed? Is Rosie Sharp sick, as well? Does Luther not have a car? Can he not drive? Whatever the case, the boy is startled to learn that his mother can drive a car.

Not then, when his unasked question certainly would have been answered, but years later when the boy expressed his first curiosity about his parents, he learned that his mother had been driving since she was first married at age eighteen. She drove a Whippet car to carry the mail on days when his father, a mail carrier, worked their farm in Yell County. The boy was equally amazed by his mother's worldliness and by the name of the car. He was never fated to see a Whippet car.

The father carried the mail on horseback before he owned a car, before the boy was born. So did the young wife who would become his mother. This further amazed the son when he learned of it, and he felt proud of her for the first time. What he felt for his father was customary. But he had never expected heroic behavior from his mother. This might have been the first time that she surprised her son.

Back in Hot Springs, the boy is ten years old. He has discovered *Tom Sawyer* and has read it several times. One day, full of Tom Sawyer and hoping to impress a girl named Catherine, he decides to jump across a ditch in the street. It is ten feet wide and ten feet deep. Seventy-one years later, he carries a memento of that adventure near the top of his forehead. It is a small red bump containing a fragment of gravel like one of those bits of shrapnel that soldiers brought home from World War II.

Memory plunges on.

The boy is in seventh grade at Fordyce, Arkansas, where his father has taken a job selling insurance. Uncle Odell Reed and his wife, Lois, also born a Reed, a very distant cousin, live there. Aunt Lois is beautiful. She has a delicate face, large brown eyes, and long, black, curly hair. When the boy sees his mother and Aunt Lois in the same room, he realizes that his mother is also beautiful. The two women dislike each other.

It is the day when the aunt regularly comes to fix the mother's hair. They are in the kitchen. The mother sits, and the aunt stands behind her working with her sister-in-law's hair. A few words pass. Then they are silent. For half an hour, until the job is finished, the women cry in anger and silence, and tears run down their cheeks.

Memories come fast to a man in his seventies when he sets out to recreate his childhood on paper. They are prompted mainly by remembered places: where we lived when I was six, when I was ten, etc. I have not yet touched other bases. I imagine I will find different memories when I ask myself to remember the joys of childhood, the problems and fears, the heroes and villains. The day I first killed a chicken. The day I first drove a car. The day I became a racist. The day I first took a drink. (I was about to forget that, thanks to the involuntary censorship that obtrudes to save a person from trouble.)

Uncle Ernest and Aunt Lola—my mother's sister—had no children. Maybe that's why they paid a lot of attention to me. Uncle Ernest was a sandy-haired man with attributes that not everyone liked. He was quick to take offense, I think because he feared being looked down on. His mind was better than his station in life. He never earned his living at anything more exalted than carrying the mail and jackleg carpentry. With a university education—far beyond the reach of him and his kind—he might have been a lawyer or an economist. He felt the unfairness of it keenly. Sometimes he eased the pain with liquor.

One fall day when I was twelve, several men of the family drove to cousin Ernest Meredith's farm in northern Garland County to spend two or three days hunting squirrels with him and his boys. I was invited. It was late in the day when we left Hot Springs. Uncle Ernest and I, bundled in warm clothes, rode in the open bed of a pickup while other relatives sat in the cab. About the time the sun went down and the road changed from pavement to rough gravel, Uncle Ernest pulled

a pint bottle of whiskey from his coat pocket. He took a drink, and then, to my surprise, he handed the bottle to me. I got the whiskey down. It scorched my throat in the same way that the tobacco smoke scorched my lungs the first time I inhaled from a cigarette. When the pain subsided, I felt an immense satisfaction. A little later, Uncle Ernest began to sing. He didn't so much carry the tune as muscle it along, mournful as a hound baying at the moon:

> Life's evening sun is sinking low;
> A few more days and I must go
> To meet the deeds that I have done
> Where there will be no setting sun.

Presently, I joined him, and we sang that old song all the way to Mount Tabor. Someone had a fire going at our camp. We ate supper. The men talked a long time. I fell asleep and missed the closing chords of the evening.

Later, during the closing months of World War II, Uncle Ernest finally joined the several thousand Arkansas men who went to the West Coast to work in the defense industry. They were too old to serve in the military, but the aircraft and weapons factories needed able-bodied men. The war was almost over when Uncle Ernest gave in to family pressure to do his part—and earn very good wages—by finding a job in one of the California plants. He bought a one-way bus ticket. Two days later, he got off at the bus station in Los Angeles, walked across the lobby, bought a ticket to Arkansas, and got on the next bus headed east. He never saw anything of Los Angeles outside of the bus station. We never asked any questions.

My friend Margaret Bolsterli grew up on a four-hundred-acre farm in the Arkansas delta a few hours' walk from where the Arkansas River runs into the Mississippi. The topsoil there is bottomless. It was cotton country in those days, and four hundred acres of it could support a large houseful of children, aunts, unmarried schoolteachers, and other long-term guests with enough left over to provide a patina of privilege. She wrote about the intricacies of the class system in that region in her memoir *Born in the Delta*. One thing that set her people apart from those lower on the ladder was snuff. Her people did not dip it. They looked down on those who did and considered them "common."

Snuff was looked at differently on the thin, rock-peppered farms of the hill country of western Arkansas where my family lived. The hills had no rich farmers and only a handful who could be called well fixed. I hesitate to suggest that snuff had something to do with that, but both of my well-fixed Meredith grandparents dipped. So did several others among the Merediths and Meltons who made up half of my gene pool. Even my gentle old great-grandmother Melton, a Christian saint, widow of the leading Baptist preacher in the community, who was so modest that her skirts brushed the floor, kept a spit-can next to her chair. The old folks gave me the empty Garrett snuff tins to play with. In the hills of Garland County, no one looked down on the Merediths or the Meltons for dipping snuff or for anything else. Those families sat at the crest of the slope that passed for a class system in Powell Holler. If any looking down was done, they were the ones who did it. This was my aristocracy. An old tombstone in Gloucestershire spells out the attitude that my folks brought to North America:

> Judge, then, what he did lose who lost but breath,
> Lived to die well, and dyed a Merideth.

My people dipped snuff. The people they considered "common" were the neighbors who let weeds grow in their corn rows. They also looked down on rowdy neighbors, moonshiners, snake handlers, and holy rollers who spoke in tongues.

The class system in the rural reaches of Garland County was not the same as in Hot Springs, where we moved when I was four. In the country, we were the heirs of privilege, the children, grandchildren, and great-grandchildren of Baptist preachers. One could aspire no higher. Then we moved to town and overnight fell into the lower middle class. Listen to the contempt that drips from that adjective. Suddenly we learned where we stood in the larger world. In Hot Springs, we saw people with finer houses, finer cars, finer clothes. Worst of all, we saw people with finer education. That was especially painful to my mother. In Powell Holler, her eighth-grade education was not just adequate but unsurpassed. Nothing greater was available there. It pained my father, who grew up a few miles away in Yell County, that he had never quite finished the eighth grade. He married

above his station. Moving to Hot Springs equalized things between them to some extent. In the cosmopolitan town, there were people who had graduated from high school and even gone to college. Dad worked for a man who had sent his kids to college. Sending his own children to college became my father's aspiration.

Meanwhile, he suffered from being near the bottom of the caste system. He dealt with the humiliation by working hard, not with the expectation that he himself would climb out of the abyss but that his children would. His greatest satisfaction, I think, was living to see his daughter and son move into the larger world without the demeaning adjective in front of "middle class."

Our family and others like us handled our low status partly by clinging together. We were close in the same way that I imagine Jewish immigrant families were in the early nineteenth century in New York. We all went to the Baptist church, in our case the Second Baptist, the dominant congregation of South Hot Springs. We buried our dead in the same cemeteries back home at Mount Tabor and in the neighboring graveyards where our people had come from. We sent our sick to St. Joseph's Hospital and steadfastly ignored the fact that it was run by Catholic nuns.

Some of those nuns grew old alongside our parents and grandparents. They accommodated to the belief of the Merediths and the Meltons that no family member should be left alone in the hospital. They trusted the nurses well enough, but it was the practice of all of the country people who had moved to town to have somebody from the family at the sick person's bedside all the time, even through the night if the illness was cancer—as it often was—or some other life-threatening ailment. I often visited aunts, cousins, and grandparents at St. Joseph's. When my mother was there, I would sometimes walk into her room and find one or both of her sisters, a cousin, and maybe some total stranger who had seen a gathering and decided to join it. If the sickness was not severe, these visits became social events. The nuns and nurses took it in stride.

To fast-forward this American story: Two young families—the Reeds and my wife's family, the Pendletons—left the farms early in the twentieth century and moved to the nearest towns. The fathers established themselves in business—one, my wife's father, successfully,

thanks to long hours, hard work, and a head for merchandising; the other, my father, tenuously, relying on long hours, hard work, determination, and pride. Owing entirely to the head start provided by their parents, the several children of those two families moved easily into the middle class and stayed there. The offspring of that second generation away from the farm settled into lives of reasonable comfort. Their hands were uncalloused. Their leisure hours were plentiful. Their interests spread far beyond merely earning a living.

Now we are watching the fourth generation out of the farm come of age. In my own branch, we see four young men studying at university for careers far removed from the soil. One aims to be a writer, one a composer, one a political scientist, and one a foreign service officer or something else in international affairs. The youngest, a granddaughter, is in high school and knows that her world is wide open. Their great-grandmothers would be surprised and pleased. Their great-grandfathers, always fretful about earning a living, would worry that the blood might be running thin.

CHAPTER 2

Some People Who Improved Me

Nineteen-forty-four, the last full year of World War II: My father was in the navy. His service pay was meager. My mother had put aside her pride and got a job as a cleaning woman at a downtown medical center. She rode a city bus to and from work. One day on the ride home, an elderly man struck up a conversation. It developed that he lived near our house on St. Louis Avenue in South Hot Springs. His name was William T. Morgan. People call me Major Morgan, he said. That was his rank in World War I.

Major Morgan was in Hot Springs to take the baths. Many older people came to our town from all over the country to soak in the hot mineral water from the springs above Central Avenue. There were bathhouses all over the downtown, some elegant and dating from the nineteenth century. Major Morgan had rented a small house near ours for a few weeks. He had come every year for many years to take a course of baths. On that first brief visit, Mother learned only that he was from Alabama. For his part, he learned a considerable part of her life story. He had once been a newspaper reporter and still had the reporter's knack for extracting information. Among other details of Mother's life, he learned that she had a son. A son in his early teens who, she said, was smart. A son who wanted to be a writer.

The Major, as we called him, took it on himself to see that I became one. He apparently saw signs of a flickering intelligence in the shy, bookish boy and plotted quite deliberately how to guide it. He bought me a second-hand typewriter. If I meant to write, I had to own a typewriter and know how to use it. Then he paid for typing lessons at the

Hot Springs Business College the summer I was thirteen. As for an occupation, that was clear: newspapers, he said. That's the way to work with words and still earn a living. So he put it in my head to go to the University of Missouri School of Journalism. If I had known at age seventeen what I knew at age forty, I would not have had the courage to aim so high. Even in the late 1940s, Missouri's was the finest journalism school in the nation, and getting in was not easy. But I had the courage of the innocent. With my friend's encouragement, I made it. As I would learn later, my two journalism degrees from Missouri would ease my way onto some of America's best newspapers.

The Major remained in my life as long as he lived. He had been a foot soldier in the Spanish-American War, an army officer in World War I, a Presbyterian preacher, a newspaperman, a lecturer, and a writer. All the skills and personal lessons he learned in those pursuits were brought to bear in advising and guiding me. He advocated and practiced self-discipline. Even as a very old man, he had the straight-up posture of a soldier.

Major Morgan brought memories and attitudes from a South far removed from *Gone With the Wind*. Warrior, Alabama, was a coal-mining town and a rough one. His father had been a mine foreman. Those were hill people, scorned by the planter class of south Alabama. They returned the scorn with interest.

The miner's boy was schooled in the racism and religious Puritanism of the aftermath of Reconstruction. He clung to the Puritanism, but he overcame the raw racism of that time and adopted a view that was considered far too progressive for most white Southerners. He believed in and preached a theory of parallel development of the races. They should remain separate, he said, but Negroes should be lifted up and offered economic and cultural opportunities. That was similar to Booker T. Washington's teaching that the races were like separate fingers on the hand. As I learned more about the race problem during my student days at the University of Missouri, I clashed with my old friend. My integrationist views troubled him. However, I came to understand that his views were, for his time, advanced and perhaps even dangerous.

I saw him for the last time a few months before he died in his daughter's home in Warrior. His hair, much too long to suit the old

military man, had he been in his right mind, spread over the pillow. His beard was long. I don't think this was from his daughter's neglect. I suspect that, even in his nineties, he was a difficult patient.

The daughter was one he did not know he had for more than fifty years. When he found out about her, he told me the story. He had taken leave from his government post in Washington to go home to Alabama to visit his dying father sometime during the 1920s. When I knew him as an older man, his jaw was still square and his blue eyes penetrating. I rather imagine that he cut a dashing figure in his early manhood. A young woman of the town had been hired to nurse the father. On the last day before heading back to his post, the girl caught his eye. Without a word from either of them, they fell into bed. He left and never saw her again.

He returned to his hometown as an old man and bought a modest house. A woman came one day and with some trepidation introduced herself. She was his daughter. Her mother was the young woman who had cared for his father. When the girl had realized she was pregnant, she chose not to notify the gentleman from Washington. She reared the girl alone. Now, nearly a lifetime later, that offspring—sibling to a brother and sister she never met, siblings who were estranged from their father—came forward and offered to look after the old man in his last years. A man of his stern religious belief must have been tormented by guilt. But the guilt was overwhelmed by gratitude for the child he finally knew. He loved her in a way that only a lonely old father could feel.

■ ■ ■

Dad bought the only store at Piney, five miles west of Hot Springs, when he got out of the navy toward the end of the war. The armed forces had not been a career choice. He was almost thirty-eight years old, the maximum age for the draft, when they called him and assigned him to the navy. He was as tough as any eighteen-year-old, having been reared on a farm in Yell County. Boot camp held no horrors for him. He came home on liberty tanned and muscled. It was only when he went to the base at Newport, Rhode Island, that it was decided that he should be discharged for medical reasons. He had refused to jump

from the deck of a ship to the water thirty or forty feet below, on the grounds that only a damned fool would do such a thing. So the brass scratched their heads and decided that he must be crazy. In any event, his attitude made him unfit for military service, they said. That suited him. They sent him home.

He had yearned for years to own his own business. He had had his first taste of business when he and my mother moved to Hot Springs from the farm in northern Garland County when I was due to be born. Mother had had at least two miscarriages in the almost four years they had been married, and she needed to be near a doctor. My first home was a boardinghouse on Fourth Street. Dad got a job selling clothes in old Mr. Massey's store on Central Avenue. He liked the old man, and he liked the work. I think the yearning to own a business began there. There was a sojourn on a farm, and when we moved back to town four years later, he sold groceries and hardware for Stell and Adams, a store owned by old Mr. Adams and his really old father-in-law, Mr. Stell. Dad took a turn selling furniture for the Wilson family. Then came another two years trying to farm near the hamlet of Buckville, and finally the family returned to town for good.

When he came home from the navy, Dad learned that the main store at Piney was for sale by the Matthews family. He bought it. I fell in love with their fifteen-year-old daughter before the deal was closed. She eventually decided that she could do better, and did. She married into a family of timber barons. The store handled groceries, livestock feed, and gasoline. A small tourist court was attached and provided a small, steady income from people who needed an inexpensive place to spend a night or a week. Sometimes they stayed only a couple of hours, which struck me, at age fifteen, as an extravagant but interesting use of money.

I learned to pump gas and add oil to car motors. Most of the motors were well worn because no new cars were sold during the war, so we did a brisk business in cheap oil. A few of the older models burned a quart every hundred miles. My first car, a 1930 Model A Ford, was highly thought of in the neighborhood because it burned so little oil.

My friends were country boys who mostly aspired to be mechanics and craftsmen, never farmers. The oldest was L. E. Ward. He was a navy veteran, but he was young enough to spend time with us younger boys

tinkering with cars, swimming in the river, and flirting with the girls. He worked in an older brother's auto repair shop. He bought a worn-out Model T Ford, manufactured about 1925, and rebuilt the motor and transmission. He removed the body and the seats and stripped the car down to its chassis and wheels. The driver sat on a board. This was a poor man's convertible, and we all admired it.

I missed its maiden run because I had to tend the store, to my annoyance. L.E. picked up every other male kid in the neighborhood above the age of thirteen, six or seven in all, and headed for our favorite swimming hole in the Ouachita River. All except L.E. were perched like blackbirds on a tree, clinging to the axles and the steel chassis wherever they could find a bare spot.

Half a mile before they got to the river, a tie-rod fell off the steering mechanism. The runaway rig left the road and climbed the side of a hill at full throttle, scattering boys in all directions. It stalled about fifteen yards up the slope and started back downhill. L.E. fell off just in time for his head to scotch the left front wheel and stop it. Otherwise, the rig would have sped across the road and caused untold damage.

He patched up the steering, probably with haywire, and they drove back to our store. The boys were dirty, bruised, and proud in the manner of adventurers everywhere who have survived and are ready to tell their story. Only L.E. was unscathed, except for the abrasions and tire marks on his head. Not long after that, he parked the Model T and got a motorcycle. He gave free rides to all the boys in Piney. Our mothers, the ones who knew about it, objected, but we were not to be denied. I regret to say that I have not been on a motorcycle since.

My wife was once transported through the midnight streets of London in a motorcycle sidecar by the future publisher of the *New York Times,* young Arthur Sulzberger. She remembers that the experience was thrilling. Nevertheless, to this day, she has forbidden me to own a motorcycle. I have promised my family and friends that if I should outlive her, I intend to buy a Harley-Davidson and a high-born bulldog. I shall load the dog into the sidecar and drive to Fayetteville, Arkansas, every Saturday morning, and we shall ride once around the square accepting the applause of the crowds. Then I shall drive home and park it until the next weekend. You don't want to be on the highway with one of those things any more than you have to.

In the Piney store, all of us, including my little sister Hattie, helped the customers. They were an exotic bunch. For example, there was the family that ran the local whiskey still and sold on the black market. Since their whiskey was untaxed, they could undercut the competition in the liquor stores. Their business thrived and had done for two generations, beginning at least as far back as Prohibition. Their facility was believed to be the oldest permanent floating whiskey still in Garland County, although the competition for that title would have been lively in those days.

The war brought rationing of food and gasoline. The average family was allowed four gallons of gasoline a week, as I recall, and similarly meager shares of food staples. Sugar was in especially short supply for some reason I never understood. Since sugar is vital to making whiskey, the distillery family was put under more stress than usual. They had always dealt with the predictable pressures of evading or bribing the authorities, but the sugar shortage was a new challenge. How did they get their hands on enough sugar rationing coupons to buy large quantities of sugar? We never knew.

Once every couple of weeks they bought one hundred pounds of sugar from us. They paid cash. We asked no questions. This was less a matter of turning a blind eye to an illegal enterprise than it was looking to our safety. Everybody knew the family's history. There was talk that there had been a killing or two. All four members of the family, parents and two sons, had served time, mostly for violation of the liquor laws. There seemed to be some extraordinary arrangement with the authorities. We noticed that one member of the family was in the penitentiary nearly all the time, but always just one. That left the others free to tend to business.

The rest of the customers were a study in diversity. Most were Baptists, ranging from true believers to slack. One of the best customers was a deacon of the Piney Baptist Church a hundred yards from the store. He was also, I learned later, his best friend's wife's lover. About 20 percent of the customers were black. These were the latest generation of three or four old extended families that had been removed from the Ouachita River valley, along with dozens of white families, to make room for the new Lake Ouachita. The lake became a small inland sea that covered thousands of years of Native American

history and a couple of hundred years of European and African history.

The black customers were as diverse as the white, ranging from church-going solid citizens to sorry and downright frightening. A sour old man named Bob was said to have been a hired assassin in an earlier life. His job, the rumor had it, was to live as the only black man in an otherwise all-white town in the Ozark Mountains. When the occasional black person got off the train there, looking for a job or just a cup of coffee, Bob made sure he got back on before the train pulled out. A sign at the station spelled out the city's policy: NIGGER DON'T LET THE SUN SET ON YOU HERE. Bob even in his later years was a man of few words. He did not waste many on the men he was hired to run out of town. He just busted them in the head and carried them onto the train. If the man lived, all right; if not, that was not Bob's problem. He was not more than five feet three inches but built like a stump. I never heard him speak more than a few words. I never saw him smile.

I was fifteen years old when I became a member of the civil rights movement. I did not know that I had joined it; in fact, I never heard of such a movement until years later. I became a follower inadvertently. I had learned to drive, and part of my job at the store was to deliver groceries and feed to customers up and down Highway 270, the road to Mount Ida. Several customers were black. They were just customers at first. Then I began to learn about their families, the names of their children, their schools and churches, their likes and dislikes. One or two members of the family usually rode with me in my old Model A Ford sedan. Over time, they became my friends. That was the beginning of my interest in the way the black minority lived.

Two of the black customers were special to me. One was Buddy Guinn, who worked at the Reynolds Aluminum Plant on the other side of Hot Springs. He remembered the forced relocation from the rich river valley to the stony little farm he bought at Piney. He was a pillar of the black Baptist church and a leader in the community. He and my father were minor functionaries in the local political system. During election campaigns, they huddled and settled on a slate of candidates and worked to get them elected, Buddy Guinn in the black community, Dad in the white.

I had come to Piney with generations of family prejudice lying not quite dormant in my young mind. My people were not serious racists; they were what would later be called moderates, meaning they never used the word "nigger" in front of a person who, in private, was never called anything else. Stunning as it might seem today, that display of manners was an important difference between good white people and bad ones. I'm not sure I was able to spell "Negro" until I was in high school, but I was given to understand that only white trash showed open contempt for black people. That was an important component of the class system in the Upper South. In the Deep South, where blacks sometimes outnumbered whites, the use of language was more complex. I once met a white gentleman of good pedigree in south Alabama who had killed a number of uppity black men, I was told, and routinely called all blacks "niggers." One of his murders made news during my tenure on the Southern beat for the *New York Times*.

I remember with more astonishment than shame a day when I was ten years old and working as a newspaper delivery boy in South Hot Springs, quarreling with a black girl of the same age in her front yard. She called me something, and I responded with the cruelest name I could come up with: Chocolate Drop! I meant it as an insult, and she accepted it as such. She produced a gusher of invective that I did not know a mere child was capable of.

Before that, when I was about four years old, I was with some of the women of the family visiting old Aunt Suze in Hot Springs. One of the women called me to the front window and pointed to a poorly dressed man walking past. "That's the sack man," she said, "and he'll get you if you don't behave." The man looked different somehow. His skin was a color I had not seen before.

My father's friend Buddy Guinn was the first black person who was fully human in my mind. I realized later that at some point I could not define during the years when I saw him several times a week—in the store, delivering groceries and feed to his house, talking with his wife and his children—he decided to favor me with his trust.

Leroy Samuels was different. While Buddy was openly friendly and might have been thought of as an Uncle Tom among some young black people, Leroy Samuels was openly angry. He was a combat veteran of World War II. He had seen his second-class citizenship on display in the army. He came home enraged. His chief relief was alcohol. One

day, half drunk, he drove his car into a ditch, and I was somehow involved in rescuing him. I don't know how he escaped arrest for that and other drunken driving escapades.

Besides the alcohol, he seemed to find some small comfort in talking. He probably vented freely among black friends and relatives, but even so angry a man as Leroy Samuels was too cautious to speak openly in the white community. He found out by careful probing that I was a curious youngster. His people, he told me, were systematically kept down because of their color. I had never heard that before. Had never even thought about it. Colored people were the way they were because—well, who knows? Leroy took pains to spell it out: the long years of bondage, the generations of segregation, the everyday insults. I listened with keen interest, but I'm not sure I believed him entirely.

I realized only later that he was taking a risk in talking about race to a callow white boy. How did he know that I wouldn't repeat his talk to some member of the white community—maybe to that deacon of Piney Baptist Church? That he willingly risked opprobrium, maybe even violence, was a considerable investment of trust in me. My friend died too young—drank himself to death—and he probably never knew that he changed my life.

I clung to a last, withering shred of my bias until I went off to the University of Missouri in 1948, and there it was obliterated, at least to my satisfaction, during my first semester. A white sociology professor undermined with scholarly skill all of my carelessly thrown together defense of segregation. A white roommate from New York finished the job by arguing me into the ground without mercy every night for weeks. But who knows what the outcome might have been if I had not been blessed with the friendship of Buddy Guinn, Leroy Samuels, and a dozen other black citizens of that small rural community. Even murderous old Bob contributed to my education. I doubt if he could carry a tune, much less dance and grin and play a banjo. He was an unsettling refutation of the white myth of the happy nigger.

Leroy was just one of the many friends and relatives who had gone off to the war. I was eleven when Japan bombed Pearl Harbor and catapulted us into the conflict on the side of Britain, France, Russia, Canada, Australia, and other members of the British Commonwealth and various other smaller nations. We were the Allies. The enemy nations, Germany, Italy, and Japan, were the Axis Powers. Morale-building propaganda

began at once. The newspapers, the movies, even the comic books were filled with anti-Axis stories. The Germans were portrayed as evil Huns, the Italians as buffoons, and the Japanese—the Japs—as little yellow, slant-eyed simians. Benito Mussolini helped our cause with his looks. His face, a cartoonist's dream, was equipped with a huge chin, which he liked to thrust upward as he spoke to the Fascist rallies in Rome. The word "strut" might have been invented to describe the way he walked back and forth in front of the microphones. Hitler was the easiest to hate, and I hate him still with an intensity that has not diminished in these seventy years. But how can you go on hating a buffoon like Mussolini? I never felt threatened by the likes of him.

The Japanese were a different matter. The propaganda aimed at them was brazenly racist. Most white Americans were brazenly racist, so no effort was required to hate this enemy. Their attack on Pearl Harbor was always described as "cowardly," and December 7, in the words of President Franklin D. Roosevelt, was "a date which shall live in infamy." Yet, the hatred that I and other Americans felt for the Japanese was somehow of a different order from that felt for the Germans. I think we saw the Germans, white Europeans, as people like us—equals, that is. We hated them with a deep and lasting hatred. I have met a number of thoroughly decent and likable Germans since the war. I think of two newspaper friends who came home from Europe with German war brides. They are wonderful women. Yet I still feel a faded, smoldering hatred for their country and what it did to us, and sometimes I have to struggle to keep from embarrassing myself in civilized company.

I now believe that the antagonism I had for the Japanese was more contempt than hatred. Because of that, my feeling dissolved a few years after the war. I have just realized that most of the cars that my wife and I have bought for the last thirty years have been Japanese made. I don't remember pausing for an instant before we bought the first one. I reckon the anti-Japanese sentiment that I harbored had already gone away by the time I was in graduate school in the mid-1950s. I remember fondly a Japanese student at the University of Missouri who shared living quarters with me one summer. He hectored me relentlessly over the way I abused my eyes. You must not read from a page that is in shadows, he said. You will ruin your eyes. I heed his advice every day.

CHAPTER 3

Gazette *Days*

My friend Stanley Slaten got me a job at the *Arkansas Gazette* in 1956. He and I had grown up together at Piney. We double-dated on the rare occasions when we both could persuade girls to go out with us. The girls were almost always fellow members of the Piney Baptist Church, strictly raised and daughters of our parents' friends. Stanley and I could not misbehave with those girls no matter how hard we tried.

One Saturday night, I had a date with Dolly Coker from our Sunday-school class. Stanley came along because we didn't have the heart to tell him no. Besides, he needed a ride from some gathering on the river where several of us youngsters had gone. I asked him to drive my Model A Ford while I sat on the other side of Dolly and tried to start a petting party. Stanley suddenly joined the party. He turned loose of the steering wheel and threw an arm around Dolly's shoulder. The car, left to its own devices, crossed the center line and plunged down a thirty-foot embankment, miraculously missing the larger trees and riding the smaller ones to the ground. It came to rest in a shallow creek bed.

Stanley and I abruptly lost our ardor and set to work devising a plausible explanation. A tie-rod came loose, we decided. We spent the next half an hour trying to make that happen. Wrenches, hammers, stones—nothing would dislodge that exquisitely manufactured Ford part.

I think we hitched a ride home and somehow delivered Dolly to hers. The memory is an embarrassing blur. Our fathers took us to the gully the next day and helped us tow the car out. They were clearly angry but asked surprisingly few questions.

It is possible that Stanley believed that he owed me a favor, so that

many years later when he learned from his friend the managing editor of the *Gazette,* A. R. "Arlie" Nelson, that the paper had an opening for a reporter, he put in a good word for me. Stanley was a printer and therefore a source of sound advice. I was just leaving the air force after the dullest two years of my life. I had a wife and two small children. Norma and I were grateful to Stanley and Arlie and quickly moved our belongings from Michigan to Arkansas.

My first job at the *Gazette* was the North Little Rock beat. I inherited it from Charles Allbright, who had been moved to the "Our Town" column, where he could exercise his wit without restraint. North Little Rock was supposed to be temporary, an assignment just long enough to acquaint me with the paper's style and other customs. Temporary turned into two years. Before I moved on to other assignments, my responsibilities in North Little Rock cost me a chance to help cover the huge story over the desegregation of Central High School in Little Rock in September 1957. That was left mainly to other reporters who, no doubt, were better equipped.

My only encounter with violence at North Little Rock had nothing to do with race. An alderman called me to his home and beat me up on the justifiable grounds that I had held him up to public opprobrium over some questionable deal, which I had. He called the cops after he attacked me, and they went along with the gag. Their report noted that they had found a knife on me. The suggestion seemed to be that I was a dangerous man. The report did not mention that the knife was a penknife about two and a half inches long. It would take half a day of hard work to kill a man with a weapon like that. That is the entirety of my criminal record unless the FBI has something on me in its secret files.

The school desegregation story that I had no part in resulted in two Pulitzer Prizes for the *Gazette.* One went to Harry Ashmore, the executive editor, whose eloquent editorials denouncing his one-time friend Governor Orval E. Faubus and pleading for following the rule of law in breaking down racial barriers earned him a national following. It also earned him a year of hostility and threats, and he finally moved to greener and more peaceful pastures.

Freed at last of combative aldermen, I took over the Little Rock schools story in mid-1958. For the next few years, I helped to cover the unending fallout from Governor Faubus's failed effort to stall, limit,

or avoid the inevitable desegregation. Little Rock's four high schools were closed for a year, with the governor's ambitious connivance, to avoid further "race-mixing." They were reopened in the fall of 1959 after a group of strong-willed white women led by Adolphine Terry, a doyenne of the establishment, shamed the city's business leaders into asserting themselves and standing up to Faubus and the legislature.

Faubus became practically unbeatable in his reelection campaigns of 1958, 1960, 1962, and 1964. I covered all or part of those campaigns and came to know the governor as well as any of us in the press were allowed to. I missed much of the 1964 campaign because I spent the 1963–64 school year at Harvard University on a Nieman Fellowship, and when I got home the election season was well under way.

One event was memorable for a joke. Faubus was addressing the state convention of the Democratic Party. He knew that he had lost virtually all of the liberals in the party, and he had to try to win some back because he was facing an unusually strong opponent in the general election. He began by appealing to their sense of humor.

A stranger was riding his horse along an Ozarks road one day and met an old mountaineer. They stopped to chat. The old man pulled a jug of whiskey from his saddlebag and offered the stranger a drink. The stranger declined. The old man insisted. Finally, the mountaineer pulled a shotgun from the other side of his saddle and leveled it at the stranger. "I said take a drink," he commanded. The stranger did. He came up coughing and choking, and then he said, "That's the worst whiskey I've ever drunk in my life." The old man replied, "It shore is." He handed his shotgun to the stranger and said, "Here—you hold the gun on me while I take a drink."

I covered some of Faubus's campaign later that year against his wealthy Republican opponent, Winthrop Rockefeller. Orval's father, Sam, was an enthusiastic member of the Socialist Party. That was not public knowledge at the time, but the son remembered his roots. He portrayed his opponent as the spoiled grandson of the despised robber baron John D. Rockefeller.

His favorite anecdote, saved for the end of the standard stump speech, was a childhood memory. When the Faubuses went for their weekly supplies at Combs in remote Madison County, it was young Orval's task to walk home behind the wagon carrying the gallon can

of kerosene, or coal oil. They dared not risk having any slosh out in the wagon, so precious was it because of the price-fixing policies of Winthrop's ruthless old grandfather, the shameless head of Standard Oil. Then the concluding sentence, every time delivered with the same passion and still-smoldering anger: "If we owe the Rockefellers anything, we've been paying it a long time." The old men in overalls at the back of the crowd would nod and harden their eyes.

The early 1960s were growth years for me. On general assignment, I learned to handle a wide variety of stories, most of them on deadline. All of us on general assignment became accustomed to turning in four, five, even eight or ten stories a day. These were mainly short items, sometimes including a luncheon speech at a civic club—a free lunch with the Rotarians in exchange for half a dozen paragraphs reporting what the speaker of the day had to say. But the *Gazette* was a serious newspaper, and we regularly devoted the time necessary—a day or three or four, even several weeks now and then—to in-depth reporting on important stories about business, culture, interesting people, government, and politics.

Before my Nieman Fellowship, I was assigned to assist the intrepid Ernest Valachovic on the capitol beat. As the senior reporter, he covered the governor's office and other choice stories of the day. I made the rounds of the state supreme court, the Justice Department, the Game and Fish Commission, the Highway Department, the Employment Security Division, and a host of other agencies. I went back to the paper at the end of every afternoon with a notebook full of stories, and I was expected to turn them in, clearly and thoroughly written, before the 7:00 p.m. first edition deadline.

Bill Shelton, the city editor, looked over every story with some care before handing it on to the copy desk. Almost without fail, he asked each reporter to fill in some gap in a story. Sometimes he became a teacher and demonstrated how to write a lead with more punch or fewer words. At the end of his day, he often passed out typewritten notes of gentle and not-so-gentle criticism of our stories. And at the beginning of our workday—hours after he had come in and read the *Gazette* and the rival *Democrat*—we could expect to see with unsettling regularity a clipping from the *Democrat* attached to his handwritten note, "Why we not have?" The only person who hated being beaten by

the *Democrat* worse than Shelton was the reporter whose negligence had allowed it to happen.

My friend and colleague Patrick J. Owens spent a year at Harvard as a Nieman Fellow in the early 1960s. He returned home so pleased with the experience that I decided to apply. Harry Ashmore, who had been executive editor when I went to work at the paper and had moved on, wrote a letter supporting my application. He himself had been a Fellow during the program's early years. I made the interview stage but was turned down. I applied again for the 1963–64 year, and this time Ashmore wrote a stinging rebuke to the selection committee for rejecting me the year before. Perhaps cowed by this scolding, the committee let me in.

CHAPTER 4

History Lesson

There's a long tradition in American life of politicians using newspapers as whipping boys—and vice versa. That was especially true in the South when race was the big issue during the middle years of the twentieth century. In Georgia, for example, segregationist governors campaigned against the *Atlanta Constitution* and its publisher/columnist Ralph McGill when he crusaded for equal rights for African Americans. Hodding Carter Jr. and his *Greenville Democrat Delta-Times* engaged in a running battle for years with the men who ran Mississippi, and they fought back. The legislature once passed a solemn resolution declaring him a liar.

The *Arkansas Gazette* had its enemies among the state's politicians going back to territorial days. Duels were fought between politicians and editors over personal slights when they weren't busy dueling with each other. But the most consequential confrontation between any Arkansas public figure and the press was in 1957 and the years afterward. Governor Faubus declared war on the *Arkansas Gazette*. That came about because the paper, which until then had been friendly to the governor, immediately and sternly condemned him for using the National Guard to stop the desegregation of Central High School in Little Rock. The Supreme Court had ordered an end to state-sponsored school segregation. The governor flouted the decision and threw in with the white supremacists whom he previously had shown no affection for. Those people had made up their minds, against all evidence, that the Court's decision was illegal and unconstitutional, and they vowed to defy it to the end. The *Gazette*'s editorial page had done nothing more than point out the absurdity of that. That the page had done so with an eloquence that few of the

opposing camp were capable of probably contributed to their fear and hatred of the newspaper, which had presumed to inform and instruct the citizens of Arkansas since 1819.

Faubus understood that it would be difficult to incite animosity against a faceless institution, especially one as old and respected as the *Gazette*. He quickly moved to personify his enemy. Harry Ashmore, the witty, sophisticated, and erudite executive editor of the paper, was ideal for the role. It did not matter that the two men had had a cordial relationship until then. From the onset of hostilities, Faubus held Ashmore up to public scorn. The editor was everything that Faubus's followers feared and despised. He was well educated and did not mind demonstrating it. He had made a serious study of the race issue, and the Supreme Court had in fact received copies of his scholarly book, *The Negro and the Schools*, in time to peruse it as it considered the ruling in 1954 that would put an end to legal segregation of public schools. He had spent a year as a Nieman Fellow at Harvard University, a perfect symbol of Eastern elitism. He had a magical way with words. He was a decorated World War II combat officer. As it happened, the governor was also a decorated combat officer. Major Faubus had been an intelligence officer in Europe. He somehow managed to leave the impression that he had spent the war in the mud and foxholes with the dogfaces.

The fight got ugly. Both sides profited from it. The paper won two Pulitzer Prizes, and the governor won six terms in office. Nevertheless, there were hard feelings between the combatants for many years afterward.

I watched all this from the vantage point of my beat across the Arkansas River in North Little Rock until 1958, when I was finally sprung from that job and put on general assignment and a little later on the capitol beat with Ernest Valachovic, the chief reporter there. I had most of five years to watch Faubus from a little distance; Val kept an eye on the governor's office every day while I roamed the outer offices of the state government—almost all of which Faubus controlled. I helped cover the gubernatorial elections every two years. The downside of my assignment was not seeing Faubus every day. The advantage of it was an easy detachment from the old rascal's personal charm, which could catch reporters unawares and draw them into his

orbit. That served me well years later when I began working on a biography of him. He knew me, but during the scores of interviews we held, he did not know from one day to the next whether he had finally succeeded in charming me. Neither did I.

As for Ashmore and the *Gazette*, I don't think Harry minded being singled out by the governor. He gave as good as he got. His editorials were eloquent and full of fire. Day after day, the editor took the governor to task, grasping every opportunity to hold him responsible for the city's turmoil and its economic losses. It would be a toss-up as to which side paid the greater cost. The *Gazette* lost 20 percent of its circulation. The governor lost his good name in the nation's history.

Ashmore adopted an interesting perspective on Faubus long after the big confrontation. He told me in an interview some years later that he thought Faubus was motivated partly by class resentment, not racial prejudice. I share that view. Harry said that Faubus rightly perceived that the Pulaski Heights crowd running the town wanted to finish a new high school on the western outskirts as soon as possible so that their children could leave downtown Central and have an unintegrated school to go to. The working-class kids in the older parts of town would end up doing all the integrating. Harry said, "This is the one thing I give Orval. This is the old populist point of view: 'You're putting it on my people; you're making the poor folks integrate. The Cadillac brigade out in the Heights doesn't have to.'"

Ernest Dumas, a *Gazette* reporter who covered Faubus for several years after Val and I were gone, told me that Faubus eventually came around to a more favorable assessment of the paper. He remembered a rally at Heber Springs in 1970 or 1974 when Faubus was trying to make a comeback. He reminded the crowd how the *Gazette* had worked against him all those years before. Then he said, "But, you know, I always liked the *Gazette*." He said that in its news coverage it was the best paper in Arkansas. He said the paper always told things fairly, and its reporting about him was accurate and balanced and fair.

Dumas remembered a private conversation that he and I had with Faubus after a party at the governor's mansion one night a few years after the Central High crisis. Faubus told us that he was the real Southern liberal, that he was the most progressive of all the Southern governors. He talked about what he had done for poor people and the

state hospital, about starting an employee retirement system, about improving benefits for teachers, and a long line of other things that his administration indeed had accomplished.

Then I had to bring up the sore subject of Central High. I didn't have time to get it out of my mouth. I just said, "But, Governor, what about . . ." He knew what I was going to ask, and he said, "Well, you can't do great things unless you are in office. . . . And you have to trim your sails to the wind." That may be the closest he ever came to admitting that he blocked Central High's desegregation in order to win a third term. And, as it turned out, a fourth term, and a fifth, and a sixth.

Except for Little Rock's Central High, Arkansas has generally been shoved to the periphery in the histories of the civil rights movement. The media of the time necessarily had to devote most of their energy to the Deep South simply because the most destructive and determined of the massive resistance took place there. But my state contributed a fair amount of crankiness to the new lost cause, and it deserves its share of the credit. I was not there to cover it, having been diverted to more incendiary stories elsewhere when I went to work for the *New York Times* in 1965. Old friends from the *Gazette* were on hand, and some of them were bruised and bloodied in the same way that national reporters and photographers were in other parts of the South.

The state's Ku Klux Klan, for example, found its voice during the 1960s after years of slumber. It never matched the violence of its counterparts in Mississippi, Louisiana, and Alabama, but it burned some crosses and made a nuisance of itself in several lowland counties. It had been only a trifling distraction in Arkansas until Faubus put the race issue in play in 1957. Then the Klan began to rouse up and creep out at night, like Dracula, in several towns in eastern and southern Arkansas. El Dorado, an oil boomtown in the 1920s and home to plenty of citizens still nursing a roughneck mentality, had between 150 and 200 Klansmen in the 1960s.

Floyd Thomas was an FBI agent in Arkansas, and it fell to him to deal with the El Dorado Kluxers after President Lyndon B. Johnson put out the word that he had had enough of their night-riding. Thomas recalled in an interview with me many years later that blacks and whites were shooting into each other's houses all over north Louisiana and south Arkansas during the mid-1960s. He learned that

large numbers of city policemen in the area were Klan members or sympathizers and could not be counted on for help.

"I was kind of the Lone Ranger around here for a while," he said.

His first move was to quietly hire two informants in the El Dorado Klan. After he learned the names of the other members, he called on them one at a time and let drop that he knew what they had been up to. Then he explained the law to them.

"Now, I want you to understand there's a statute on the books that [if] you are in a meeting and they agree to burn down someone's house . . . and someone's in that house and they lose their life, in the meantime you say that you didn't want to participate in it—well, according to that statute, you're as equally guilty as they are even though you backed out of it because you were there when the agreement was made between two or more persons. [They would say,] 'Oh.' Then they wouldn't show up any more. It was a long, drawn-out process to interview them. Most of them, they'd fall by the wayside."

Thomas's interview program, as he called it, was effective. The Klan membership in Union County shriveled. All it took for most was exposure to public scrutiny, limited as it was. They preferred to work at night; the daylight did not agree with them.

But a sizable group believed they were made of sterner stuff. Thomas found out that they planned to set fire to a school one night and blame it on the black folks. He and two state troopers drove to the leader's house as the Klansmen gathered for the evening's work.

"Here came a guy walking up toward us. So I got out, and he had a pistol in his hand. I laid my pistol down across the rear of the car, and I just called him. I knew him. I called him by his name. I said, 'Just hold that by the barrel very gingerly, and go back and give it to the lieutenant in the back seat of the car.' He did. And here came a guy on some crutches who had been in a fight before that and got his leg broken or something. He was on crutches. He smarted off, and I said, 'You better get back in the house or I'm going to kick those crutches out from under you and make you go back there on that sore foot.' He went back in the house. After a while, here came twenty-five or thirty of them."

Their leader asserted his property rights, to which Thomas offered to whip him "right here in front of all your boys."

The boys drifted away. The school burning was postponed. The last I heard, they never got around to it.

It put me in mind of a scene in *Huckleberry Finn*. A mob in a dirty little town in Arkansas has come to old Colonel Sherburn's house to lynch him because he has shot to death a drunken lout who, in the colonel's judgment, needed killing. He greets them from the roof of his porch armed with a double-barreled shotgun and a dripping scorn. "The idea of you thinking you had pluck enough to lynch a man. Because you're brave enough to tar and feather poor friendless cast-out women that come along here, did that make you think you had grit enough to lay your hands on a man? Why, a man's safe in the hands of ten thousand of your kind—as long as it's day-time and you're not behind him." He tosses the shotgun across his left arm and cocks it. The mob leaves.

After Little Rock in the fall of 1957, the most lurid episode in my state's contribution to racial disorder occurred in the late 1960s in the east Arkansas town of Forrest City—named for General Nathan Bedford Forrest, a Confederate hero and one of the first members of the Ku Klux Klan. It's a pretty little town sitting on a string of hills that rise disconcertingly from the surrounding delta because of an ancient geographic upheaval. Forrest City's resistance to integration lacked murders, but it had a full-throated anger that caused a lot of hard feelings along class as well as racial fault lines.

Wayne Jordan of the *Gazette* spent a lot of time in the town in 1968 after black students rioted and damaged the black high school. Jordan felt the brunt of the paper's unpopularity. He was spat on and threatened repeatedly. The FBI called him one day and said, "It's best if you don't go back into Forrest City because the White Citizens Council is going to kill you." He went back, but always looked over his shoulder.

Almost all of 1969 was consumed in playing out the drama. Governor Winthrop Rockefeller, one of the last liberal Republicans, used his office to broker a settlement. The segregationists had the last shout. After the federal government ordered the schools there integrated, the resisters opened a private school for whites and named it for General Forrest.

CHAPTER 5

Moving South

I was not there for any of that because I had embarked for the New World. I had no more idea where I was going than Columbus had when he pushed off for India.

I looked up one day in 1965 and found myself in the intimidating newsroom of the world's best newspaper. In my fuzzed recollection, that newsroom was about a mile wide and populated by thousands of people who sounded funny when they talked. The paper had hired me precisely because the people who ran it thought *I* talked funny, and they needed such a fellow on the staff then.

That there are many Souths has become a commonplace among scholars, but for the purposes of my story I choose to stay mainly in just two: upland and lowland, the hills stretching from Virginia to Arkansas and the plantation country south of them. Those are the regions that I have studied, experienced, worked in, and lived in. If there is a strong thread that binds all Southerners together, upland and lowland, it is a belief that government should be limited, meaning that it should not waste money on sick people or welfare for needy children. There are Southern men who believe that the only proper function of government is to wage war and to do so as often as possible. A war allows a gentleman to get mad and kill somebody without going to the pen.

Not counting a few months after college spent at the *Globe* in Joplin, Missouri, my first serious work in journalism was at the *Arkansas Gazette* in Little Rock. After eight years at the *Gazette*, I worked fourteen years for the *New York Times*, and for nine of those years I traveled the South, with periodic forays into other regions. Here is an odd thing: I always felt at home in the Upper South, from the

Ozarks to the Appalachians. But when I dropped below the Thirty-fifth Parallel, I became a stranger. The race story that occupied much of my working time during those years was to a great extent a story of the Deep South. The editors who sent me there assumed that I was fully familiar with it because I was after all a Southerner. I never told them any different.

I went into a stall in the men's room on my second or third day in the *Times* newsroom in 1965. The stall was equipped with a partial door that swung about a foot above the floor, leaving a gap that a thin man might crawl under if he desired. Someone had left a message printed neatly in ink just above the bottom of the inside of the door: BEWARE OF LIMBO DANCERS. This was a style of wit that I had never before encountered. I suddenly knew that I was a stranger in town—not unwelcome, just a stranger.

Before my first year with the paper was out, I found myself covering a story in Greenville, Mississippi. I was invited to a party at the country estate of Betty and Hodding Carter Jr., the owners of the *Delta Democrat-Times*. The crowd spilled onto the lawn in late evening, and one of the Carter sons, either Hodding III or Philip, produced a bar of some kind, maybe a broomstick. People began to bend backward and duck-walk under it as the men holding the ends lowered it further and further toward the ground. I struggled under it once or twice, enough to make me understand that you have to be young or drunk to dance the limbo.

Again, I knew that I was a stranger in town. The Mississippi Delta is as different from the Arkansas hills as Milwaukee is from Shreveport. I had heard of the limbo, but I had never known anyone who had done it. The traditional dance of the hills is stately. The partners face each other but don't touch. Sometimes it is performed by just men after the fashion of the Greeks or the Russians, but with more restraint. They move no part of the body from the knees up. The face is solemn. Not frowning, just solemn and unsmiling, totally concentrated on the subtle movement of legs and feet. Sometime after the rise of Nashville and the Americanization of country music, the old hill dance became something different, adulterated with laughing and wild swings of the body and with men and women clinging to each other. We saw it coming in Hot Springs when I was a boy. A dance called the jitterbug

moved into our schools. I never got the hang of it, maybe because my genes rejected an unseemly public admission that I was having fun.

The Deep South fascinated me, and I jumped at every chance to go there, as I did to Scandinavia or Great Britain or Southeast Asia in later years. This was exotic country to a young man who had grown up in Hot Springs and the surrounding hills. It was not just the language that was different. The people, the climate, the landscape, the very air, everything about the lower region was different. Even the water was different. In the hills, rivers and creeks flow fast. A stream of fast-moving water reflects the light and becomes a living, shimmering being. Water in the Mississippi Delta is slow. It is murky. It captures the light and overwhelms it. The Ouachita River, which runs fast and drains a large part of the Arkansas hill country, has always invited men and boys like me. It tried to drown me once, but even after that I could not stay away from it. Years later, I waded into the dark, still water of a swamp in Florida to gather material for a story. I wanted out as soon as I left the open sunshine at its edge. My guide was a young man who had grown up in and around the swamp. He was at home there. I liked the fellow, and I liked his grizzled old daddy, but we understood that we were different creatures and that we could go only so far in reaching a commonality. They would have been as uneasy in the hills as I was in the swamp. A good place to visit, they would say, but they wouldn't want to live there.

The reader should be interested in any fraud in the life of an author he is investing his time in. So here you have my more or less full disclosure. The reporter who ventured into Selma, Bogalusa, Faulkner's Mississippi, Margaret Mitchell's Georgia, and the rest of the Deep South to inform the trusting readers of the *New York Times*—that fellow traveled on false credentials. He was not a Southerner as the nation perceives the beast. He was a tourist—a really anxious tourist. My first experience in the Deep South was in the Black Belt of Alabama, a region as exotic to me as Germany and filled with not dissimilar apprehensions. People were killing people there, not impersonally as appeared at first blush but in deeply personal ways born of the deepest hatred and fear.

CHAPTER 6

A Stranger in New York

Sometime during my middle years, I realized that my position in the world had changed. I had begun life as an aristocrat, had descended a little later into the lower middle class, and then, in a moment of uncharacteristic alertness, had slipped into an open slot in the unmodified middle class. At about age thirty-five, however, I found that I had joined the ranks of the nobility again—the nobility of storytellers.

We were a motley crew in the original sense—fools and jesters arrayed in clashing colors and with little to show in the way of taste. A few of us had money, but most did not. Some were of good character; some were not. We comprised a worldwide brotherhood. Set one of us down after sundown anywhere and prime our tongues, and we were ready to spin yarns in all the languages of the earth. Joining this nobility required no vertical movement from me, just a sidling motion. No exertion was demanded. I displaced no barons or earls. I just said, "Scoot over a little, will you?" and made myself at home.

I had settled comfortably into storytelling at the *Gazette* and might well have spent the rest of my career there. But a period of restlessness set in during my middle thirties, and before I had time to give it much thought or exertion I found myself in the newsroom of the *New York Times*. I don't remember having much to do with it. My friend Claude Sitton, the Southern correspondent for the *Times*, who had befriended me during his many working trips to Little Rock, had unearthed evidence of my restlessness and had taken it on himself to make a place for me at his paper. As it happened, he was being promoted to national editor, and he needed someone to fill in at the Southern beat until the new chief Southern correspondent, Gene Roberts, could untangle himself from the *Detroit Free Press* and move south.

So there I was, one day in January 1965, standing in that huge, intimidating newsroom trying to stay out of the way until they figured out what to do with me. (Here's how big that newsroom was: Years later, after the building was sold, the room that once was occupied by hundreds of reporters' desks, typewriters, clattering wire machines, and dozens of support columns was turned into a bunch of bowling alleys.)

It was understood that I would spend the first two months in New York before heading to my destination in the Atlanta bureau. They put me up at the Manhattan Hotel a couple of blocks from the paper, which was at 229 West Forty-third Street. The rooms in the Manhattan were the smallest I had ever seen in a hotel. Years later, while searching for a cheap hotel in London, I landed in a room even smaller, but in 1965 my sense of space was offended.

I realized a few years into my career at the *Times* that New York intimidated me in other ways. I began to dream about the place. A fellow alumnus of the national desk told me not long ago that he had had a nightmare in which he had missed a deadline and disappointed our editor one more time. My own nightmare was less straightforward. It had little obvious connection to the paper; it was about my anxiety in the city. The dream recurred so often over so many years that I gave it a title. I would tell Norma when I awoke that I had had my "Lost in New York" dream again. That was no literary reference to a lost soul or the poor Southern lad thrown among the urban intelligentsia. In the dream, I was walking in Manhattan looking for something and couldn't find it because the geography was incomprehensible.

That is ridiculous on its face. Any third grader can memorize the handful of avenues that run uptown and downtown—Eighth, Broadway, etc. The cross streets are numbered running from downtown to uptown—Forty-third (where our office was), Forty-fourth, Forty-fifth. The north-south streets are so close together that you could hit a pitching wedge up Third Avenue at Thirty-fourth Street and land a golf ball in the middle of Thirty-fifth Street. If a pedestrian is lost in thought and forgets where he is, he has only to glance ahead a few yards and read the sign. No one can get lost in New York. But I did in my dream, over and over.

Far into my retirement back in Arkansas, the dream added a bit of geography that made it plausible to be lost. I spent my last two years

with the paper in London, where the streets have no pattern. They look as if they had been laid out at midnight by a drunk Cockney in a pea-soup fog. For a very few months after we arrived there, I tried driving to work from our house in Hampstead to the office near Fleet Street. I never found the same route twice. I would just keep going downhill toward the Thames River and eventually would recognize a landmark. New York is nothing like that. But in my dream, beginning after I left London, New York's beautifully regular streets became a moil of twists and bends, wretched narrow little paths that wound up and down hills, defying all sense of geographic logic. In one regular scene, I could see my destination off in the distance on the side of a hill, but I could never reach it. That dream bedeviled me well into my seventies.

I looked forward to a leisurely get-acquainted period when I was hired at the *Times.* The paper's policy for new reporters from elsewhere in the country was sound. We were to get used to the idea that we now worked for a New York paper. Two months in the city was the standard orientation. That time was to be spent getting to know our fellow reporters and the various levels of editors in the newsroom. It also gave us a chance to learn a little about the city, its geography, culture, pecu-liarities, ethnic groups, restaurants, theaters, street names, habits, speech—all that goes into making a big city what it is.

The other reporters befriended me at once. They took me to the restaurants, both fancy and greasy, in the Forty-third Street neighbor-hood. They talked about the editors—who was easy to get along with, who was not. I noticed that they all seemed to like and admire Turner Catledge, the executive editor. The *Times* had always hired many Southerners, perhaps because the great Adolph Ochs was himself one, a Chattanooga boy. Now the Mississippian Catledge was the paper's biggest Southerner. It was said in praise of his light touch that he had his hand in everything but never left a fingerprint. He was a friend and mentor to the young publisher, Arthur Ochs "Punch" Sulzberger. He was equally at ease with the lowest copy boy. If a reporter or an editor had to be reprimanded or fired, the bruise that was left could never be traced to Catledge.

I noticed that the several Southerners among the reporters tended to cling together. That didn't mean they stood apart from the Northerners. They certainly had friends across the paper's Mason-Dixon

Line. But when I arrived, the Southerners went out of their way to assure me that I was not alone in this infernal big city. The Southerners included a few black reporters. As they came around one by one to introduce themselves, almost the first thing they told me was that they, too, were from the South. It was almost as if the bond of our common birthplace overrode our racial difference. That was strange and comforting to a young white man who yearned to become better acquainted with those who until fairly recently had been simply strange.

I got to know Charlayne Hunter, who had integrated the University of Georgia only a few years earlier. She had learned to cuss in a soft drawl, and she eventually took that skill with her as a longtime correspondent for National Public Radio in South Africa, a place that still needed an occasional cussing even after the end of apartheid. When I met her in the 1960s, she was a rising star on the *Times* reporting staff.

She took me to lunch one day at a *Times* hangout around the corner on Eighth Avenue. As we reached a spot on Forty-third Street, she stopped and told me of an incident there a month or two earlier. She had been assigned to have lunch with a visiting ambassador from an African country. As they walked down the sidewalk, they came upon an ugly scene. One man was viciously attacking another and had him down in the gutter pummeling him. Charlayne stepped into the fray with mouth blazing. "Get off of him, you goddamned motherfucking son of a bitch!" she said. After settling the dispute, she turned to the ambassador, a proper, stately man, and found him shocked and silent. She was mortified.

As I call up that conversation with Charlayne, I remember a ten-year-old girl in Hot Springs standing in her yard addressing the passing scene.

Years later, a *Times* man, John Darnton, wrote a novel set at a thinly disguised *New York Times*, a murder mystery he called *Black and White and Dead All Over*. I recognized many of the men and women even though he had given them new names. And I recognized Gough's, the greasy-spoon bar and café across Forty-third Street from the paper. It was there that I learned the most about my new colleagues in 1965. They were unfailingly friendly and helpful. They saw no threat to their own jobs or ambitions from this hick-talking Arkansawyer, and they seemed genuinely curious about my species. I fielded a lot of questions:

What was it really like in Arkansas? Was the South really as bigoted as it seemed? A few of them had been sent south to cover the unfolding civil rights story and knew quite a lot about the region. In person, not one of them showed any sign of that annoying habit that so many New Yorkers have on the phone, not letting you finish a sentence.

The new national editor, Claude Sitton, was the main reason I was hired. He had covered the South for several years and had set the standard for national coverage of the civil rights story. Claude was a Georgian and sounded like it. He hired me partly because I was an Arkansawyer and sounded like it. He believed, as did Turner Catledge, that it was important to have Southerners covering the South at that time. It was felt that a stranger from the North would have trouble negotiating Southern speech and Southern behavior, although some of the Northern reporters had done exemplary work.

At the end of my first month, Claude and the managing editor, Clifton Daniel—a North Carolinian— cut short my get-acquainted lessons in New York. The civil rights story had broken out with renewed urgency in Selma, Alabama. John Herbers, the Mississippian who was covering it for the paper, had been reassigned to Washington. He was needed there. His family had gone ahead from Atlanta, the base of the *Times* Southern bureau. Meanwhile, the Selma story was heating up and needed immediate coverage.

I had already moved my family to Atlanta, and our children, Cindy and John, had started school. I had stayed only long enough to help move into a rented house before flying to New York. Now on the return trip I stopped at our new home only long enough to pack a fresh batch of clothes before flying off to Alabama. I would see my wife and children only a day or two at a time for the next several months. So little time did I spend at the rented house that one day, after we heard a noise from below and investigated, we discovered that the house had a downstairs apartment and that a man and a woman were living there. They turned out to be drunks, uncommonly quiet ones.

I was heading south from Birmingham to Montgomery in an Avis rental car one day in 1965 when I saw a woman running down a hill toward the highway. She waved her arms and shouted, clearly alarmed. I stopped. She told me that she had been threatened by someone and needed urgently to get to the next town. I gave her a lift for a few miles,

let her out at her destination, and went on my way. I can't remember what her story was, or even what color she was, just that she was in a state of alarm and needed help.

That evening when I phoned Claude on the national desk, I told him about the incident. I was shocked when he upbraided me for stopping to pick her up. It might have been a trap, he said. She might have been setting me up for a false charge of sexual assault or some such snare.

I was shaken by Claude's reaction. Only later did I appreciate why he felt so strongly. He had covered Alabama during an even darker period, when the state authorities, some in league with the Ku Klux Klan, saw the *New York Times* as an enemy, as part of a new Yankee invasion of the South.

Alabama had made the *New York Times* officially unwelcome in 1960 through a series of criminal and civil actions. First, the *Times* had published an advertisement soliciting funds for the Reverend Dr. Martin Luther King's organization and beseeching Congress to listen to the protest marchers in Alabama. The ad was promptly denounced for its "lies" by indignant state leaders. Shortly afterward, the veteran *Times* foreign correspondent Harrison Salisbury, newly reassigned to New York, flew to Alabama to investigate conditions. His report from the state's leading city, headlined "Fear and Hatred Grip Birmingham," further inflamed not only political leaders but also local editorial writers. The *Times* was quickly hit by a twin legal assault: one libel suit stemming from the ad and another in reply to Salisbury's story. In addition, the reporter was indicted for criminal libel. The result was that no *Times* representative, certainly not Salisbury, could safely enter Alabama.

Sitton, then the chief Southern correspondent, later complained half seriously to Salisbury, "Your damn stories kept me out of Alabama for over a year." Needless to say, the libel actions did not stand, and Salisbury never served time in the Birmingham jail. One of the libel judgments from the Supreme Court established an important standard for proving libel, a decision still protecting news media today from malicious suits.

As it happened, I spent most of those early months not only in Selma but also in two or three other south Alabama towns. That part of the state was called the Black Belt, ostensibly because of the color of the soil. More to the point, many of the counties in the Black Belt had majority populations of African Americans. Selma got most of

the attention because that's where King and his Southern Christian Leadership Conference (SCLC, which we called Slick) had chosen to make a stand.

If you don't believe I was in Selma that winter, take a look at the *Times* of February 6, 1965. My byline is on page 1, but that Roy Reed might have been some interloper. On the page where the story is jumped, you'll see a picture of King on the steps of the Dallas County jail, needing a shave. Standing next to him are two white men: Wilson Baker, the city's top cop, and me. I am freshly shaved and looking young and seemingly wondering, "What the hell am I doing here?" That's the only time my picture ever appeared in the *Times*. I hope no editor was reprimanded for that. The paper never liked to publicize its own people unnecessarily. I'm guessing that they couldn't crop me out of the picture without losing Baker's upraised arm as he calls for quiet. He was not demanding it, just asking for it. That was the first indication I had that Wilson Baker was not cut from the same cloth as a great many other law enforcement officers in the South.

King had been arrested four days earlier for leading a demonstration to dramatize the drive for voting rights for black people in the Deep South. More than three thousand people had already been arrested for trying to register to vote in Selma. The jailing of a Nobel Prize laureate made news around the world. But four days behind bars was judged sufficient to make his point, and now he figured his release would trigger a new round of publicity for his cause. It did. The black-and-white United Press International telephoto showed his stubble of beard. It did not show a smudge of lipstick from a woman admirer on his other cheek. My story, the first I had written in Alabama, noted that his imprisonment had reached the point "where it was more dramatic to come out than to stay in."

King left almost at once for Washington. He and his people were already arranging appointments with President Johnson and congressional leaders. This was the moment the civil rights campaigners had been working for. Legislation would soon make its way through the House and Senate, and by late spring the president would sign it, and then the world as seen from the American South would change forever.

■ ■ ■

The Student Non-Violent Coordinating Committee was younger and more daring than King's organization. The typical member was not a pastor or an old-line leader but a student or a recent graduate or drop-out of one of the South's several black colleges. SNCC, or Snick as everybody called it, worked in Selma, but it also ran an operation of outriders in neighboring counties, notably in Lowndes County— Bloody Lowndes, they called it with brutal honesty.

The most visible leader of SNCC when I came on the scene was Stokely Carmichael. He had some of the bearing and appearance of old Emperor Haile Selassie of Ethiopa, the lion of Judah, except that he was a foot taller and built like a running back. While Stokely's head was that of a monarch, he had the mouth of a revolutionary and the charisma of a rock star.

Carmichael was born in Trinidad and came with his family to Harlem when he was two. He graduated from the prestigious Bronx High School of Science, then got a degree in philosophy from Howard University.

I first met him on the lawn of the Lowndes County courthouse in 1965. I liked him. He sat and ate a sandwich with me and Virginia Durr, a white activist who by then was so old that she was barely able to get down on the grass and back up again under her own power. Virginia Foster Durr had social credentials that protected her from ordinary racist violence. She was a niece of the late Supreme Court justice Hugo Black's first wife. Her husband, Clifford, was one of President Roosevelt's young New Dealers. He had high positions in the Reconstruction Finance Corporation and the Federal Communications Commission. The Durrs, staunch civil libertarians, were hounded by J. Edgar Hoover's FBI and the communist-hunting congressional committees. Back home in Montgomery, Clifford defended civil rights activists, including Rosa Parks in the bus-segregation case. I believe that the Durrs were able to get away with outraging Alabama sensibilities because of their position in the patrician class. They had deep roots in the state's moneyed, land-owning, and professional circles. She undoubtedly knew that she needed all the protection she could get in Bloody Lowndes.

Stokely charmed us both with his easy talk and big smile. Even so, I sensed some of the hidden rage that would eventually propel him from the American shores and back, as he saw it, to Africa. I'm not sure what

the three of us were doing in Lowndes County, but it had something to do with SNCC's continuing campaign against the oppression of the county's big black majority. I wonder whether Stokely had any inkling how near he was to death that day. Not only did he presume to lounge on the sacred lawn of the white man's courthouse. He had the effrontery to do it in the company of an elderly white woman. There was at least one man inside the courthouse that day who might have killed him, and perhaps Virginia and me as well, on the spot. That man demonstrated what he was capable of a few weeks later.

There must be something about black Americans of Caribbean heritage that makes them different. I think of my friend Bob Maynard, whose parents were from Barbados. He grew up in New York but seemed always to have been free of the old emotional heritage of slavery that damaged so many native-born American blacks. It never would have occurred to Bob that he might say "Yassuh, boss" to any white man. He was so confident, in fact, that when he found himself dissatisfied with being merely a reporter for the *Washington Post,* he went out and bought his own newspaper. The *Oakland Tribune* was his until he died. He and his wife, Nancy Hicks, bought it 1983, making the *Tribune* the first big American daily to be owned by Americans of African descent.

It was Stokely who, some years later, raised the call for "Black Power," to the fearful astonishment of white America. He had already helped found the Lowndes County Freedom Party, which had stirred white anxieties in that old feudal outpost. And before he died too young, he would leave America in disgust, move to Africa, and take a new name that carried no baggage from the English-speaking world.

Nicholas von Hoffman, then a reporter for the *Chicago Daily News*, and I drove to Hayneville, the Lowndes County seat, one day during a slack time in Selma. We arrived at the stately old courthouse during the lunch hour. All the offices were empty, and the doors were open. We heard voices and drifted to the back, where a group of men sat eating sandwiches and playing dominoes. One middle-aged man got up to greet us. He welcomed us warmly, then gave us a tour of the building and a thumbnail history of the town. His is one of the voices I can still hear in my memory. The accent was cultivated, one heard only among a certain privileged class. Not at all like the grating nasal accent associated with unlettered Southerners. His thrifty sounding of

the letter *r* reminded me of Franklin D. Roosevelt's accent. The man's name was Tom Coleman.

A short time later, Tom Coleman came to my attention again. There was a murder in Hayneville. It happened at noon on the porch of a store with numerous witnesses. A white man wielding a shotgun shot to death a young white man from the North who was known as a civil rights organizer. An outside agitator, as such were called. The white people who came south to work for racial equality were considered even worse than the home-grown black agitators, in the eyes of the true-believing white supremacists. The man with the gun, the defender of the faith, was Tom Coleman. He was charged, tried, and very promptly acquitted.

That event brought me to a new level of understanding regarding race. My own youthful racism was based mainly on fear of the other and the unknown. Some of my young friends had picked up a more advanced form, the type that taught a kind of mindless contempt for people obviously less fortunate than themselves. But Tom Coleman's racism, and that of many other white people in the Deep South, was of a different order. Coleman and his kind believed sincerely that black people were a lower form of human life, that they were inferior to whites in mind and character. I once met a scholarly old man in Alabama who was versed in the defining characteristics of half a dozen African tribes and the presumed inferiorities of each. He was especially talkative about blue-gummed Ibos. That kind of intellectual support being easily obtained in Alabama, it became the white man's obligation to be alert to any sign of advanced intelligence or undue ambition in black men and to put a stop to it. Only a few were prepared to murder for the belief, strongly held as it might be. Nevertheless, the sheer monstrosity of the Alabama brand of white supremacy made its believers abhorrent in the eyes of civilized society. An unintended consequence of Tom Coleman's brazen action was to horrify and jolt awake huge numbers of white Americans in other parts of the country.

CHAPTER 7

Marching to Montgomery

My own awakening to a new level of reality had begun just days after my arrival in Selma. On March 7, a Sunday, a few hundred marchers, mostly black, had crossed the Edmund Pettus Bridge on the Alabama River to begin what had been billed, a little tentatively, as a march to the state capital, Montgomery, some fifty-four miles east. King, their most important leader, was not there. He was in another part of the country that day. The marchers headed out without him, going to see the governor, they said. Their repeated attempts to register to vote had been rebuffed—firmly, you might say—so they wanted to press their case with Governor George C. Wallace in person. The governor, always attentive to the desires of the citizens, went to see them, instead, in a manner of speaking. He sent his personal emissary, Colonel Al Lingo, head of the state police, and several dozen armed troopers. The state men were accompanied by a sizable band of Sheriff Jim Clark's deputies and ex officio helpers on horseback. The sheriff referred to the horsemen affectionately as his "posse."

Men and horses blocked the highway on the Montgomery side of the bridge. Colonel Lingo got out a bullhorn and ordered the marchers to halt. They went a few steps farther. They stopped, hesitated, then knelt to pray in the grassy median that divided the four-lane highway. At the head of the column were John Lewis, the young chairman of SNCC and many years later a congressman, and Hosea Williams, a chief organizer for King's Southern Christian Leadership Conference. Mrs. Amelia Boynton, a local leader, knelt beside them.

Quite suddenly, Colonel Lingo ordered the troopers to advance. They rushed forward in a flying wedge. I described what happened next in my story for the *Times:*

> The wedge moved with such force that it seemed almost to pass over the waiting column instead of through it.
>
> The first 10 or 20 Negroes were swept to the ground scream-ing, arms and legs flying, and packs and bags went skittering across the grassy divider strip and on to the pavement on both sides.
>
> Those still on their feet retreated.
>
> A cheer went up from the white spectators lining the south side of the highway.
>
> Then came the pop of a tear-gas canister, and a venomous cloud covered the highway. Through the mist I heard coughing, the sound of clubs on flesh and bone, and cries of pain. The men on horses sped through the fleeing marchers wielding whips on faces, backs, and legs. The spectators whooped and cheered.

I hope never again to see such hatred in the eyes of men, women and, yes, children.

Tear gas was not new to me—I had tasted it once in Little Rock when some segregationist hothead set it off at a Little Rock school board meeting—but it is not an experience that a person can become accustomed to. Inhalation is almost never fatal, but it is altogether a physical and emotional torment. You feel that you dare not breathe or, worse, that you cannot breathe. But by then it is too late because you have already got enough of it in the lungs to start the coughing. The eyes sting so intensely that you believe it may be unbearable, and you think you surely are going blind. Then comes an unreasoning fear. You are cut off and at the mercy of whatever marauders may be heading your way.

And that is just the reaction of the newsmen who happened to be there watching. At the Pettus Bridge, the real targets were the hapless people fleeing for their lives back into the town, and fleeing blinded because while the newsmen got only noxious whiffs of the gas, the marchers got it all, an enormous thick mass that rolled over them just as the club-swinging officers—wearing gas masks, of course—were attacking them from the rear. I saw many outrages covering the civil rights story, but for sheer brutality I never saw anything to match the scene at the Alabama River crossing that day in 1965. They called it Bloody Sunday. Yes, there was blood as well as terror. Among those hos-

pitalized were Mrs. Boynton and John Lewis. The young man's skull was fractured. He never forgot that day, even as an old man and one of the longest-serving members of the U.S. House of Representatives.

The weapon that felled Mrs. Boynton and Mr. Lewis was a billy club. All the officers carried them, and they used them with enthusiasm. The *Times* for some reason required us to spell it as one word. I remember seeing the weapon in use a month or so before Bloody Sunday. Some of King's lieutenants had led a few dozen voting rights protesters to the courthouse. Sheriff Clark, who was angrier than usual that day, used his billy club to rough up James Bevel, a senior aide to Dr. King. He didn't use it as a club to the head but as a punch to the belly. Here's the way I described it: "The sheriff rushed outside shaking with anger. Mr. Bevel was the first Negro he encountered. The sheriff began jabbing him in the abdomen with his billyclub, then grabbed his shoulders and forced him backward down the steps."

A little later, one of Clark's deputies used the club the same way—as a jabbing tool—to chase away Ivanhoe Donaldson, a staff worker for SNCC. The billy club became a "nightstick" in the *Times* before the running story left Selma. I never knew why. I speculated that my upright editors considered "nightstick" more in keeping with the paper's tone. I still don't understand. In my experience, those clubs are put into service around the clock. Besides, the term "billy club" has an honesty about it that tells both the innocent victim and the common miscreant that it means business.

The television images that night after the assault at Pettus Bridge sickened and enraged millions of Americans. My story ran on page 1, but no newspaper account could match the television images of the assault on innocent marchers, some of them elderly women. When the injuries were tallied that day, eighty-four marchers had been hurt. Some were bruised by clubs. Some were cut by whips. Some were scraped by dirt and asphalt when they were swept off their feet trying to dodge the posse's horses.

When the march resumed days later, unobstructed, it was vastly enlarged by hundreds of black and white demonstrators from all over the country—including fifty hardy white citizens of Alabama who wanted it known that George Wallace and Jim Clark did not speak for them. Those fifty have been long forgotten, swept aside by the larger

crime of their fellow citizens, pushed into the gutter of history by the storming horsemen.

The fifty whites who were bold enough to march were not the only white Alabamians who disagreed to one degree or another with the segregationist resistance that was blackening their state's name. In Selma alone a large number, but probably not a majority, were at the very least embarrassed by their sheriff and their governor. There was a couple who had moved from the North years before to establish a cigar factory. They invited visiting reporters and cameramen for dinner and drinks. The local newspaper editor welcomed visiting newsmen to his newsroom. More important, he made sure that his staff covered the ongoing story without bias. The old Albert Hotel became our home for days and weeks at a time; the manager and his staff took good care of us. I did suffer a financial setback there. Someone stole $120 worth of travelers' checks and a substantial amount of cash from my room while I was at breakfast one morning. Nonetheless, I grieved when the place was demolished several years ago. The Albert might have been the only building in the Deep South modeled after the Doge's Palace in Venice. Fat chance of seeing another in this age of Philistine styling for small-town lodging.

Then there was the Tally-Ho restaurant. It still exists and apparently is prospering, as it should. In 1965, the Tally-Ho was a private club nestled in the woods just outside the city. The hours were flexible enough to accommodate reporters and television crews with late deadlines. I think the Tally-Ho introduced me to the gin martini. The chef had a taste for Louisiana cuisine. The owner was a mouthy old broad whom we knew only as "Mama." She did not encourage flirts, but a TV cameraman named Earl became a close enough friend to exchange confidences and commiserations. All of us loved the place. Daily reporting requires a person to start the day slowly and build to a crescendo in the minutes before the evening deadline. If the day's work has included bedlam and violence, the deadline becomes something more than merely a time of tension. It becomes an affliction of the mind and the body. Mama's martinis were the cure for that.

There was one other thing about the Tally-Ho. It had no black members. A public restaurant faced the likelihood that any day in the 1960s might bring sit-ins and protests and maybe lawsuits to force it

to integrate. As a private club, the Tally-Ho did not have that anxiety. We knew that. We were ashamed of it. But we were desperate for respite from the tumult. We shoved our guilt aside and kept it at arm's length until we had time to deal with it. So I'm dealing with it. I was wrong. But I'm still grateful for Mama. She was there for us, bearing gin, in our time of need.

■　　■　　■

If the Albert and the Tally-Ho were relief, murder was the reality. A constant possibility of violent death had hung over the voting rights movement since the drive began in Dallas County in 1963. The motive for the drive was obvious to everybody except the white supremacist power structure that controlled not only Dallas County but virtually all of the Deep South. Blacks constituted a majority of the county— as was the case in dozens of counties on the southern rim of the United States—but only 1 percent of them were registered to vote. Among the activists who set about changing that was a young SNCC member named Bernard Lafayette. He became prominent enough that the Kluxers tried to beat him to death one day in June 1963. They failed, but not out of some fit of compassion.

Another band of thugs finally succeeded in killing someone on March 9, 1965. Bloody Sunday, two days earlier, had prompted several hundred angry citizens, black and white, to descend on Selma to attempt a second march to Montgomery. It was led by King, the injured John Lewis, and numerous other prominent people from labor and the civil rights movement. By prearrangement, the marchers' leaders agreed to obey the state troopers' order to stop at Pettus Bridge and return to Browns Chapel Church. That evening, the Reverend James J. Reeb, thirty-eight, a white Unitarian minister from Boston, and two white friends had supper in a predominantly black café. As they walked down the street afterward, five white men were waiting outside a seg hangout. They attacked Reeb and his friends with clubs. Reeb died two days later at a hospital in Birmingham.

Speaking of Browns Chapel, modern historians and journalists have corrected our spelling to "Brown Chapel." They may be right. When we were there in 1965, all of us—journalists and members of the

church—called it and spelled it "Browns," plural and unpossessed. I try never to argue with revisionists.

The tension between Alabama and the federal government intensified. For the second attempted march, Governor Wallace had ordered a much larger force of troopers to stop it. When a third march was scheduled for March 21, the federal government called Wallace's bluff.

First, there was stern action by federal judge Frank Johnson, a hill country Republican and a classmate of the governor's at the University of Alabama. When he was asked to enjoin King and the demonstrators from marching, he ruled that the protesters had a right to march. Johnson became a hero of the civil rights movement for that and numerous other decisions down through the years. That probably annoyed him. He was not much for showing off, in or out of the courtroom. His old college friend came to despise him.

I had my own personal encounter with the federal authorities one day. I walked into the U.S. district attorney's office in Selma and heard someone say, "Hi, Roy Reed." It was Jim Turner, one of my roommates at the University of Missouri. He had gone to law school, married his college sweetheart, and joined the Civil Rights Division of the Justice Department in time for the big enforcement push of the 1960s. We got reacquainted and have stayed in touch since. We occasionally meet in neutral territory to play golf, and I take more pleasure than I should in beating him.

Acting on Judge Johnson's injunction, President Johnson, another Southerner with a sturdy spine, backed up the order by sending two thousand men from his own army, which was stouter than Governor Wallace's, to Alabama. He rubbed it in a little by federalizing nineteen hundred members of the Alabama National Guard and ordering them to the scene. Then, just to show who was boss, he sent in a large band of FBI agents and federal marshals. Some of us remembered when President Dwight D. Eisenhower sent federal troops to put down Faubus's insurrection at Little Rock's Central High School. It had become necessary to demonstrate once again that no state, no matter how angry and obstreperous its citizens, could bully the national government and get away with it.

Almost half of the front page of the March 22 edition of the *Times* was devoted to the beginning of the fifty-four-mile trek.

"Backed by the armed might of the United States," my story began, "3,200 persons marched out of Selma today on the first leg of a historic venture in nonviolent protest." For some reason, the *Times* preferred "persons" to "people" in those days. Newspapers have always been eccentric.

King sent the marchers off from Selma in high spirits. "Walk together, children, don't you get weary," he told the thousands massed in front of the movement's main church, Browns Chapel, "and it [your marching] will lead us to the promised land. And Alabama will be a new Alabama, and America will be a new America."

I smarted off in the next paragraph. "Dr. King's sense of history, if not his optimism, seemed well-placed. The Alabama march seems destined for a niche in the annals of the great protest demonstrations." I turned out to be right about both the history and the misplaced optimism. My story noted, ominously, that two men had already been killed since the beginning of the Black Belt campaign and that, for what it was worth, thirty-eight hundred "persons" had been arrested.

After his speech, King and a large component of famous people, including Dr. Ralph J. Bunche, an under-secretary in the United Nations, took their places at the head of the column, and the marchers stepped off.

They spent their first night just over seven miles from Selma, in tents pitched in a black farmer's field. The celebrities found more comfortable lodging back in town and in Montgomery.

The goal of the march was said to be to present a petition to Wallace asking him and the state of Alabama to start treating its black citizens fairly. The wording was fancier than that, but that was the gist. The real motive of the march was to raise a commotion and create a spectacle so overwhelming that the government of the United States would have to respond. A few weeks later, it responded resoundingly. As for the governor, he had already sent word that he wouldn't be in his office to receive the petition. Said he was going to be "in Michigan or some place" making a speech. In the end, even he couldn't resist the spectacle. He stayed in Montgomery.

The *Times* treated the story as a significant turning point in Southern history. My assignment on the march was to write the main story every day, an overview of the day's events, the miles traveled, a

broad picture of the countryside, the marchers, the bystanders on the side of the road—some hostile, some friendly. Additional stories, sidebars, were written by other *Times* reporters, in particular by a footsore Paul Montgomery from the city desk in New York. It rained for two straight days, and then it turned cold. The marchers slept in the mud, and so did Paul. But he had asked for the assignment, and he never complained.

I moved up and down the highway in a car, stopping sometimes ahead of the march and marching alongside it a while before getting back in the car and moving along. Sometimes I stopped to chat with onlookers or people in the little businesses that were the convenience stores of the time.

Sitton had risked much in assigning me to this story. I was the first reporter he hired after he took over as national editor in the fall of 1964. His judgment as an editor was being tested. He had joined a distinguished company of national editors. His immediate predecessor was Harrison Salisbury, one of the giants of twentieth-century journalism, a fabled war correspondent and one of the ablest of the American reporters who covered the almost impenetrable government of the Soviet Union during the worst of the Cold War. It was not enough that Claude came to the job with his own shining record as the Southern correspondent considered the best that any paper had ever had on that beat.

He told me bluntly more than once that I had to do a good job because I was being tested along with him. I understood that, and I was determined not to let him down. More than a year after the Alabama march, Claude was still keeping a close eye on me. James Meredith, the first black student at the University of Mississippi, returned to Mississippi during the summer of 1966 vowing to march alone through the middle of his home state. A white man put a load of buckshot in his back outside Hernando. I missed the shooting because I had stopped for a cold drink in a little roadside store. That meant I was not visible in any of the wire photos that emerged in the *Times* newsroom minutes later. Two or three witnesses on Forty-third Street saw fit to record the scene: Sitton standing over the wire-photo machine, scanning the pictures, and demanding, "Where's Roy Reed!?"

Meredith was only slightly injured. I redeemed myself with an exclusive interview in his Memphis hospital room the next day.

President Johnson had little patience with Wallace, but he gave the governor the small comfort of a cover to explain why the federal troops were on hand. Mr. Wallace said the state couldn't afford the expense of protecting the marchers, so the president obliged him by picking up the tab. All in all, it was strange to see the state troopers who had clubbed, horse-whipped, and tear-gassed the marchers two weeks earlier now assigned to guard their enemies from spectators who might give in to an urge to pull a gun or grab a club.

White protesters were there, but mostly keeping a low profile. A couple of signs were held up for the cameras at the end of Pettus Bridge. One said, TOO BAD, REEB. The other said, I HATE NIGGERS. Down the road a way, a car of envoys from a neighboring state carried a sign proclaiming solidarity: MERIDIAN, MISS., HATES NIGGERS.

A white minister with the march was knocked down and slightly hurt, but that was the only report of violence. State and local authorities repeatedly urged white citizens to stay away. Those who declined the advice were simply too curious or too angry to ignore the march, and who could blame them? This would turn out to be the most important event in Alabama for years to come. What were you going to tell your grandchildren? "What did you do in the big civil rights march, Grandfather?" Who would want to admit that he cared so little that he wouldn't drive a few miles to get a peek at it? And if he happened to be packing a pistol or a blackjack—well, you never know when you might need to protect yourself from some marauding preacher.

The visiting preachers were everywhere, along with union members, students, and public officials. Paul R. Screvane, president of the New York City Council, was there representing Mayor Robert Wagner "and, we hope, the people of New York."

Describing the scene before the march got under way, I smarted off again: "At 8 a.m., 400 or 500 persons milled in the street. Milling has become the style of the movement in recent weeks, and the character of the milling has changed as hundreds of whites from the North, East and West have come into town to add their protest to the Negro's. The outsiders mill with a greater air of purpose." Our son John, a New

Orleans boy, left the Big Easy and went off to Yale University a few years after that and found a similar air there. He complained that the Northern kids were always in a hurry. They even stand in line in a hurry, he said.

My story included a bit of history that probably did not appear in most other reporting that day. I quoted the Reverend Andrew Young, one of King's main aides, as saying the Alabama movement had actually begun in 1963 when the Ku Klux Klan bombed a black church and killed four little girls. He said, "At that time, we began to ask ourselves, 'What can we do to change the climate of an entire state?'" SNCC moved into Selma that year and started holding meetings and demonstrations. Those young people were outside agitators and proud of it. King's organization, SCLC, did not come to town in any big way until early 1965.

Speaking of the Klan, you have to wonder how much time its leaders devoted to long-range strategy. Did it occur to any of them that killing children—no matter how justified it might be in their minds— would at the very least bring a strong reaction from saner members of the community and that somewhere down the road it might call down God's own wrath on their heads? I know a Baptist preacher named Will Campbell who has befriended members of the Klan and whose heart is big enough to see them not just as murderers but as fellow human beings in need of God's forgiveness. Another preacher I used to know preached a sermon one Sunday on God's grace. He explained it in intricate and stimulating detail, not a one of which I can remember now. Will Campbell explained it in a single sentence: "All men are bastards, and God loves them, anyway." Maybe the Kluxers were relying on Will's theology to pull them through.

Just east of Selma, the marchers passed a billboard containing a piece of historical fiction that would take on a life of its own for years to come. It showed a photograph of King at the Highlander Folk School in Tennessee and the message, MARTIN LUTHER KING AT COMMUNIST TRAINING SCHOOL. Those billboards eventually would number more than eight hundred on Southern highways. I think the one in Dallas County was the first to go up. Highlander had a few communists, as did other self-help schools where students

earned their tuition by working on the schools' farms and other enter-prises. It was also supported by the likes of Eleanor Roosevelt.

As to the suggestion that the civil rights movement was rife with communists, King addressed the question as he marched past the sign. "There are as many Communists in the civil rights movement as there are Eskimos in Florida," he said. That was disingenuous. The movement always had a few card-carriers. But the notion that the Communist Party invented the civil rights movement, and that it was all a plot to drive a wedge in the United States and enable the Party to take over the govern-ment, was absurd.

The march lasted five days. The armed troops were there every step of the way. There was mud and rain. There were minor scrapes and bruises and blistered feet and sunburn. Even King limped into camp with a sore foot the second night. He rested his foot the next day by flying up to Cleveland to make a speech. On that second day, he had been joined by his wife, Coretta Scott King, and by LeRoy Collins, a former governor of Florida, who had become the director of the Federal Community Relations Service. Several other federal officials were on hand, including Ramsey Clark, the deputy attorney general. President Johnson wanted to make his point not merely with armed soldiers but also with a government presence that said, "Don't mess with me." Maybe he was thinking, "How many times do you people have to be shown?"

The procession crossed into Lowndes County on the second day at 12:13 p.m. I was at pains to make the reader understand the dreadful sig-nificance of that crossing. As if to underline it further, the highway—officially named by the state the Jefferson Davis Highway—narrowed from four lanes to two at the county line. Judge Johnson had ordered that to make it easier to protect the marchers, only three hundred of the thirty-two hundred who had started from Selma could continue until they emerged onto four-lane highway near Montgomery.

All of us reporters made note of that requirement. Several of us also found ways to describe the psychological setting. I referred to Lowndes County as "lonesome." Houses were seen only here and there, and only black occupants came outside to watch. Even the landscape looked lone-some. Swamps and marshes were visible from the highway in Dallas

County, but those in Bloody Lowndes looked more ominous. We would be gazing out on beautiful rolling farmland and pastures, and abruptly, or so it seemed, there would be a dark patch of woods with enormous trees planted in water the color of dark copper. Copperhead snakes liked to come up from the swamps and sun themselves on the shoulder of the highway on warm spring days. The marchers had been warned to watch where they stepped. But they were considerably more alert for men who might be lurking in the shadows of those trees and bushes. The soldiers paid a lot of attention to the woods.

Andy Young, marching at the head of the column, talked about Lowndes County's majority-black population and its systematic subjection. "Not a single Negro in Lowndes County had even tried to register in the last 65 years until two weeks ago. In Lowndes County, all the Negroes are either school teachers or sharecroppers, which means that the whites have strings on them all, one way or another." He did not consider it necessary to point out that Lowndes was simply an especially vivid example of the condition of the political underclass across the South, especially in the Black Belt. That was not going to change until Negroes got the right to vote without restraint. Just how much that right meant to them, after a century of denial of that right, and another century before that of outright bondage, was evident in the fact that more than a handful of them were willing to risk death by showing their defiant faces in one of the most brutal places in the nation. Every marcher knew that Lowndes County, like many others, boasted white enforcers—men who were unofficially delegated by their fellows to shoot "uppity niggers."

On the evening of the fourth day, the victorious, foot-sore demonstrators set up a stage on the campus of the City of St. Jude, a Roman Catholic social service organization, on the outskirts of Montgomery. They were entertained by Harry Belafonte, Tony Bennett, Frankie Laine, Sammy Davis Jr., Joan Baez, Nina Simone, and Peter, Paul and Mary.

On the fifth day the march had swelled to twenty-five thousand people. They included hundreds of celebrities and enough musicians to form the biggest band in history. There were labor leaders, preachers, civil rights heroes, and civil rights foot soldiers. I don't know how many reporters and photographers were there, but we were numerous

enough to form a pretty fair combat force if we decided to take matters into our own hands. The sun was shining, there was no tear gas, and everybody, reporters included, had seemingly decided to enjoy the spectacle.

The whole crowd swept up to the steps of the capitol. George Wallace watched his humiliation from behind a curtain in his office (with the *Times*'s intrepid Ben Franklin, down from Washington, watching him from a few feet away). There on the steps, dangerously near the sacred spot where Jefferson Davis had taken the oath of office to become president of the Confederacy, there was one last triumphant rally. Martin Luther King delivered one of his best speeches: "How long? Not long!"

Then it was all over, and the happy demonstrators scattered, some to the airport, some back to Selma.

CHAPTER 8

Getting Away with Murder

I was having a late supper that night at the capital's Elite Café—pronounced EE-lite—with some other reporters. John Doar, the Justice Department man in charge of security for the march, was there. John was tough. He was about as talkative as Gary Cooper in *High Noon*. He had once stood alone in a Mississippi street and faced down a white mob with a speech of about twenty words. In the middle of dinner, John was called to the Elite's telephone. He came back grim-faced. He went quickly from one table of reporters to the next and told us what had happened. A civil rights helper had been gunned down on the highway between Selma and Montgomery.

The victim was Viola Liuzzo, a white housewife from Michigan. She had been seen by a carload of Ku Klux Klansmen driving a car with a young black man by her side. Her job was to ferry marchers back to Selma. She and her companion had deposited one load and were returning to Montgomery for more when the Klansmen pulled alongside and opened fire.

Mrs. Liuzzo's murder reverberated in ways the Klan could not have foreseen. First, President Lyndon B. Johnson declared war on the Klan in an address to the nation. The FBI made arrests within hours. In 1960, it had hired an informant named Gary Thomas Rowe to join the Klan in the steel-manufacturing town of Bessemer, near Birmingham. Luckily, he was in the carload of Klansmen who had driven south that day looking for a chance to cause trouble. His five years undercover paid off. He was able to give a minute-by-minute account of the fatal mission in court.

In spite of his utterly damning testimony in the first murder trials,

the defendants were acquitted. It was only after the federal government tried them in a federal court with a tough federal judge that they were convicted, and then only of violating Mrs. Liuzzo's civil rights. There was no federal law against murder. They were sentenced to ten years in prison. Two got out in seven years; one died earlier. All are now dead, along with Rowe, who died in 1998 at age sixty-four. He had been in a witness protection program living under another name.

Rowe's career became a model for the pluses and minuses of the government informer program. He became a hero for a time among civil rights activists. His testifying in open court in one of the most violently racist sections of the South was an act of great courage. Just how worried he was was made clear to my friend Jack Nelson of the *Los Angeles Times* one day outside the Lowndes County courthouse. Rowe had been there testifying before a grand jury. Jack followed him out, hoping to ask a few questions. He somehow squeezed past the armed government men who were protecting the witness and ran to the car where Rowe was seated, shouting that he wanted to ask him something. Rowe pulled a pistol and aimed it at Jack and apparently was ready to pull the trigger when Jack skidded to a stop, threw up his hands, and backed away.

The rest of Rowe's life was spent in and out of controversy, often spilling out of the privacy of the witness protection program. He was accused of planning and participating in some of the violence he was reporting to the FBI. In 1975, wearing a cotton hood that resembled a Klan headpiece, he told a Senate committee that the FBI had known of and condoned his participation in violence against black people. He said the agency had ordered him to sow dissent within the Klan by having sexual relations with members' wives. He admitted to having taken part in a baseball-bat assault on Freedom Riders in Birmingham in 1961. He said he had told the Alabama police that he had fatally shot a black man, never named, in a riot in 1963. He said the federal authorities knew about these incidents.

As late as 1983, Mrs. Liuzzo's children brought an unsuccessful $2 million suit against the FBI, charging that through its negligence in recruiting, training, and controlling Mr. Rowe, it bore responsibility for their mother's killing. As Mr. Rowe made his often boastful disclosures, figures inside and outside the government debated the proper

use of informers. Some demanded greater oversight. Others contended that good intelligence could not be obtained if infiltrators had to take the Boy Scout oath.

Rowe lived thirty-three years after fingering Mrs. Liuzzo's murderers. He died bankrupt.

Here's how hard it was in those days to convict a white man of killing a black man: When the first of the three Klansmen in the Liuzzo case, Collie Leroy Wilkins, came to trial in Lowndes County, the prosecution examined thirty-two white men on the jury panel as to their views on race. Twenty-five of them declared forthrightly that they were white supremacists. Only two flatly denied it. William Bradford Huie, a hardened old Alabama journalist, filed his story twenty-four hours before the trial ended, saying the defendant would be acquitted, and left town. He bid goodbye to the rest of us and said he had enjoyed our company, but he happened to know how the trial would come out, and he had work to do back home. I admired his chutzpah but lacked his nerve. I stayed to the end.

The acquittal of Viola Liuzzo's murderers was one more announcement to the world that as late as the mid-1960s, precious little justice was to be had from racist juries in the Deep South.

Far more important was what happened in Washington. Congress, already edgy from the national reaction to the televised images at Selma, immediately rushed through a bill to end discriminatory practices against black voters. Discrimination had been built into the system of white supremacy in parts of the Deep South since the end of Reconstruction. Sometimes a ludicrously difficult test given only to black voters was enough to limit the ballot to whites. Sometimes more strenuous measures were used—beatings and threats by nightriders, occasionally kidnapping and murder. After President Johnson signed the bill, which became the Voting Rights Act of 1965, blacks began to vote in unprecedented numbers. Black officials were elected across the South. In many black-majority counties, they became the dominant office-holders. And the Klan found itself under governmental pressure so severe that it was forced even further underground. It finally dissolved into a little band of sullen old men.

The segregationist resistance made a lot of men famous. They were heroes in the eyes of many Southerners and more than a few

Northerners. But it's hard to imagine that men like Jim Clark attracted many fans outside the Deep South. Even there, millions of white people who called themselves segregationists were appalled by the extremists who pursued their beliefs with bricks, ax handles, guns, and dynamite. Sheriff Clark's weapons were the billy club and the cattle prod.

The bully of Dallas County became one of the best-known public faces of the resistance for a short while. He and Bull Connor, the equally violent police commissioner of Birmingham, were as famous in their time as ambitious governors like George C. Wallace and Orval E. Faubus, who lent their names to this newest lost cause.

Even so, I suspect that some ordinary white supremacists were quietly sickened when word got around Selma late one Saturday about what Clark had done to some black children. About a hundred of the kids, thinking to get in on the movement that was the talk of their part of town, decided to hold a march of their own. The sheriff obliged them by leading them himself in his official car. He led them right out of town and several miles down a country road, moving at a brisk pace. I followed the procession in a rental car. When the smaller kids couldn't keep up, deputies shocked them with cattle prods. The kids finally swarmed into somebody's yard and lay panting and crying, some vomiting, while the sheriff and his men drove away laughing. I was close to vomiting myself as I drove back to town and phoned in my story.

Clark died June 4, 2007, in a nursing home. His obituary mentioned that he had been voted out of office in the next election after his fame had peaked in 1965. He made a living selling mobile homes for a while, then went into a new line of work. He was convicted in 1976 of conspiring to smuggle marijuana. He served nine months in prison.

The obituary also noted that he was divorced from his wife, Louise. I never met her, but I was aware of her because of a bold piece of reporting by a *Times* colleague, Gay Talese. He had flown in from New York to write a story for the Sunday magazine about the sheriff and his county. He had cannily traded on the fact that he had studied at the University of Alabama. That got him into the sheriff's confidence in spite of his New York style and speech. He became so friendly with Jim and Louise that they invited him repeatedly into their apartment above the county jail. He had eaten meals with them. No doubt he had

exchanged confidences with them. They trusted him so much that they both left the apartment one day and invited Gay to stay there until they returned. Then Louise came home earlier than expected.

A group of reporters were gathered around the sheriff a few days later at the courthouse when he recalled what had happened. He was still furious.

"When my wife got back to the apartment," he said, "she found him in our bedroom. The son of a bitch was counting my underwear!"

Gay was one of three *Times* reporters sent to help me cover the march. Ben Franklin of the Washington Bureau, a gifted con artist, somehow inveigled his way into the governor's office the day the march concluded. Wallace had taken a liking to him in an earlier encounter, and he ordered his staff to let Ben in. Ben watched as Wallace stood behind a curtain and watched the throng make its way triumphantly up the street toward the capitol. Our coverage had the rare advantage of the governor's minute-by-minute reaction as the march ended and as one speaker after another stood on the governor's own front porch and denounced him.

The other reporter flown in to help was Paul Montgomery. He wangled the assignment from Claude Sitton, the national editor, and somehow forgot to tell Claude that he didn't have a driver's license. As a native of Manhattan, he had never learned to drive. Claude learned that only after Paul landed in Montgomery. The normal routine for a traveling reporter is to head straight for a rental car desk after arriving at an airport.

By the time Paul had cadged a ride to the Albert Hotel to join the rest of us, he had already confessed to Claude and been chewed out. Claude sentenced him to walk every step from Selma to Montgomery —all fifty miles. Instead of returning to a comfortable hotel bed at night, he was condemned to sleep on the ground with the marchers. If it rained—and it poured for two days straight—tough luck. He slept in the mud with everyone else. But like Br'er Rabbit in the briar patch, he quickly found himself envied. Camping with the marchers gave him an insider's view. He turned it into some of the best reporting of that extraordinary week.

■　■　■

Most of the attacks on newsmen during those years were by freelancers, although police authorities joined in often enough to let the press know where their sympathies lay. Bull Connor and Jim Clark loved harassing reporters and photographers, and they were not alone. Right across the South, far too many law enforcement men cast their lot openly with the segregationist elements. Some police officers in Bogalusa, Louisiana, were members of the Klan. We knew when we went into such towns that we could expect little protection from the law.

A television cameraman named Laurens Pierce—a tough Alabamian—designed a camera harness with a steel bar that he could quickly detach to defend himself when he needed to, as he frequently did. Some newsmen carried guns. Pierce and his crew had pistols at hand wherever they went, and they made sure the word got around. Once near Birmingham, a segregationist shoved a shotgun into Dan Rather's ribs and said he would pull the trigger if Rather went any farther. One of Pierce's soundmen responded by thrusting his own pistol against the fellow's head. The man and his toughs backed off.

Pierce carried his half-glasses pushed over his hair as he worked, a wise precaution in case an opponent got in the first lick and struck him in the eye. His fighting reputation was well established before I met him. He had got the best of it in a fight with Alton Wayne Roberts, one of the killers of the Neshoba County, Mississippi, civil rights workers Michael Schwerner, Andrew Goodman, and James Chaney. When Pierce photographed Roberts and some friends outside a courtroom in Meridian, Mississippi, an argument ensued. It began with curses and escalated to fists. Pierce had the last word with a club.

When I arrived in Alabama in 1965, the perils for newsmen were somewhat less serious than those that journalists had faced two years earlier at the University of Mississippi. At Ole Miss, newsmen and federal marshals became substitute targets of a murderous mob. What the killers craved was the blood of James Meredith, the man who had come to destroy their Way of Life. When they found themselves thwarted by the marshals, they used guns, clubs, and firebombs against the hated federal men and the equally hated journalists. Dozens of marshals were wounded. Several journalists were beaten. One hardy fellow filed his story by phone while a doctor removed pellets from his back. Paul Guihard, a French reporter sent by Agence France Presse,

never filed his final report. He was shot in the back at close range, execution style.

The Guihard case was closed without finding his killer. Maybe the man who did it died in his sleep somewhere. Maybe he is still walking around Mississippi. Does he still feel good about the greatest deed of his life? Does he dream?

It would be easy for reporters, photographers, and television journalists to feel heroic about what we endured during those years. We were not heroic. We were merely alert. We only rarely feared for our lives and our safety; mostly we just tried to stay out of harm's way, or at least out of the direct line of fire. It helped that most reporters are by nature content to be spectators. For myself, I never felt very heroic when I was spat on by an angry black girl in Atlanta or slammed in the shoulder by an angry white man in Bogalusa or when I became thoroughly frightened in half a dozen ragged little towns. We in the news trade were paid witnesses. An honorable enough calling, perhaps, but not heroic. With a little effort, we had to remind ourselves periodically that the heroes were the people who put their lives at risk to force an entire society to change its stubborn, hateful ways. Scores of them gave their lives for the cause. Their names are inscribed on memorial tablets here and there across the South. Paul Guihard's name is on one of them, but I doubt that he would have claimed to be a hero. He went to Mississippi as a witness.

We had to be alert not only to avoid injury but also to understand the strange unfolding circumstances. Most of us were young. The civil rights story was new to us. We had to learn how to cover it day by day, sometimes hour by hour. We knew instinctively that it was historic, but history took a back seat in the daily coverage of marches, rallies, speeches, and violence. I found myself agreeing with George Wallace on one point. He told his first biographer, Marshall Frady, "Naw, we don't stop and figger, we don't think about history or theories or none of that. We just go ahead. Hell, history can take care of itself."

So history has now taken care of itself. And the daily unfolding of events that confronted the young reporters in the 1950s and 1960s turned out to be a story of great magnitude, nothing less than the beginning of a wholesale remaking of the South, a giant step toward its Americanization. First, there was a national ass-kicking administered

by those other Americans who were finally fed up. It was a matter of sickening rage to the last of the big-time bigots, already suffering from the larger nation's scorn, that the chief ass-kicker was a Southerner, Lyndon B. Johnson. He and an equally maddening army of nonviolent African Americans finally whipped the holdouts into submission. Drove old Dixie down, again.

You will look in vain today for an open, avowed racist anywhere in the South. Plenty of secret ones, hiding and sulking because even they understand that they are despised outcasts. I enjoy the mental vision of little cadres of the old racists meeting in dark rooms talking about the old days and their lost dreams of a pure Aryan nation—little suspecting that at least one of their number is probably a government agent, just keeping tabs to make it easier to nail the bastards when they occasionally can't stand it any longer and bomb a school or a church or a synagogue.

Even the bitter old never-enders know now that their time has passed and that the rights movement they fought so desperately half a century ago was one more gasp in the long dying of slavery. Just a gasp, not the perverse satisfaction of a resounding death rattle that they dreaded and stoutly opposed then, even as they grudgingly went along with the new name for slavery, white supremacy. But every time the Klan bullies and the deputies of Jim Clark and Bull Connor and Leander Perez asserted the ancient ownership rights of the white masters, the day of the coffin moved a little closer.

■ ■ ■

One of the first people I met at Selma was another Southerner who had just moved from a first-rate Southern newspaper to a national one. Jack Nelson, who had won a Pulitzer Prize for investigative reporting at the *Atlanta Constitution*, had been hired by the *Los Angeles Times* at the same time I had been hired by the *New York Times*. His editors, like mine, had rushed him to Selma to cover the erupting story. I was sitting on the grass during a break in the action one day when Jack walked up and introduced himself. Thus began a long friendship.

It was not uncommon for competing reporters to cover the story together. Aside from the companionship of like-minded people, the

arrangement offered a measure of safety. There was comfort in knowing that we were not alone in hostile streets. Jack and I often exchanged bits of information, checking for the accuracy of quotes, the spelling of names, middle initials, and other such details. Only when one of us had a clear scoop would we fail to share what we knew. That was understood and accepted without rancor. My paper competed briskly with Jack's; both were read every day by the public officials in Washington who made and enforced policy on civil rights. Along with the *Washington Post*, the *Washington Evening Star*, the *Baltimore Sun*, and the *Wall Street Journal*, ours were the papers that mattered in the White House and in Congress. The television networks were beginning to be influential, but in many cases they took their cues from the big national newspapers. It was common at Selma, for example, for a reporter for one of the three networks to tip me to a story so that it would appear first in the *Times*—which had the most extensive national coverage—and prompt his New York bosses to allow him to get on it, the story having been legitimized for the cautious TV managers.

Jack and I often traveled together from Atlanta to hot spots around the South. Jack had the same arrangement with Gene Roberts after Gene arrived from the *Detroit Free Press* to become the Southern bureau chief for our paper. They had been friends since their days as Nieman Fellows at Harvard. Gene, who later became known as the best newspaper editor in America for his extraordinary tenure at the *Philadelphia Inquirer*, was full of eccentricities that made him the target of good-humored fun. He resisted going to bed as stoutly as any high-strung child. He usually read books until well after midnight and as a consequence was hard to rouse up the next morning. One night in New Orleans, Gene stayed up until about three o'clock. Knowing that he and Jack were due in the federal courthouse early, he slipped a note under Jack's hotel door that said, "Jack—Get me up somehow."

Jack and I found ourselves in New Orleans several times during the mid-1960s. The usual reason was to cover this or that hearing involving the Ku Klux Klan in federal court. The courthouse was half a block from the Hotel Royal Orleans, where we always stayed. The hotel was luxurious. The restaurant was good. A rooftop bar was perfect for sipping gin-and-tonics and watching the ships go by in the Mississippi as the sun went down. It was also a good spot for trying to

unravel the incomprehensible geography of the city. Residents simply speak of uptown, downtown, river side and lake side. North, south, east, and west have no meaning except to puzzled visitors; no location in New Orleans lends itself to normal directions.

The French Quarter offered an array of entertainment, most of it innocent by the degraded standards of the twenty-first century. One night Jack and I strolled into a Bourbon Street club that featured go-go dancers. That was a new craze featuring scantily clad young women who danced on the tables. Jack and I drank salty dogs and admired the dancers at close range far into the night. I suspect that our tips were listed on our expense accounts. That was our first experience of go-go dancing and the salty dog, a kind of poor man's margarita.

He and I were in New Orleans on another occasion to cover a hearing in federal court for members of the Klan and some of their police buddies at Bogalusa, Louisiana. The hearing was abruptly adjourned so that we could get ready for Hurricane Betsy, which was roaring across the coast and headed for the city. A hurricane traditionally is— or was before the sobering disaster of Hurricane Katrina—an excuse for a party in New Orleans and along the Gulf Coast. People all over the French Quarter huddled and waited, drinks in hand and spirits high. Jack and I spent the evening in a Royal Orleans bar that sat a foot or two below street level. The threshold was already packed with sand bags. A piano player named Monique played "Milord" and comforted us against the rising wind.

I went to bed about ten o'clock. Jack lingered in the main doorway of the hotel lobby and watched the swinging signs and garbage cans hurtling down Royal Street. The wind had reached full force. As he watched, an auxiliary policeman came in from the fury and joined him. They stood chatting, and suddenly they saw a young woman running barefoot down the middle of the street. The policeman went out and stopped her and led her into the lobby. She was dressed up but was thoroughly disheveled. When they calmed her down, she told them she had gone out to get milk for her baby—dressed to the nines, which both men skeptically noted—and that a man had grabbed her and dragged her under a magnolia tree on the lawn of the federal courthouse and had tried to rape her. The policeman took her back to the lawn and, sure enough, there lay her purse and shoes. He brought

her back to the hotel and asked Jack to see her home. She lived a block or two away. She led Jack into her apartment building and started up the stairs. On the third-floor landing, a man opened a door and shouted in what sounded more like anger than anxiety, "Is that you?!" Jack fled and left the mother to her own devices.

The city was a mess the next morning. Businesses and houses were without power. Jack and I had rooms on the top floor, the seventh, and the elevators were not running. As we made our way down the stairs in semidarkness, we overtook a middle-aged couple in time to hear the woman say, with sharp chagrin, "I don't know why I came down here in the first place. I should have stayed in Akron."

Both Jack and I had been assigned to fly from New Orleans that day to a Southern governors' conference at Sea Island, Georgia. We picked up our wives in Atlanta and flew on to the resort. Our editors understood that this was to be more holiday than work, a reward for working too many sixteen-hour days. As we checked in at the hotel, the clerk handed me a message from Claude, my national editor. I phoned, and he ordered me back to Louisiana as fast as I could get there. The Associated Press had moved a bulletin saying that the death toll in the storm had passed three hundred—a major disaster. I was on the next plane back. I phoned Claude when I landed at New Orleans and learned that the report was a mistake. People had died—several dozen—but nowhere near three hundred. As long as you're there, Claude said, give us a second-day story.

I hitched a ride on a seaplane headed for the lower Mississippi River town of Venice, which had suffered quite a lot of damage. The pilot put me off and said I was on my own for the return; he had to get back in a hurry. I had only about an hour to interview survivors. One old man told me about spending most of the night tied with a rope to the top of a utility pole, watching dead cows and pieces of houses sweep by in the water only a few feet beneath him. He was finally rescued and led to a nearby dredge, where he remained soaked and miserable until daylight. I got a ride on an oil company plane back to New Orleans and somehow met my first-edition deadline of 6:30 p.m. It had been one of the most fretful but entirely satisfying days of my career. I was in a good enough humor about it until I remembered my friend Nelson, who had spent the day playing on the beach at Sea Island.

After the violence declined in the 1970s, I occasionally traveled with Jack on other stories. George Wallace ran four unsuccessful campaigns for president, and we covered parts of those together. Wallace's populist appeal was not entirely quixotic. He attracted millions of votes of disenchanted Americans who were fed up with various problems that they blamed on elitist liberals, the National Association for the Advancement of Colored People (NAACP), the American Civil Liberties Union (ACLU), labor unions, college professors, antiwar demonstrators, and—when they were at a loss for words—the federal government. Wallace invented a crowd-pleasing new target, "pointy-headed bureaucrats."

In his 1968 presidential campaign, Wallace hit on the apparently brilliant idea of naming as his running mate a World War II hero, the retired air force general Curtis LeMay. The general became famous as the first effective commander of the Strategic Air Command. His pilots had incinerated the major cities of Germany and Japan. When the Vietnam War continued to drag on seemingly without end, he caused considerable dismay by suggesting that the way to end it was to use nuclear weapons and "bomb them back to the Stone Age."

Wallace called a press conference in Washington to announce his choice. After he introduced the general, he stood aside and turned the microphone over to his new running mate.

LeMay, blunt-spoken and not given to lengthy speeches, made a few remarks and opened the press conference to questions. The first reporter on his feet was Nelson. What about bombing them back to the Stone Age? he asked. LeMay started answering. It quickly became obvious that he had no political skills. He was digging his hole deeper. Wallace watched in distress and anger; then, two or three minutes into the ordeal—with Nelson and other reporters on their feet demanding answers—Wallace took the microphone away from LeMay and called an end to the press conference.

The two candidates left town and headed across the country to different destinations. All of us assigned to Wallace joined him on his campaign plane. He hated flying and was said to fear airplanes, but he was in his seat at the front, game for anything if it would advance his campaign. Jack and I were toward the back, he next to the window and I on the aisle. As soon as the seat belt sign was turned off, Wallace leapt out of his seat and hurtled down the aisle. He leaned across me, jabbed

his finger into Jack's chest, and started shouting. Jack, who relished a disturbance of any kind, rose partly out of his seat and shouted back. It occurred to me that I was in the middle of what was about to become a fistfight. If blows were struck, I was in a fair way of suffering collateral damage. I remembered that the governor in his youth had been a Golden Gloves boxer, and I worried a little for my friend.

I phoned Jack many years later when he was in his last illness. "Those were wild times," he said. It was just after his eightieth birthday. I was pleased to find his voice and spirit strong. I asked whether he remembered the episode on the plane with Wallace. He did. I told him that I had worried that the governor, who had been a Golden Gloves champion, might beat up on him. Jack replied, with some heat, "Hell, I was a boxer, myself, when I was young." I couldn't see him, but I'm certain that he rose up off his pillow and that his eyes were full of fight.

The pancreatic cancer got him. He died a week later, on October 21, 2009.

■　■　■

As I review my work in the faded clippings, I am struck by how much of what we now recall as high drama in the civil rights movement was actually pedestrian and even tedious.

"Negroes Suspend Selma Protests," says the one-column headline on February 7, 1965. The demonstrators were taking a breather, and rather than record that simple fact I led the story with this featurized nongrabber: "A slow shower of rain that hinted of spring fell on Selma today and with the change in the weather came a lull in the Negro voter drive that has rubbed the city's nerves for the last three weeks."

Then there were the periodic arrivals and departures of the movement's most famous figure, Martin Luther King. Already, the nation's chief editors made sure that his every appearance was covered. It was almost a certainty in the editors' minds that sooner or later someone would try to kill him. The major news organizations dared not take the chance that the deed might occur on the one day they had no one on hand. Only the president got that same kind of around-the-clock coverage.

Between the dramatic marches and outrages, there were periods

of news that could hardly be called eye-catching. "Aide of Dr. King Sent to Natchez to Weigh the Next Rights Move." "Rights Unit Quits Parley in Capital." "TV Widens Crack in a Racial Wall; Jackson Station Has Brought Rights Hearings into Home."

Then, on April 2, a one-column headline in the *Times* read: "3 Bombs Planted in Birmingham." Any story with the words "bombs" and "Birmingham" in the lead was bound to appear on page 1. Eleven days earlier, six unexploded time bombs had been found in the Negro neighborhood. In this second round, only one exploded. It caused minor injuries to a black teenager. Two more bombs were found unexploded outside the homes of two white moderates, Mayor Albert Boutwell and City Councilwoman Nina Miglionico. Both bombs were big enough to level a house. They were also a timely exclamation mark by the Klan to mark the end of the Selma-Montgomery march.

The bombs got the attention of Governor Wallace. He interrupted a trip to Washington and returned to Birmingham to offer a $5,000 reward. After pointing out that bombings had occurred in other places outside of Alabama, notably in Chicago and Youngstown, Ohio, he said there was no excuse for it in his state. "We are not used to this," he said, with no hint of irony. "We are not going to tolerate it." He did not mention that this latest was Birmingham's twenty-third bombing or attempted bombing since 1956, that more than thirty bombs had been planted there since 1951, and that one in 1963 had killed four little African American girls in a church.

Once again, racial violence had entered the headlines during a short lull in the civil rights movement. King was tied up planning future activities, and nothing much was going on elsewhere in the South. I figure that the Klan, whatever else its shortcomings, had an eye for slow news days.

Then there was this headline that got my attention: "Negro Is Adviser to Faubus on Hiring." That might have gone unnoticed by a lot of readers, but I saw it as filled with ironic portent. Governor Faubus's stealthy return to his boyhood liberal ideals was one of the little-noticed stories of the civil rights era. The world knew of his apostasy in 1957 when he called out the National Guard to stop nine black students from integrating Central High School. The world followed the story for a year or two as he played out his part the way the ancient

Greek dramatists would have written it, the slow progression from early idealism into pragmatism and then finally the surrender to tragedy. What the world lost interest in was the next stage as he regained his foothold on reality. I went to Little Rock and wrote the story about his taking on as an unofficial adviser L. C. Bates, publisher of the city's militant black newspaper and, more to the point, husband of the civil rights heroine Daisy Bates.

Mrs. Bates was the bete noire of the segregationists in 1957 and for years afterward. Faubus had used her to frighten the white supremacists, and she had returned the favor by using him to rally her troops and raise money for the cause of integration. Her husband, the quiet mover and shaker in the marriage, saw practical advantages in making peace with Faubus as soon as the storm abated in the early 1960s. He knew that black Arkansawyers needed jobs, and he knew that Faubus could help provide them. Faubus worked in private with L. C. Bates for some years during the 1960s. Daisy Bates never gave the game away; she continued to speak nationally for integration, and when she needed to invoke Faubus's bad name she did so. Toward the end of their lives, Faubus reached out to her publicly, and she responded, not warmly but civilly.

When calm threatened to spread across the Deep South, more violence could be counted on. "New Violence Breaks Out in Negro Area of Atlanta as Several Fires Are Set." And now and then the totally unexpected: "Kennedy Cheered in Ole Miss Talk by Crowd of 5,000." That was the assassinated president's brother Robert, by then a senator from New York. Here's the opening paragraph of my story datelined Oxford, Mississippi, March 18, 1966: "Senator Robert F. Kennedy, once an object of general hatred in this state, was greeted with brimming cordiality today at the University of Mississippi."

He was destined to live two more years before being assassinated in Los Angeles during his campaign for president.

CHAPTER 9

Learning to Speak Times *Talk*

I spent all of 1965 and 1966 on the Southern beat before moving to Washington to help cover the White House. A large part of those two years was spent on normal political coverage. Stump speakings were becoming rare in South Carolina. Orval Faubus missed the filing deadline for a seventh term in 1966, signaling his retirement from the governor's office in Arkansas. The Democrats of Tennessee were split between friends of President Lyndon B. Johnson and those of his least favorite politician, Senator Robert F. Kennedy.

In Louisiana, one of the last of Huey P. Long's political associates, Senator Allen J. Ellender, was running for a sixth term. My story mentioned that Ellender had been presiding over a session of the state House of Representatives in Baton Rouge when Long was assassinated in a nearby corridor on September 8, 1935. His challenger in 1966 was Camille Gravel, a suave, well-spoken man who was known as a friend of the late President Kennedy and, not coincidentally, of Huey's younger brother Earl. Earl's man came in second. Both Longs were still revered, but Huey carried the mantle of martyrdom.

The civil rights story began to shift during my Southern tenure. Although we were barely aware of it at the time, our stories began to tell of African American victories along with the stubborn and often violent white resistance. With the political victories came the inevitable stories of petty corruption among some of the new black mayors, legislators, and county officials. I saw my old editor and friend Harry Ashmore not long after the new guys started showing their venality. "It's like I've been telling people," he said. "They're just like us, and we're no damned good."

Meanwhile, the job with the *Times* changed me. I realized sometime during my first year that I was becoming bilingual. I was starting to speak a form of standard American English. I had to learn the new tongue in my daily telephone conversations with my colleagues and bosses in New York. Claude Sitton and I spoke more or less the same language, but almost everyone else on and around the national desk spoke another tongue, the Northern version of English, the one that had been the national standard for many years.

I spoke the new language with the same difficulty that anyone encounters when he studies a foreign language. I reckon my accent gave me away in spite of my efforts to sound all my syllables and make myself understood. My daily encounters with the recording room in the newsroom, where three or four New Yorkers took phoned-in stories from around the world, were studies in comedy. The rule was that one of them monitored dictation from all the correspondents to make sure they understood all the words clearly. If he doubted a word, or was puzzled by a pronunciation, he interrupted and asked us to repeat it. I could count on half a dozen such requests during the dictation of every story of seven hundred words or more. (We had to get permission from the desk to exceed seven hundred words, the length of a standard column of type.)

One day I dictated a story about a river, and one line referred to "shooting rapids in a kayak." It came out in print, unchallenged by anyone from the recording room to the phalanx of copy editors, as "shooting rabbits in a kayak." Somehow, the mental image of rabbits riding a kayak was terrifically funny to my newsroom colleagues, and they took turns gibing me about it. In a less serious newspaper, the story would have been accompanied by a line drawing of a rabbit in a kayak looking nervously over his shoulder.

Speaking Southern was not just a matter of drawl or twang; it meant a different way of framing thoughts. South-speak is a mental and emotional posture. Many words are different. I used the word "reckon" earlier. Southerners, especially older ones, use the word in the same way Northerners use "think": "I reckon I'll get ready and go to town." "Proud" often means "glad" or "happy," as in "We're proud you could stop by." My grandfather Meredith was on his deathbed in St. Joseph's Hospital in Hot Springs with a cancer killing him. He was

in agony. My aunt Lola, who was attending him as he neared the end, said that he got up one last time and walked slowly to the bathroom. He came back, then lay down and said, "I'm going to die and I'm proud of it." Minutes later he did.

Dropping the final *g* in a word is not considered an affectation in the South. Indeed, sounding it often is. "Good old boy" was a term of affection in the South until the North picked it up and made it semi-pejorative. People who study the subject have suggested that language is more than a means of communicating thoughts, that it can identify a people and help define who they are. I won't get into that, but I suspect that Southerners historically have been different from other people partly because of the way they talk. As the language of Southerners has changed to accommodate to the national speech, perhaps the Southerners themselves have edged along toward a grudging accommodation to the national culture.

When I went to the work for the *Times* in 1965, regional differences were pronounced. I noticed it in an odd way in the newsroom on Forty-third Street. I was always sought out by the Southerners there, like Molly Ivins and Charlayne Hunter, when I visited the city. I think their mouth muscles were tired, and they needed someone to rest with.

Molly was already known at the paper for her humor and for padding around the newsroom barefoot. Her writing style, which was never fully appreciated in the upper reaches of the *Times*, would make her one of the nation's most popular columnists after she went home to Texas. After she and I had left the paper, she flew up from Austin to speak to the ACLU in Fayetteville, where I was teaching. I introduced her. As we sat on the speaker's platform before the program started, she noticed a video camera on a tripod aimed at the podium. She asked what it was. I explained that it belonged to the local cable station and that it probably meant the station intended to record her talk. "Does that mean I can't say 'shit' or 'fuck' or anything like that?" I told her that was up to her.

She kept it clean until halfway through the question period. Someone asked about her friend Ann Richards, the gravel-voiced governor of Texas. Ms. Richards had recently defeated a muddle-headed millionaire who had mistaken her for a demure little lady. Molly gave a straightforward answer to the ACLU questioner, then couldn't resist

telling this story, and the camera be damned: She had been at a dinner party in Austin a few weeks earlier, and among the guests was Ms. Richards. A man arrived late and explained to the table that he had passed a striking beauty on the way and that he had circled back for another look. "She had a pair of titties that were like this." He demonstrated with his cupped hands. "They were the size of cantaloupes." The next voice heard was the governor's foghorn drawl: "You girls seen any good dicks lately?" Molly said that she was searching for an appropriate answer when another woman beat her to it. "No," the woman said, "but I saw a great pair of balls the other day. They were as big as watermelons!"

I assumed that the cable station would edit out that story. It did not. They ran the whole thing. Over and over.

CHAPTER 10

The Murky Pearl and Other Graveyards

I inherited a considerable body of running stories on race and civil rights when I moved into the Southern beat for the *Times*. Some were still alive and needing my periodic attention. Others had seemingly faded into history. You could stand blindfolded and throw a dart at a map of Mississippi and hit a place where some outrage had been committed during recent years.

One old story with uncanny staying power was a lynching that ended in a river. The Pearl River starts in Mississippi, loops briefly through Louisiana, then returns to Mississippi and empties into the Gulf of Mexico. It is quite pretty. In its lower regions, near the coast, it takes on the brownish cast common to coastal rivers throughout the region. In the South, these coastal rivers tend to be shaded by cypresses, oaks, and other lowland trees that we associate with days of languor and nights of mystery.

The official records list only two bodies of black men dumped in the Pearl. The first lynching had been misted over in the memory of the press by the time I started covering Mississippi. A black man named Joe Rodgers of Canton was murdered because he refused to allow $5.50 a week to be deducted from his wages to help pay for a company-owned cabin that he never used. The mob shot, tortured, and slashed him with knives, then dumped his body into the Pearl near Canton, north of Jackson. That was in 1939.

The second lynching occurred in 1959. The blameless stream that received the body that time became known from then on as "the

murky Pearl." Mack Charles Parker was arrested on suspicion that he had raped a white woman as she waited for help in her stalled car on a rural road in Pearl River County, Mississippi. A mob took him from the county jail and drove away. Days later, his bullet-riddled body was found in the Pearl near Bogalusa, Louisiana, a few miles south of the Mississippi border. No arrests were made. The "murky Pearl" returned to print every time a news organization remembered the case for years to come. In 2009, someone remembered that no one had ever been brought to justice and said that time was running out. Once again, the Pearl was identified as "murky." Most likely, the angel of death had already meted out justice. Even murderers run out of time eventually.

When I arrived on the scene in the mid-1960s, Mack Charles Parker's name was still vivid in the nation's memory. So was the river where his body was found. The Pearl enters the Gulf a few miles east of New Orleans, and after I moved to that city in 1969 I found myself driving east to the Mississippi coast one day. Suddenly I was crossing a river and realized that I was looking down on the murky Pearl.

For every Mack Charles Parker, the South has uncounted numbers of other victims whose names appear on no museum plaques. I'm thinking of a father and son I encountered in some woebegone stretch of piney woods in Mississippi in the 1970s. The father cut and hauled pulpwood for a paper mill. Several billet haulers, as they were called, had traded at my dad's store outside Hot Springs when I was young. Most of them were black, as were the father and son I met in Mississippi. Their trucks were invariably worn out. Working in pulpwood was considered not only the lowliest but also the hardest work that a man could do. I spent a few weeks cutting and loading pulpwood one summer when I was a teenager. If I were forced to do it again, I would cut my throat.

I had sought out a pulpwood hauler to feature in a story about uneducated manual laborers. The boy, who was about ten, had gone along to help in small ways. The father and I chatted as he worked. He was not a large man; his face was older than his years. He described his work in language that relied more on gestures than words. I think he told me he could not read or write. As he reached some point in the loading of the wood, he turned to the boy and told him to do some simple task. The boy tried and failed. The man jumped down from the truck and fell upon his son and flailed him with his fists until his rage was spent. The

boy lay whimpering on the dirt. The father stood and turned away from me in shame. I turned away from him in a shame of my own.

■　■　■

I worked out of the Atlanta bureau from 1965 to 1967, but most of my reporting was from Alabama, Mississippi, and Louisiana. I have only vague memories of time spent in Virginia, the Carolinas, and Florida. I covered political stories all across the South. But the race stories that occupied me and other national reporters occurred mainly in Alabama, Mississippi, and Louisiana, with occasional forays into south Georgia and elsewhere.

Almost invariably, those stories told of desperate attempts by segregationist leaders to maintain the white supremacy that had held sway since the days of slavery and right on down through Reconstruction, Jim Crow, the lynching years, and political oppression in all its forms. Some efforts were raw, brutal, and murderous. Others were more refined and subtle. But almost always the goal was the same: maintenance of the unequal status quo. In more than a few areas of the Upper South, the status quo had given way peacefully to limited accommodation of the black minority. Little Rock was cited as an example of that until Governor Faubus and his racist supporters changed the city's reputation in 1957.

It is not necessary to recount in detail the region's moderate advances from World War II and into the 1950s. Those took place mostly but not altogether in the border and upland states. Georgia was Deep South, but its capital, Atlanta, was an island of moderation. The city had made noticeable strides toward equality by the time the civil rights movement made that city its unofficial headquarters in the 1950s. A prosperous black middle class produced many of the movement's leaders. Paschal's soul food restaurant provided a daily meeting place for the movement's planners—with the added convenience of allowing black and white movement leaders to eat and plot at the same tables in open defiance of the city's segregation laws. That was an old Southern dodge: pass a law, then ignore it if the law becomes inconvenient. Liquor was handled that way. Ban it to satisfy the devout, but look the other way to satisfy the thirsty sinners.

All of us wrote about racial progress from time to time, but the bloody resistance necessarily claimed most of our energies. And slowly the rest of the nation lost patience with Dixie's never-enders. One of the great tests of American patience came with the murder of Viola Liuzzo and the unsatisfying efforts to bring her murderers to justice.

Equally frustrating was the quest for justice for the murderers of the three young civil rights workers James Chaney, Andrew Goodman, and Michael Schwerner in Neshoba County, Mississippi, in 1964. Mississippi refused to try anyone for their murder. Until their bodies were found in an earthen dam, the governor suggested that they were probably hiding in Cuba. The feds stepped in, rounded up eighteen members and friends of the Ku Klux Klan, charged them with depriving the three of their civil rights by killing them, and held a trial. Again, the results were frustrating. Seven of the eighteen were found guilty and sentenced to terms of three to ten years. No one served more than six years. Sheriff Lawrence Rainey was acquitted, although his deputy, Cecil Price, was convicted. There is a famous photograph taken before the trial showing Rainey slouched on a courtroom bench. His jaw is bloated with chewing tobacco. The photo still adorns old civil rights posters around the country.

A determined investigative reporter named Jerry Mitchell at Jackson's *Clarion-Ledger* forced a reopening of the old case in 2005. The purported planner and director of the murders, a part-time Baptist preacher named Edgar Ray Killen, was finally convicted in a state court—not of murder, but of manslaughter. He was sentenced to three consecutive terms of twenty years. He was 80 years old when he went to the pen. He will be 140 when he gets out, barring health complications.

While we're remembering old crimes and misdemeanors in Neshoba County, Mississippi, let me bring up one more that has been almost obliterated in the national memory. Ronald Reagan was chosen by the Republican Party to oppose President Jimmy Carter for a second term in 1980. Mr. Reagan chose Neshoba County as the jumping-off place for his campaign in the South. The subject of his speech was "states' rights."

Mr. Carter, who never warmed up to Mr. Reagan after the old actor defeated him, recalled the Neshoba County speech in his late-life memoir *White House Diary*. He reminded his readers that Reagan had

been endorsed by the Ku Klux Klan. Referring to the Neshoba County speech, he wrote, "As he and his campaign staff well knew, that place had strong symbolic meaning for Southerners for whom the race issue was important."

The well-mannered Georgian was too easy on the guy. Reagan's choosing that county, the site of the most infamous racial lynching of the civil rights era, to speak on "states' rights" was loathsome. Several of the Klansmen who murdered the three young men were still alive in 1980. It is possible that some were in the candidate's audience that day. To them, Reagan's message was clear and brutal: It's all right to murder the uppity niggers and white do-gooders who are trying to destroy your Southern way of life.

■　　■　　■

Some of the segregationists of that time became famous. George C. Wallace tried several times to parlay the governorship of Alabama and his pugnacious resistance into the presidency. Faubus swapped his youthful principles for six terms in the Arkansas governor's office. Lester Maddox won the Georgia governor's office by brandishing a pistol and threatening to use pick handles to keep Negroes out of his popular Atlanta eating place, the Pickrick Cafeteria. Almost every Southern state had its segregationist hero whose light shone brightly for a moment, then sputtered and went out.

A few nourished a lasting notoriety. In Plaquemines Parish, Louisiana, an odd spit of land thrown up centuries ago by the Mississippi River where it approaches the Gulf of Mexico, a feudal lord named Leander Perez expanded his fame to national dimensions by telling the federal government to take its civil rights laws and put them where the sun don't shine. His henchmen kept black citizens firmly in their place, sometimes with violence. He kept a prison on an island in the river. Civil rights workers were routinely parked there for long periods. None dared to escape by swimming the river. That would have been suicide.

I showed up at Judge Perez's office just before lunch one day, announced who I was, and was immediately invited to lunch with him and his courthouse colleagues. Perez led the way from his office at the end of a long hall. He placed me beside him in a position of honor. As

we passed each office along the hall, his handpicked team of elected officials fell in behind us, apparently in a rigid pecking order that remained in place as we marched single-file along a graveled highway shoulder to a nearby cafe. We seated ourselves at lunch in the same order.

I sat at the right hand of the boss, and as the lunch got under way—food appeared magically, obviously preordered—it became clear that I was the entertainment of the day, provided on the sudden like a gift from God. With the judge leading the way, each official took his turn poking fun at me and the national press. Years' worth of stored-up venom was directed at my paper. I had no choice but to listen, grin, and pretend to enjoy it. I felt like a worn-out pincushion as I drove back to New Orleans.

Earl K. Long, a friend of black citizens during the last years of the segregationist resistance, was governor of Louisiana during that time. He once directed a press conference question to the absent Perez. "What you gonna do now, Leander?" he said. "The feds have got the A-bomb!"

I have wondered what would have happened if Perez's parish had seceded from the union. There was enough anger among the whites of Plaquemines Parish, and enough disgust with the parish in the rest of the United States, to make it a realistic option. I can't imagine a twentieth-century Lincoln sending troops into the swamps to keep that crowd in the union. The new nation would have consisted of a hundred-mile stretch of the Mississippi River with just its banks and adjacent marshes. Land in Plaquemines that is fit to build on is barely wider than an eighteen-hole golf course on either side of the river. The sovereign nation of Plaquemines would have had more water than land. Without the U.S. Army Corps of Engineers to maintain the river levees and fight back the encroaching Gulf of Mexico, the country would have had a lifespan of about thirty years. It would have gone under water about 1990.

Mark Twain in *Life on the Mississippi* said he had read in some learned article that the great river had been growing steadily shorter over the centuries by overflowing its curves and twists and thereby becoming straighter. He deduced that the time would come a few centuries hence when the river would be so short that New Orleans and

Cairo, Illinois, would be twin cities. He surmised that in the distant past the Mississippi had stuck out over the Gulf of Mexico hundreds of miles, like a fishing pole. There's an entertaining thought: the ancient nation of Leander Perez lying cheek by jowl with Venezuela, making him neighbor to some Latin American warlord who would have appreciated his politics and made him feel at home.

CHAPTER 11

A Funeral Oration

Selma was only the geographic core of the racial turbulence in Alabama during the mid-1960s. The efforts of SNCC and SCLC brought out predictable hostility right across the state's Black Belt in 1964 and 1965.

I was on the scene less than a month in the winter of 1965 when the nearby town of Marion produced a killing—a particularly gratuitous one by the law enforcement agency of the state of Alabama, it seemed—that was judged in later years to have been the spark that ignited the famous march to Montgomery. We in the press didn't understand that at the time, but we covered it diligently as a breaking daily story.

Jimmie Lee Jackson was a solid but seemingly ordinary citizen of the black community. He was a deacon of his church by age twenty-five. He had a girlfriend, an adoring mother, and a protective grandfather. Then the movement came to town. James Orange, one of Dr. King's workers, led a demonstration and was jailed for it. His associates used that to stir up sentiment for the voting rights campaign. There was a march to the jail the night of February 18. It met a phalanx of policemen, sheriff's deputies, and state troopers. Suddenly the lights went out, with no explanation, and the cops waded in with clubs.

I was not there. My friend Richard Valeriani, a correspondent for NBC News, was. A freelance enforcer knocked him in the head with an ax handle and sent him to a hospital. The cops beat a couple of other photographers and smashed their cameras.

But the treatment of the press was not important. The main victims that night were the black protesters. Jimmie Lee Jackson, his mother, Viola, and his grandfather Cager Lee ran into a café to try to

escape the raging lawmen. The officers cornered them there and began flailing away at Jackson's mother and grandfather. As the young man ran to protect his mother, a state trooper hurled him against a cigarette machine. Then he shot him twice. After the trooper was indicted for murder—about two generations afterward, during one of the fits of guilt that afflicted the South around the end of the twentieth century —he said Jackson was trying to take his pistol from him. I find that believable. I try imagining what I hope I would have done if I had encountered a policeman beating my mother with a club.

Jackson lived several days in a hospital, long enough to identify his assailant to agents of the FBI. More than forty years later, an enterprising reporter got the case reopened. The trooper, James Bonard Fowler, eventually pleaded guilty to manslaughter and, in 2010, was sentenced to six months in jail.

I went to Marion in 1965 for the funeral. The lead on my story was a calm enough statement: "Jimmie Lee Jackson was proclaimed a martyr and buried in a country graveyard here today."

Then I turned to the funeral sermon. Martin Luther King's eulogy was the most eloquent condemnation of evil that I had ever heard. It also put into words the rage that nearly everyone in the church felt. Listen to that still-familiar voice:

> He was murdered by the indifference of every white minister of the gospel who has remained silent behind the safe security of his stained-glass windows.
>
> He was murdered by the irresponsibility of every politician from governors on down who has fed his constituents the stale bread of hatred and the spoiled meat of racism.
>
> He was murdered by the timidity of a federal government that is willing to spend millions of dollars a day to defend freedom in Vietnam but cannot protect the rights of its citizens at home.
>
> He was murdered by the brutality of every sheriff who practices lawlessness in the name of the law.
>
> And he was murdered by the cowardice of every Negro who passively accepts the evils of segregation and stands on the sidelines in the struggle for justice.

Every sentence was punctuated by a swelling of "Amen!" from the congregation.

Few reporters carried tape recorders during those days. Those of us in the church understood that we had heard an oration for the ages, and we huddled in small groups comparing notes to make sure we had the words right. I once wrote on another occasion that I could still hear Dr. King's voice in the nautilus of my memory. I still hear it. His sentences, every one perfectly crafted, had no room for "uh" or "ah." I think he never uttered "you know" or "I mean," even in the private conversations that I had with him occasionally. I remember that he laughed. He was not a solemn man except in the pulpit. But even in his informality he used the English language with respect and love.

Meanwhile, the brutality of the resistance gathered force. And with each new outrage, the national revulsion built.

Two weeks after the shooting of Jimmie Lee Jackson in Marion, a Unitarian Universalist minister from Boston named James Reeb was clubbed fatally with an ax handle on a street in Selma. That happened just two days after Bloody Sunday, the aborted march that ended at Pettus Bridge, and after Dr. King had issued a nationwide call for white ministers to descend on Selma to continue the march to Montgomery. About 450 did so. Reeb, the father of four children, a devout man who had chosen to work in the poorest and most dangerous wards of Boston and Washington because his conscience had led him there, died in a Birmingham hospital two days after the attack. He was thirty-eight years old. President Johnson seized the highly publicized death of a white man to promote passage of the voting rights bill, and Congress passed it a few days later.

There was a good bit of bitterness that it took the murder of a white man to get the federal government off its rear end. The murder of a black deacon defending his mother was not enough. Alabama justice, however, treated the victims equally. The four men involved in the murder of Reeb got off, three with an outright acquittal and the fourth by running away to Mississippi, where he found safety.

CHAPTER 12

Bigots I Have Known

The other big civil rights story of 1965 was in Louisiana. There are people in New Orleans who claim they have never been north of Lake Pontchartrain except to travel in Europe. They see nothing of interest and little of real civilization north of the lake. Those folks have not got over the shock of being declared Americans against their will a couple of centuries ago.

The objects of their scorn are personified in the north-of-the-lake Anglo-Saxon town of Bogalusa. The town got its name from a Choctaw term, *bogue lusa,* meaning "dark water." The countryside is pine forest drained by slow-moving streams. The pines have been the economic mainstay of the area for more than a hundred years. The town was established as a colonial outpost by a Northern company that owned an immense swath of woods extending from southern Mississippi almost to Lake Pontchartrain. After the virgin timber was all cut, the company turned to paper manufacturing. The Crown-Zellerbach mill was the main employer in the 1960s when I paid my first visit there.

Bogalusa is seventy miles north of New Orleans. More pertinently, it is a ten-minute drive from Mississippi. The state border is the Pearl River, Mack Charles Parker's tomb. The jail from which he was dragged is in Poplarville, Mississippi, only a few miles east of the state border.

That same year, Washington Parish—Bogalusa is the parish seat—had contorted an old Reconstruction law that had been designed to protect Negroes to strike 1,377 of the parish's 1,510 Negro voters from the rolls. It took action from the Justice Department and eventually a Supreme Court decision to get them restored.

Washington Parish's action had set the stage for one of the most bizarre episodes in Louisiana history. Governor Earl K. Long was trying to persuade the legislature to change the old registration law so that it no longer could be used to discriminate against Negroes. He was opposed by a strong contingent of white supremacists led by a stiff-necked state senator named Willie Rainach from the Protestant Bible Belt of northern Louisiana.

At the height of the debate, the governor elbowed his way onto the floor of the legislature, probably against all the rules, and grabbed the microphone. There he delivered the most inelegant rebuke of a racist demagogue that I have ever heard. A. J. Liebling, writing for the *New Yorker*, described it.

Pointing to Rainach, Long said, "After all this is over, he'll probably go up there to Summerfield, get up on his front porch, take off his shoes, wash his feet, look at the moon and get close to God." Liebling said the governor shouted, "And when you do, you got to recognize that niggers is human beings!"

It reminded me of his brother Huey's promising a group of black leaders that he would get black nurses hired at the new Charity Hospital in New Orleans. You won't like the way I do it, he said, but I'll get it done. He defused possible white opposition by putting it about that he was not going have white nurses forced to look after black male patients.

During the days-long contretemps between Earl Long and Rainach—whom Long called "a little pissant"—the governor's mind finally came unhinged. He had to be led off by a kindly newspaper woman and shortly afterward was institutionalized for an emotional breakdown.

Margaret Dixon, on whose arm the governor was led from the chamber, had covered Louisiana's serpentine politics for years and had developed a kind of fondness for old Earl. She was editor of the *Baton Rouge Morning Advocate* and was one of a handful of women newspaper editors in the United States. Women editors are numerous now, but in those days the conventional view was that women had no place in the profane atmosphere of a newsroom. Their tender sensibilities could not stand it, and they risked being sullied for life.

I remember a couple of other exceptions in Arkansas. My friend

Tom Dearmore, whose family had deep roots in an Ozarks newspaper, found out that his young cousin Ginger Shiras had quit journalism to go to law school. He said he guessed that was all right, but he had always thought a woman's place was in the newsroom. Then there was Matilda Tuohey, who at various times was the only female reporter at the *Arkansas Gazette*. Early on, she wondered what she would have to do to fit in. She took up smoking, drinking, and cussing and discovered that those habits agreed with her. By the time I got there, the place fit her like a glove. Her nickname was "Tiger."

Maggie Dixon might have been tender-hearted, but she was also one of the toughest journalists of her generation. She had been a stringer for the *New York Times* for years when I arrived on the scene in the mid-1960s. She guided me through the political thickets of Louisiana and kept me from making silly mistakes. For good measure, she introduced me to the capital's best restaurants. A Louisiana libel that refuses to die is that Baton Rouge has no decent food. That is only by comparison with New Orleans; up against the cuisines of any other state capital, Baton Rouge is in a class of its own. It is disappointing, however, if measured against any crossroads Cajun town to its west where you can feed on crawfish, turtles, alligator meat, and other unexpected delicacies that are considered beneath the attention of city cooks.

Mrs. Dixon and A. J. Liebling were responsible for a fair amount of my political education when I began to cover Louisiana, first as a roving Southern reporter in 1965 and later, from 1969 until 1977, as the chief of a one-man bureau operating across and beyond the South from the spare bedroom of my house in New Orleans. Liebling explained to my satisfaction why Louisiana was different from all the other Southern states, not just in its French-Spanish-Balkan and all-around polyglot history but in its Mediterranean attitude to the present day. He remarked several times during his lengthy visit on how this or that political event or person reminded him of Lebanon. He sketched an imaginary map of what he called the Mediterranean littoral extending from Lebanon to North America. Louisiana, he said, was the "westernmost Arab state." He was referring to a ruthless cunning in politics and commerce that held idealism and reform impulses in low esteem.

I still treasure some of Liebling's imagery. I collect sentences the way some people collect primitive art, and I must share a couple from

my Liebling collection. Here he is describing an angry exchange between Governor Long, who is on the speaker's platform at a rally in Alexandria, and a heckler whose voice cannot be heard by most of the crowd. Long becomes increasingly agitated. Liebling writes, "It sounded like a dialogue between a man with the horrors and his hallucinations."

Later in the same speech, after he has regained his composure, Long is portrayed with these words: "The expressions on the Governor's face changed with the poetry of his thought, now benign, now mischievous, now indignant. Only the moist hazel eyes remained the same, fixed on a spot above and to the rear of the audience as if expecting momentarily the arrival of a posse."

The governor's emotional breakdown on the floor of the legislature led to several weeks of indignities. He was subjected to what he considered barbaric treatment in institutions in Texas and Louisiana before he more or less forcibly escaped. Once back in a Louisiana asylum, and within the jurisdiction of his own state, he used his position as governor to fire the doctor in charge and signed himself out. Then he left the state again, heading west, accompanied by state troopers and a flock of reporters. He patronized a string of race tracks in several states. Visiting Juarez, Mexico, long enough to pick up a supply of two-dollar champagne, he had a memorable encounter there with a gaggle of photographers and offered to shoot one with his pistol. He told a radio interviewer back home who had got wind of the episode, "I looked up at the transom and there was one of them bastards about to climb through it. I started to throw that champagne bottle at him."

He stopped at Hot Springs for a leisurely visit, during the horse-racing season, then returned home to start one more election campaign, for a seat in Congress. He won, but died before he could move to Washington. Liebling argued that old Earl never got the recognition he deserved as a civil rights advocate.

The governor never forgave his wife, Miz Blanche, for her part in having him sent to the nuthouse, as he called it. One entertaining but sensibly incomplete biography of Earl was a movie, *Blaze*. The movie picks up post-Blanche (she is never mentioned), after Odysseus's return from his adventures, as Liebling puts it, and after he has started a very public affair with a Bourbon Street stripper named Blaze Starr.

Earl is played by Paul Newman. The governor, had he been alive, could not have found a better earthly incarnation to represent his interests.

■ ■ ■

Meanwhile, back in Bogalusa, the contending forces were mobilizing. The Supreme Court had restored the black voters who had been stricken from the registration rolls. The Ku Klux Klan redoubled its organizing efforts to repel the black peril. A small group of white political moderates, notably including Mayor Jesse Cutrer, drafted a statement to be signed by large numbers and published in the paper to show the world that Bogalusa was not in the hands of bigots and extremists. The statement said that the undersigned believed in law and order. They couldn't get enough signatures to avoid embarrassment. The town's black leaders and their voting rights organization were left to stand up to the Klan almost alone.

My boss, Claude Sitton, was a genius at spotting trouble before it exploded. He had covered the South and seemed to know every country store and filling station. He somehow divined that Bogalusa was about to boil over during the spring of 1965, and he told me to get over there. I arrived just in time to see a minor traffic accident touch off a small riot.

It was April 9, 1965. James Farmer, the national director of the Congress of Racial Equality (CORE), was leading a march to protest the Klan's harassment of the town's black citizens. At the main intersection, several young white men began to shout insults at the marchers. One went after Farmer with a blackjack. He was held off by a white policeman. Others attacked an FBI agent and a *Life* magazine photographer. Things were about to get out of hand, and an assistant police chief rushed down the street in his car to help put down the disturbance. A white guy blinded by rage raced across the street and was struck down by the speeding car. He was taken to the hospital with a broken pelvis.

The victim's friends poured into the street full of wrath and beer and quickly found themselves fighting on two fronts. First, they attacked the mostly black marchers with fists, hand-lettered signs nailed to sticks, and any other tools at hand. Then they began fighting the police, who, until moments before, had been seen as friends of the

white supremacists. Indeed, several cops were later exposed as Klan members or sympathizers. The police ordered the marchers to turn back, and they did.

I was in and out of Bogalusa for the next two months as the violence ebbed and flowed and negotiations plodded on. At one point, the moderate governor of Louisiana, John McKeithen, persuaded Vice President Hubert H. Humphrey to intervene.

The talking abruptly stopped June 2. That night, Washington Parish's two Negro sheriff's deputies—the first in the parish's modern history—were ambushed a few miles north of Bogalusa. One was shot to death and the other wounded. A white paper-mill worker was arrested an hour later a few miles across the Pearl River in Mississippi.

Protest demonstrations erupted with renewed force. And with the rise of tempers, a black organization that held nonviolence in open contempt pushed itself across my line of sight for the first time.

It was called the Deacons for Defense and Justice. I wrote what was probably the first full-length magazine story about it for the *New York Times Magazine*. The story took me to northern Louisiana, to the paper-mill town of Jonesboro, where the Deacons were started during the summer of 1964. As in Bogalusa, the Klan had effectively taken over the town. Its mission was to smother any civil rights campaign in its cradle. It burned crosses. It paraded loudly through the streets of the black community. The last straw was one such parade, twenty-five cars driven at full speed led by a police car. It was the police escort that pushed the men of the neighborhood into action. A group of Negro veterans, men skilled with firearms, quietly gathered and made an inventory of guns and ammunition. Members were signed up. They named their organization Deacons because those are the men who support and protect a church congregation. From that day on, any marauding Klansmen could expect to be greeted by gunfire, and some were.

The immediate result was grimly comical. I described it in the magazine article. The formerly leisurely ritual of a cross-burning had been modified to speed it up. Two cars were now used. In the first, a man in the passenger seat planted the cross, presoaked in kerosene, on the chosen lawn. The second car surged forward, and one of its passengers struck a match to the cross. Then they all roared off to safety.

I interviewed the Bogalusa leader of the Deacons, Charles Sims,

in his car. The first thing I noticed was a very large pistol on the bench seat between us. Sims had a police record that included assault and carrying a concealed weapon. Once the Deacons got under way in Bogalusa, his gun came out of hiding. The news quickly flashed across the racial divide.

Sims made one of his first public appearances at the funeral of the slain deputy, O'Neal Moore. James Farmer flew in for the occasion, and Sims, with his pistol at the ready, escorted him from the airport.

The Deacons drew blood during a Bogalusa demonstration July 8. A white spectator was apparently incensed by the sight of a white nurse getting into a car with two Negro men and an injured Negro girl. He began pummeling the two men in their faces, managing somehow to strike both of them through the open car windows.

One of the men pulled a pistol and shot him. He survived but came close to becoming the next fatality in the Washington Parish race war. The two black men in the car were tentatively identified as Deacons. The police chief sounded frustrated when he explained to out-of-state reporters that he had no authority to disarm the Deacons. Under Louisiana law, he said, anyone could carry a gun in his car. The gun toters of Louisiana still enjoy that right.

While the outnumbered moderates struggled, the segregationist vanguard found still another way to fight. Someone dug up an old state statute prohibiting common-law marriages, which were common in the black community. The law provided up to a year in prison and a fine of $1,000 for each violation. The head of the New Orleans–area Citizens Council happily predicted that thousands of black outlaws would soon fill the prisons. To show they meant business, the Bogalusa Citizens Council swore out warrants for the arrest of "three prominent niggers" in the equal rights movement. The three were not named, but one was believed to be Charles Sims.

A muddy lot on the edge of town was the local Speakers' Corner for racist harangues. Two prominent speakers there were J. B. Stoner of Atlanta and Connie Lynch of Riverside, California. The two men traveled the country together promoting white supremacy. They held forth there night after night that summer. Stoner was a lawyer from Georgia who specialized in defending Klan members who had run amok. He eventually became an appeals attorney for James Earl Ray

after Ray had been convicted of assassinating Martin Luther King. Lynch was a preacher. One night when I was in the audience, they took turns addressing about fifteen hundred mad white folks. The message was that it was time for whites to start fighting back.

The Deacons, with some logic, took the position that it was black folks' turn to fight back. The local blood feud had been going in the Klan's favor for a long time. Stoner's words seemed to suggest that he could see into the future, though, and he was not optimistic. His advice was explicit: arm yourselves and stock up on ammunition. Meanwhile, before armed hostilities began, he advised using the law. He endorsed the Louisiana Citizens Council's plan to jail the thousands who were breaking the common-law-marriage law. He said he intended to export the idea all across the South.

Stoner's philosophical underpinning was this: "The nigger is not a human being. He is somewhere between the white man and the ape. We don't believe in tolerance. We don't believe in getting along with our enemy, and the nigger is our enemy."

And then, the clincher: "What the nigger really wants is our white women."

African Americans were not his only targets. He believed that "being a Jew [should be] a crime punishable by death." Hitler, he said, was too moderate.

Earl Long had been dead about five years when Stoner showed up in Louisiana. I wondered how the old man would have taken the news that niggers were not human beings. But basic science, then as now, is not considered reliable in much of the South, and Long's assertion of the black man's humanity was seen in some quarters as dangerously avant-garde. Stoner knew that his followers were in sync with his own more skeptical scholarship.

He had other credentials that added authority to his message. In 1964, he had run for vice president on the National States Rights Party ticket. Before that, he had been the imperial wizard of the Christian Knights of the Ku Klux Klan. He had a proven record of effectiveness. The same year he ran for vice president, he and his friend Lynch had stirred up white mobs in St. Augustine, Florida, that provided violence in the streets for several months. I had missed St. Augustine—it was

before I started to work for the *Times*—so Bogalusa was my first encounter with him.

I have never seen so profound a hatred in the breast of so ordinary a man. I had witnessed true believers in Arkansas, but they seemed to lack the will to murder for the cause. A few had toyed with bombing the homes and offices of their enemies, but their incompetence had saved them from homicide. Some others had been swept up in the passion and anger of the moment and had used fists, feet, and clubs. Their leaders except for a gifted few had shown none of the rhetorical skills of the man I heard that night in Bogalusa.

Stoner died in 2005 at age eighty-one. His obituary noted that he had been indicted for involvement in the bombing of an empty church in Birmingham in 1958. He dodged justice for twenty-two years but was finally convicted in 1980. He served six years in prison. He lived his last years in a Georgia nursing home partly paralyzed by a stroke. He never repented of his sins, but he publicly admitted toward the end that his side had lost.

Maybe he died with that bitter regret on his mind. I take solace in believing that he did, and if I happen to make his acquaintance in Hell, I'll tell him that. He will no doubt reply that he left plenty of his seed behind.

I remember an editorial written by Jerry Neil for the *Arkansas Gazette* when Senator Joseph R. McCarthy died in 1957. Jerry recounted the senator's long list of offenses and concluded, "Joe was a bad guy, and the evil that he did will live after him." Jerry was right. Joe's kind still thrives, and so does Jesse Benjamin Stoner's.

The federal government finally stepped in and called a halt to the anarchy in Bogalusa. The Justice Department's argument was that, contrary to popular opinion in southeast Louisiana, the authorities in Washington still had some voice in what went on in the territory between Canada and Mexico.

It was judges who took the first step in restoring the rule of law in Bogalusa. That was the case in one jurisdiction after another in the South during the 1950s and 1960s. Local authorities dropped the ball. State authorities dragged their feet. Finally, the federal judiciary stepped in. The same pattern was followed in every state of the old

Confederacy. The judges did good work, but at the cost of inciting a deep hatred of the "dictatorial" federal courts among the never-enders.

The beginning of the end in Washington Parish came with a lawsuit by CORE. The suit complained that the Klan was running rampant in the parish and that the local lawmen were doing little to stop it and in fact were abetting the violence and harassment. Federal district judge Herbert W. Christenberry of New Orleans, a normally genial old gentleman, ordered the cops to do their job and protect people's constitutional rights.

When there was no sign that the police were paying attention, President Johnson sent John Doar, the Justice Department's Lone Ranger, to Bogalusa. On his motion, the police chief and his assistant were ordered to New Orleans to explain why their men had not obeyed the judge's order.

The hearing began with a motion picture showing Bogalusa policemen standing by doing nothing while white men attacked and harassed civil rights demonstrators. One out-of-state demonstrator was beaten almost unconscious, then was arrested and jailed by a nearby cop.

The gentlemanly old judge got mad. He cited the police for contempt. He went on to say that the trouble seemed to be caused by a small group of white people "who simply will not recognize that Washington Parish is part of the United States and that its inhabitants are subject to the laws of the United States." And, he said, he was saddened to see that white women, "who ordinarily would be expected to show compassion, apparently were enjoying the beating of a defenseless man."

Then he rubbed it in.

"We have seen, too, the use of the Confederate flag, which once in the South was almost sacred, to foment trouble and encourage people to attack and assault individuals who were merely seeking to exercise their constitutional rights."

Six weeks later, the Justice Department went after the Klan in earnest. The outfit was hauled into federal court, and this time it faced not only Judge Christenberry but two others, a three-judge panel. One of the others was the redoubtable John Minor Wisdom, one of the two or three most courageous judges in the South during those days—all

appointed not by the supposedly liberal President John F. Kennedy but by his conservative predecessor, Dwight D. Eisenhower. That was a luxury enjoyed back then by the South's minority party. It could afford to send its best and brightest to the federal judiciary because it was beholden to no pack of local demagogues.

The Grand Dragon and his lieutenant, the Grand Titan, had a lot of trouble on the stand with their memory. They also regretted to inform the court that all the organization's records had been destroyed. Also, they said, the Klan had developed such an unfortunate reputation that it had disbanded and had been succeeded by the Anti-Communist Christian Association. The Grand Dragon, Charles Christmas, testified that the Klan had been a pretty "loose-knit" organization and that he didn't really know much about it. Judge Christenberry observed, "I think the Klan has a very loose Grand Dragon. I think you can answer some of these questions if you will." Judge Wisdom weighed in with a warning that "this court will not be trifled with."

The Kluxers were accused of violating the year-old 1964 Civil Rights Act, which protected people who presumed to take to the streets for their rights. Robert Owen, the young lawyer representing the Justice Department's Civil Rights Division, clearly enjoyed this early use of the new law. He was a good lawyer, and he needed all his skill. The defense had hired one of the best criminal lawyers in the state, Ossie Brown of Baton Rouge. That gent understood that he had his work cut out for him in front of those stern Eisenhower judges. The third judge, Robert A. Ainsworth Jr., enjoyed the same reputation for probity and impatience with nuttery as the other two. None of these men were to be trifled with, as dozens of malcontents, thugs, massive-resisters, recalcitrant public officials, foot-draggers, reckless demagogues, dynamiters, murderers, and plain damned crooks were to discover during the coming decades.

The Dragon, whom I described as "a calm man of considerable bulk," sounded a little aggrieved as he explained why the Klan had shucked its name. He said it was because of its bad reputation. "Every act of violence that was committed any place was put at the door of the Klan."

Dragon Christmas was a salesman at a Ford agency in Amite, near Bogalusa. His deputy, Saxon Farmer, was a distributor for the

Continental Oil Company at Bogalusa. I described the Titan as "a nerv-
ous little man who said 'sir' in every sentence." The pair put on a good
show, and I admit that I enjoyed it more than I should have. It was the
squirming that I liked best.

However, the Klansmen abruptly stopped the show, entertaining
as it was, the next day by admitting most of the government's allega-
tions. Their cunning lawyer obviously persuaded them that they would
fare better if they just owned up to the whole thing on paper rather
than have their crimes pulled from them, one assault and battery at a
time, in open trial.

A couple of witnesses testified anyway. One was Mayor Cutrer. He
told about going to a Klan meeting to try to persuade the Klansmen
against a demonstration. It was unnerving, he said. When he got there,
all the 150 or so members were sitting with hoods over their heads. "All
I could see was their eyes." A government lawyer asked if he had been
frightened. "I was frightened, yes," he said. "You can't be too comfort-
able talking to a group of eyes." The mayor did not have to remind us
that for some of the Klan's victims, those were the last eyes they saw.

The treasurer of the Anti-Communist Christian Association (aka
the Ku Klux Klan) was called to tell the court about the organization's
finances. John Magee was the treasurer, yes, but he didn't know any-
thing about the finances. Those were handled by the vice president.
Judge Christenberry called him a liar, in only slightly more judicious
language.

Judge Wisdom threatened Magee with contempt of court and sent
him outside for ten minutes to refresh his memory. It was a little better
after the refreshment, but he still couldn't remember whether he had
been at the meeting where Mayor Cutrer spoke. By then he had the
foresight to see a contempt citation coming, so he asked for a nitro-
glycerin pill for his heart. That brought his memory around, and he
said that yes he now recollected that he was at that meeting.

One more Klansman was called in to produce the group's mem-
bership records. Saxon Farmer, the Titan, said he didn't have any, but
that he and others had compiled a list from memory. Their memories
came up with only forty-eight names. It was widely known that
Washington Parish had at least one hundred Klan members. At the
mention of forty-eight, Farmer was immediately put under the threat

of contempt. He and his buddies huddled in the hall, while back inside the judges talked over an urgent new situation. Hurricane Betsy was bearing down on New Orleans. The judges called a recess until the storm had passed, thereby providing a reprieve for the forgetful Titan.

I filed a hurricane story the next day. It said the storm had killed at least twenty-three people in three states, only three in New Orleans as far as the authorities knew at the time. The story pointed out, as we always did in such situations, that the city was largely below sea level and that a lot of neighborhoods were water-logged. In 2005, Hurricane Katrina demonstrated just how vulnerable the city was. In 1965, Betsy did not have much impact. Nevertheless, the president flew down— old Lyndon never missed a chance to show up at a calamity or an important funeral—and inspected the damage.

Betsy took me away from the Bogalusa story, and I never made it back. Claude told me to ignore the mop-up of the storm story, which was being covered adequately by the wire services. Then the AP moved a wildly erroneous story saying three hundred people had been killed. I hurried back from my Sea Island vacation and spent the next few days reporting on the storm's aftermath. The death toll turned out to be seventy-six statewide. By the time I finished with Betsy, it was time to move on to other subjects besides Bogalusa.

I learned later that when the hearing resumed after the storm, Christmas and Farmer managed to come up with the names of 87 men in their Klavern. Their list was supplemented by another 151 names from the Justice Department—for a total of 238—indicating that the government's paid informers either had better memories or better math skills than the people they spied on.

On December 22, the court issued an injunction against 234 Klansmen (the missing four were not accounted for; maybe they were all informants), threatening them with fines or jail if they went on terrorizing and beating up black citizens. That pretty well shut down the Klan in Bogalusa for several years.

Lance Hill, the author of *The Deacons for Defense*, speculates that the feds could have shut it down a lot sooner if President Kennedy had not been reluctant to alienate Southern voters and their powerful representatives in Congress, whose cooperation he needed to pass any legislation. He may be right. I do know that Kennedy's successor, the

Texan Lyndon Johnson, was more successful in dealing with the problem. He did it with craft, cunning, arm-twisting, and threats, never shrinking from whatever it took. He shouldered through the 1965 Voting Rights Act, which forever changed the political landscape of the South. He also alienated a majority of Southern voters and handed the South to the Republican Party for decades to come. He knew the cost, but he did it, anyway. *Cojones*, they call them in Texas.

As for Bogalusa, I am still reduced to tremors of melancholy when I read my account of one old man's attempt to save the honor of his beloved little hometown at the height of the killing and hating. It happened when Bogalusa's band of moderates still believed they had some influence, before their hope was dashed.

His name was Vertrees Young. He had run the big paper mill until he retired. I referred to him as Bogalusa's number-one elder citizen, still valued for his solid advice and inspiration. He was in torment over what was happening in the town and went to see his friend Mayor Cutrer. With tears in his eyes, he pleaded with the mayor to tell him what he could do to help. The mayor was equally tormented but could offer no satisfactory answer.

Young left City Hall and drove to the mud lot where the National States Rights Party was holding a rally. Mssrs. Stoner and Lynch were speaking, rousing their listeners against "the niggers." The old man stood shaking his head in anger and disagreement. Finally, he walked up to the platform and asked the men in charge for permission to speak to the crowd for two minutes. Just two minutes.

"They turned him down," I reported, "and he hung his head and went home."

CHAPTER 13

Resisting the Resisters

The thugs and demagogues got most of the attention, but there were quieter men and women in the South who had the courage to oppose this last wrongheaded lost cause. We reporters seemed to gravitate toward those folks everywhere we went. I think of Mike and Patt Derian in Jackson, leading citizens, he a physician and she a former nurse, seemingly ordinary parents and concerned citizens. Patt jumped into the fight against segregation, and Mike spoke out fervently against it. Patt's friend Winifred Green, a daughter of a powerful, well-connected lawyer, joined the fight about the same time. Winifred parted company with her father on the race issue and never looked back. She spent the next fifty years fighting for justice and equality. Her friend Constance Curry, a colleague in the American Friends Service Committee, traversed the South endlessly and fearlessly, hard at work against the established order. These were all white people of the substantial middle class. Right across the South there were newspaper editors and reporters who understood the stakes and reported honestly. There were also courageous clergy, educators, and civic leaders.

In Birmingham there was Cecil Roberts, an English-born woman whose husband, David, a coal-mine owner, had the conscience and the wealth to support his wife's liberal habit. Mrs. Roberts was not satisfied just to run the city behind the scenes, as she apparently did. She knew every officeholder at the state and local level, starting with Governor Wallace. I think he was afraid of her, but he understood who she was and made sure to stay on friendly terms with her.

Cecil and David invited me to stay at their house when I visited Birmingham on stories, many of which had been more or less assigned

to me by Cecil. The *New York Times* was her favorite newspaper. She
saw herself as its ex-officio representative in darkest Alabama. She
loved boosting her adopted hometown while improving it with tough
love. She was a big force behind the arts. Theater and music were her
main interests, and no one knows how much of her family's money
she invested in them. She saw to it that the city had a first-class pro-
fessional theater.

When Martin Luther King came to town in 1963 and wrote his
"Letter From the Birmingham Jail," everything changed in Cecil's life.
The civil rights movement had already come, and she was an early sup-
porter, but it seemed not to have affected most of the people in her
social circle. She changed that in one bold stroke. She integrated a sym-
phony concert. She walked into the auditorium one night on the arm
of a prominent black man and in a matter of minutes managed to
offend Birmingham sensibilities on two or three different levels. I don't
remember whether David was with her. He probably was not. Cecil
was a public relations genius. She might well have persuaded him to
stay home so as to raise the dramatic effect of her entrance with not
just a black man, but a man who was not her husband.

Cecil was an irresistible force. Harry Ashmore phoned her once
from Little Rock and asked whether she might be able to keep the
Reverend Fred Shuttlesworth, a famous civil rights activist and fire-
brand, from coming to Little Rock to further inflame the city during
the powder-keg months after the Central High School crisis. She
replied that she could ask her friend Bull Connor to put him in jail
long enough to keep him away. Ashmore, not quite sure that she was
joking, declined the offer.

For a white person of liberal tendencies, even for such a towering
personality as Cecil Roberts, Birmingham was quite a horrible place
during those years. Here's the way Charles Morgan Jr., the civil rights
lawyer, described his hometown as it was when he began his practice:

> Birmingham closed its parks, de-seated its park benches,
> drained its swimming pools, poured concrete in the holes of its
> public golf courses, witnessed the beatings of countless blacks
> and the castration of one, suffered scores of unsolved bombings,
> and voted its habit for Police Commissioner Bull Connor and his
> designees. Birmingham had seen preacher Fred L. Shuttlesworth

and singer Nat ("King") Cole slugged, the latter onstage. It had sued *The New York Times* for libel, denied all, denounced the world, and fought in courts and in the streets to maintain "the old-South" way of life it had never known.

This same Chuck Morgan became one of the heroes of the opposition, although it would be a mistake to call him quiet in any sense. He was large and loud. He used flamboyance as a weapon, in and out of court. He sued the diehards everywhere he could find them, and he almost always won. His most important victory was in *Reynolds v. Sims,* the 1964 Supreme Court decision establishing the "one man, one vote" rule. He had challenged the malapportionment of the Alabama legislature, which had been in the clutches of the feudal lords of the sparsely populated countryside for generations. Later, as a high official of the American Civil Liberties Union, Chuck led an almost successful effort to impeach President Richard M. Nixon. He fought in court to get the boxer Muhammad Ali out of trouble with the military draft during the Vietnam War. And on and on.

Away from the halls of justice, Chuck was in the top tier of Southern drinkers, eaters, and storytellers. I can still see his long, overweight frame propped on pillows in his motel bed in this or that Southern city. He would be holding court—in his pajamas as often as not—for as many men and women as he could corral at the end of a hard day's work. There would be a cigarette in one hand and a glass of whiskey in the other. We would discuss the day's events and argue over the main villains of the time (Nixon was a favorite entry) and settle on a restaurant for that night's dinner.

One day he dropped by our house in New Orleans for a quick visit before rushing to catch a plane to Atlanta. He used the toilet, and when he came out he was embarrassed to tell us that his zipper was hopelessly stuck—broken, he surmised. There was no time to disrobe and try to fix it. These characters always arrived at the airport minutes before their flight. Norma grabbed a needle and some thread, knelt on the floor, and sewed his fly shut. He made the flight. We never heard how he got out of his britches when he got home, or what he did if he needed to open his fly before then.

As I write this, I notice that the date is January 9, 2010. And as I look at his *New York Times* obituary, which I wrote, I see that Chuck

died one year ago yesterday. Done in and dragged to earth finally by Alzheimer's disease.

There was another good guy who deserves to be remembered not for his integrationist sympathies—I don't know that he had any—but because of his professionalism in the heat of battle. Wilson Baker, the public safety director for Selma, made his reputation by defying Jim Clark instead of the feds. While Clark was hot-tempered and impetuous, Baker was calm and reasonable. He tried without success to reason with Clark, but the sheriff preferred angry bluster and brutal confrontation. Baker disciplined one of his policemen for firing a shot in the air to force black demonstrators to walk faster. A few days later, Baker persuaded one hundred black kids to stop marching and go home. It was growing dark, and that meant the kids would be in greater danger.

"Now listen," he said to them as they left Browns Chapel, "a march at this time of evening is a dangerous thing." Governor Wallace had outlawed night marches a few days earlier after the bloody one at Marion. Baker didn't mention Wallace. He just said, "To do this will be unlawful. I am asking you not to do this thing." No one had to tell the kids what Sheriff Clark would have said. In fact, Clark was already waiting for them at the courthouse, along with a force of his deputies and seventy-five state troopers, all armed with billy clubs, cattle prods, tear gas, and guns. Clark and Al Lingo, head of the state police, had issued stern warnings that the marches would be dealt with if they came to the courthouse. Baker, acting as diplomat, had talked with the two men and persuaded them not to act precipitously.

But Baker, a tall, portly, bespectacled man who wore a felt hat instead of a policeman's cap, understood that the better part of diplomacy was preventing confrontation before it happened. He went back to the marchers and intercepted them after they had walked only three blocks. He picked up a bullhorn, stepped into the street in front of them, and called for attention. The youngsters probably thought they were going to be arrested, which, they understood, was all right. Better to go to Baker's jail than Clark's. They stopped and knelt. Then they sang "We Shall Overcome" and prayed. Baker waited patiently, the bullhorn in one hand and a cigar in the other. When they finished, he spoke into the bullhorn.

"All right now, go peacefully back to your church."

I think all of us reporters were fairly amazed to see the kids turn around and head back to the church. They walked slowly at first, seeming to consider what they were doing. Then they started singing, with no hint of irony, "Ain't Gonna Let Nobody Turn Me Round."

When about fifteen broke away and ran down a side street, two or three policemen started after them waving their billy clubs. Baker shouted, "Let them alone!" The cops came back.

My story that night pointed out that night marches were a deliberate tactic to provoke white racists into violence. It had happened several times. The movement had asked a federal court to overturn Wallace's ban on night marches, but King had pledged to renew them after the court acted, no matter what it ruled. The story also pointed out that King was not just putting other people in jeopardy. He had told a group of us earlier that day that a plot had been uncovered to kill him. He seemed almost unconcerned. I remembered my paper's policy of never leaving this man unreported on, even for a day.

Dallas County had an election a year or so later. Jim Clark was voted out of office. The man who beat him was Wilson Baker.

■ ■ ■

Then there was Sheriff P. C. Jenkins in next-door Wilcox County. He was illiterate in the language of bombast. One day in March, John Lewis, who had already had his skull cracked in Selma, led fifty Negroes in a march to the courthouse in the county seat of Camden. They were stopped by Mayor F. R. Allbritton and a force of city cops, along with nine members of the town's "Rescue Squad." All but the mayor carried billy clubs. The mayor told the demonstrators they couldn't march. Backing up the seriousness of the mayor's order were a couple of dozen white men with no official connection, but, as I casually surveyed their hip pockets, sufficiently armed. I spotted two blackjacks, a pistol, and a pair of pliers. And a little more: "A young man of seemingly sound body leaned on a heavy wooden walking stick. A shabbily dressed middle-aged man carried a wooden cane with a heavy steel bolt screwed into the end."

The marchers left, then came back later in the day. The second

time they were met by Sheriff Jenkins. After the demonstrators finished praying and singing and stood waiting to decide on their next move, the sheriff spoke to them in his aging, gentle voice.

"Y'all go home now," he said to them, not loudly, just a little pleadingly. The Negroes stood their ground. Lummie, as everyone called him, looked pained. He was about sixty and had been sheriff for a long time and clearly was on friendly terms with many of the older black leaders of the county. He walked over to the little knot of reporters and unburdened himself.

"This is the first time we've had anything like this," he said. He tried on a small chuckle, but it went down his throat and lost its volume. "Some of them I know. They agree with me, that I'm right, that they ought to go on home. But it's their leaders." His deep Southern drawl trailed away, and he shook his head. He seemed sad and genuinely baffled.

He had been sheriff since 1939. And this was indeed the first time anybody among the 78 percent black majority of the county had tried in any systematic way to break down the voting barrier. Without a critical change in the rules, there would be no black voters any time soon. Wilcox County had what was known as the voucher system. Before a person could register to vote, someone already registered had to vouch for him or her. No white person had come forward to vouch for the first black voter. And not a single black person was already on the voting rolls, so no one was there to vouch for the others.

Two weeks earlier, the sheriff had met with Dr. King, who had driven to Camden, the county seat, to lead a similar march for voting rights. At that time, he had told the famous preacher, "I'm not against their voting. We just want everything orderly. We love peace and quiet."

I believe that Lummie Jenkins was far more representative of Southern white officeholders than Jim Clark, Bull Connor, and Leander Perez. The loudmouths got the headlines, but the lawmen who just wanted peace and quiet outnumbered them by huge majorities. That had been the Southern attitude since the official end of slavery: just keep things quiet; don't rock the boat; if racial passions heat up, try to keep them from boiling over. It's not hard to understand the reason for that. The time for extremists to be elected to office was when public emotion was at a boil on one side or the other. That held true

on the reformist side as well. Does anyone really believe that Lummie Jenkins would have been elected sheriff in 1939 if he had been seized in a fit of Christian conscience and had run for office on a platform of equal rights for Negroes and an end to discrimination in Wilcox County?

In 1965, I believed him when he said it was all right with him if Negroes voted. For one thing, he had warm relationships with a large number of his black constituents. Lay aside the one-sided nature of such relationships in those days. As a political fact of life, Lummie Jenkins would have received a big slice of the black vote if the voter rolls had been opened up to that 78 percent majority. He was not alone in that position. The South had hundreds of such white officials who, in the peculiar way of those times, got along fine with black people. As African Americans began to vote by the tens of thousands across the South, before they began to win offices in places like Wilcox County, those sympathetic white officials were the first beneficiaries of the relaxed rules.

CHAPTER 14

You Want Your Power Black or with Cream?

The civil rights movement of the 1950s and 1960s had more white sympathizers in the South than has been acknowledged in many of the printed and televised retrospectives. But the core of the movement was black. It had to be so. There had been white activists for many years, and there had been black activists for at least a couple of generations. But in the '50s and '60s the South saw for the first time a mass uprising of black people that spread right across the old Confederacy. It was as if in the 1850s there had been a simultaneous uprising of millions of slaves, all somehow coming to a telepathic understanding from Texas to the Carolinas that the black underclass was mad as hell and was not going to take it any longer. In the 1950s, that telepathic understanding came about not by some mysterious message carried on the wind but because gifted black leaders meticulously gathered the massive rage of black people and thrust it with great force against the massive resistance of their white oppressors. That meant that for the first time the black resistance was able to gather a critical mass of leadership, not in one or two places but right across the South. Some came from black universities. Some were young preachers. Some were young teachers. Some even came from the servant class. Think Fannie Lou Hamer of the Mississippi Delta, who suddenly fanned her spark into a flame and strode into the fray.

The bulk of the leadership coalesced in the civil rights organizations, new and old. There was the National Association for the Advancement of Colored People, which had been active for generations. It still had great strength, but its leaders tended to use its strength with a measure

of caution. There was the Congress of Racial Equality (CORE), which had been around long enough to accumulate battle scars. Then there were the two new institutions, the Southern Christian Leadership Conference (SCLC) and the Student Non-Violent Coordinating Committee (SNCC). The latter two provided most of the leaders who became known around the South and the nation.

James L. Bevel was the most charismatic of Dr. King's colleagues in SCLC. He had come down from Nashville with a good-looking wife and a history of hell-raising at the American Baptist Theological Seminary. His wife, Diane Nash, was another young leader who remained active in the movement for many years. The so-called children's crusade in Birmingham was Bevel's idea. That produced sickening television images of children being chased by the police and knocked down by fire hoses. It strengthened the SCLC, the sponsor of the idea, at a time when it needed national support. It was Bevel who rallied the hurt and angry marchers after Bloody Sunday at Selma and sent them forth again to face the ongoing peril on the road to Montgomery. Later it was Bevel who counseled his boss to oppose the Vietnam War, which split King and the movement from the president who had strong-armed Congress into passing the Voting Rights Act.

I was astonished the first time I saw Bevel. He was a preacher, but he wore overalls over a white shirt and tie. He became known for warming up the crowd for the main act, Martin Luther King. His preaching style was fiery, and so were his words, a contrast to King's measured, low-volume, and stunningly elegant style. It was hard to reconcile the flamboyant fellow in the pulpit with the calmly rational conversationalist who spent hours with us reporters in the back rooms of churches and in the living rooms of local activists. Indeed, as the years went by it became clear that James Bevel was a seriously divided personality. The same man who so effectively led crowds of demonstrators, and who was widely believed in some white circles to be a Communist, evolved politically into a follower of Ronald Reagan. In his later years, he showed signs of real instability. He was Lyndon H. LaRouche's running mate in the presidential campaign of 1992. His personal life descended into disaster. He was convicted in 2008, the last year of his life, of having sexual intercourse with one of his daughters when she was a teenager. That was long after he had parted from

his first wife. He told the court that he had fathered sixteen children by seven women.

At the opposite end of the emotional spectrum there was the Reverend Andrew Young. I was not surprised to see him elected mayor of Atlanta several years after the turmoil of the 1960s. The reporters called him "Andy," and he called us by our first names. There you have a small but important lesson in public relations. I can think of only two or three reporters who considered themselves close enough to King to call him Martin. To the rest of us, he was Dr. King. But we routinely addressed his aides by their first names, and they responded in kind. That undoubtedly sent a signal from us to the movement leaders that we were sympathetic to their cause. We did not call Sheriff Clark "Jim" or Governor Wallace "George." It would have been an affront to our own self-respect to call any member of the Klan or the Citizens Council by his first name.

There were a few exceptions. Back in Little Rock, for example, the reporters who covered the Citizens Council called its lawyer, Amis Guthridge, simply "Amis." All of us were offended by his political posture, but we couldn't resist liking him. Unlike some other segregationist stalwarts, Amis understood the game. He would take to the podium and deliver a thunderous appeal to the worst racist instincts in his audience. Then he would huddle with the reporters on the way out and make sure they had all they needed for their stories. He could be funny. He didn't make all his living as a lawyer. He sold used furniture to increase his income. But he had a sense of humor and a sparkle in his eye.

Orval Faubus played a similar game. I was the only reporter one night at a rally of his supporters in a small town well away from Little Rock. Most of the crowd seemed to be angry white supremacists. Faubus loudly denounced his enemy the *Arkansas Gazette* and its editor, Harry Ashmore. Then he let it drop that the paper had a reporter in the audience. I immediately felt the eyes of enraged men on me, and I felt in real danger. I stayed on well after the meeting ended, partly because I figured that I was safe as long as I was in the vicinity of the governor and his bodyguards. After everyone else had left, he walked over and put his arm around my shoulder and said, "Roy, I hope you don't take any of this personally." I didn't know whether to thank him for his concern or cut him dead.

CHAPTER 15

Blurred Colors

I never met a black reporter until I went to New York in 1965 and met Charlayne Hunter. I met Paul Delaney afterward in the paper's Washington bureau, and we became friends. We stayed in touch until both of us left the paper years later. He eventually returned to his home state and became the first African American chair of the Journalism Department at the University of Alabama. I met others through the *Times* when I returned to the Southern beat in 1969. There was Reggie Stuart somewhere along the way, and Nat Sheppard, who had a long career at the *Times* and the *Chicago Tribune*. I invited Nat to speak to my students at the University of Arkansas after I left newspapering. He had the looks of a movie star and the body of a wide receiver. Fayetteville women swooned every time he came into a room.

One day in the early 1970s, a Mississippi Highway Patrol car pulled up in front of our house in New Orleans and unloaded three men—two black and one white. A Mississippi trooper hauling an integrated group of well-dressed men across the state line could only mean that someone was in trouble. This was still a time when it was rare to see black and white people together in the South except in jails and court-rooms. These men did not look like jailbirds. Then I remembered that the two black men had phoned a day or two earlier saying they would like to lodge at our house for a couple of days during that year's Super Bowl, which was being played at Tulane Stadium. They were reporters of my acquaintance and were interested in some story I've now forgotten that had nothing to do with the football game. I was expecting them but was astonished to see them stepping out of a Mississippi Highway Patrol car. And who was this white guy?

Bob Maynard, a *Washington Post* reporter I had met a year or two earlier in Washington, came to the door first. His traveling companion was the *Times*'s own Tom Johnson, whom I had met briefly on one of my trips to New York. The white man turned out to be Senator Mike Gravel of Alaska. The reporters, who were old friends, had paused on the Mississippi coast for a day of rest and play and had run into Gravel. When he learned that all three were headed to New Orleans, the senator somehow arranged for the Mississippi Highway Patrol to give them all a lift. Gravel stayed for a quick drink, then moved to a hotel.

Tom was already famous in newspaper circles for having been the first black reporter to work for a major daily. He had distinguished himself as a foreign correspondent in Vietnam, Africa, Europe, and the Caribbean. Now he was back in New York working on a variety of stories, including race-related material. Bob worked a similar beat for the *Post*.

About the only thing I could see that this pair had in common was their race. Tom was a native of Florida. He had served in the army, which in those days was just as segregated as the South. He knew the customs and the rituals of white supremacy and what they required of black citizens. Like millions of others, he knew how to game the system and move up in spite of its hateful rules.

Bob was a New Yorker, brought up on the demanding streets of Bedford-Stuyvesant. His parents were from Barbados, and the Caribbean spirit was strong in him. Many people from the islands seemingly never felt the burden of ancestral slavery as heavily as African Americans born in the United States. I think Bob never got it into his head that he might be inferior to anybody. While Tom played the system, Bob just ignored it. He dropped out of high school, probably because it bored him. A Brooklyn high school dropout of his powerful intelligence might have become a mob boss. He found another route. He somehow cultivated thinkers instead of gangsters. He numbered James Baldwin and Langston Hughes among his friends by the time he was college age. He more or less bypassed college, but got himself selected as a Nieman Fellow at Harvard in 1966. The next year he stepped directly into a job at the *Post*.

On the night Bob and Tom arrived, we all went to a party at the home of Charles Ferguson, the editor of the *New Orleans States-Item*.

Charlie had invited several up-and-coming political figures who showed promise as reformers. Historically, New Orleans had always had an opening for reformers, although they typically had brief tenures when they stumbled into office. The reform candidate at the Fergusons' party was Ernest "Dutch" Morial, who would a few years hence become the first black mayor in modern times, and his wife, Sybil. They were Creoles whose families went back several generations in the city. A lot of the so-called black Creoles passed as white when they saw fit, but many more saw no advantage in that. The city's Creoles had always been among the more substantial citizens. They shared Bob Maynard's view that there was no profit in looking up to white people. Thousands of their families had roots older than most white families in the city.

Norma fell into conversation with Sybil Morial, and Mrs. Morial saw a chance to educate this uplander from Arkansas. She told her about the paper bag test. For admittance to certain upscale Creole organizations and sororities, a young woman's skin had to be lighter than a paper bag. When Norma told me the story, I realized that I needed to pay more attention to class divisions among African Americans.

The party was in full swing about ten o'clock when I heard a commotion on the front porch. Several men, including our houseguests and Dutch Morial, had gone out there for a breath of air. By the time I rushed through the door, Tom Johnson was holding Bob Maynard by the shoulders and pulling him toward the other end of the porch. Maynard was mad, and he was struggling to get at Morial. Dutch went inside to avoid further trouble. When the atmosphere cleared and Tom had had a chance to tell Bob what was going on, our two guests collapsed in laughter. I was told that Morial had been talking amiably with Maynard and had switched from his normal cultivated voice to his second language, the voice of the ghetto—one "brother" addressing another. Bob, thinking he was being deliberately insulted by a white stranger, offered to fight and was in the act of swinging when Tom rushed in and stopped him. Tom knew New Orleans, and he recognized Dutch as a Creole. Bob was a simple New Yorker with no experience in this strange city.

Bob's education continued the next afternoon at Galatoire's, the famous old restaurant on Bourbon Street. The four of us had gone

there for a peaceful meal during the playing of the Super Bowl. We knew the place would have few customers during the game. None of the four of us was especially interested in it. Galatoire's at that time had a wait staff of very old white men, one or two of whom apparently had been there since the Louisiana Purchase. One of those old birds came to our table with menus, spotted a white couple sitting with two black men, and shot us a look of deep anger. He threw—literally threw—the menus across the table at us and walked back to the kitchen to listen to the game on the radio. We exchanged knowing glances as we studied the menus. The old waiter came back, still surly. Bob looked up and flashed a smile that came in a straight line from Barbados to Galatoire's. He asked, "What's the score of the game?" The old man's face melted. Before he thought to control it, it was lit by a smile, and he told Bob the score. The service was superb for the rest of the meal. We left a nice tip.

Tom and Bob are dead now. So is Dutch. I haven't been to Galatoire's for a while. I assume that all the old waiters are dead, but I wouldn't bet on it.

■ ■ ■

Wiley Branton's bloodlines were exotic even by American standards. According to family lore, his great-grandfather was Greenwood LeFlore, a wealthy planter and influential chief of the Choctaw nation in Mississippi. LeFlore became perhaps the best-known chief that the Choctaws have ever had. His reputation was nationwide. LeFlore County, Missssippi, is named for him, as is the county seat, Greenwood. There is even a Leflore County in Oklahoma. The same family lore has it that Branton's maternal line included a "black Cherokee" woman, the daughter of a white plantation owner and an Alabama slave with Cherokee ancestors. Branton's family moved from Mississippi to Pine Bluff, Arkansas, and established itself in business in the black community. Young Wiley grew up knowing that he was a person of substance. He also understood that his color—or rather, the absence of color— would affect who he was.

He told me once about going to Florida as a federal trouble-shooter to help settle some racial dust-up. He was invited to a civic club lunch-

eon. As he chatted with the white men at the table, one of them looked across the room and said to Wiley, "They say there's a nigger here today. I don't see him, do you?" Wiley scanned the room and replied, "No, I don't, either." He told the story with huge amusement.

The other man's confusion was understandable. Branton, with his black wavy hair and aquiline facial features, might easily have been mistaken for an Asian Indian. If he had bothered to learn a Cajun accent, he could have made a place for himself in south Louisiana. He might have ended up running a prosperous casino if by chance he had been raised in Oklahoma with other Choctaws. I could see him becoming chief of the Mississippi Choctaws in the twentieth century.

On another occasion, Wiley told me about one of his grandest moments—a trip to his ancestral home, Greenwood, Mississippi. He went there as executive director of the Southern Regional Council's Voter Education Project. The VEP had led large numbers of black Mississippians to register to vote for the first time. He was the guest speaker at an evening meeting that had been called to soothe racial tensions. Stokely Carmichael and his SNCC friends had got the town's attention with their new Black Power campaign. Young people were marching every day. The police were not friendly, and neither were the white business leaders. Emotions were nearing a boil when Wiley arrived. Hundreds of people, including the local civic and political leaders, were waiting at the city auditorium. Wiley started with a bit of personal history.

"It's good to be here in the city of Greenwood and the county of Leflore," he said. "I am the grandson of Greenwood LeFlore." There was a gasp, and then applause, and for the rest of the meeting the man from Washington was treated as an honored guest. Anyone kin to Greenwood Leflore was automatically welcome in Greenwood, Mississippi.

He first made his mark as a civil rights lawyer by handling the Little Rock desegregation case that came to the world's attention in the fall of 1957. His credentials included a degree from the University of Arkansas School of Law, where, in 1950, at age twenty-seven, he became the fifth Negro admitted. He and a handful of other determined young men had been trying for two years to break down the racial barriers at the university. That personal experience made him even more determined to remove those same barriers in the Little Rock

school system. Thurgood Marshall, already a lion of the movement, came to town to help him. A few years later, Marshall integrated the U.S. Supreme Court.

Branton moved to the national stage in 1962 as the first executive director of the Voter Education Project, which helped register six hundred thousand new black voters in eleven Southern states during the next three years. He took charge of kick-starting the 1964 Civil Rights Act and did the same for the 1965 Voting Rights Act after President Johnson put him to work in the Justice Department. Branton landed as dean of the Howard University Law School in 1977 and saw to the training of still another generation of committed black lawyers. He treated himself to a period of private practice before he died in 1988 at age sixty-five. His hometown has named a freeway for him.

CHAPTER 16

Outrage by the Book

In August 1965, the cops in West Point, Mississippi, arrested the eighteen-year-old son of a congressman and charged him with manslaughter. Michael Reuss, son of Representative Henry S. Reuss of Wisconsin, had traveled to the state along with hundreds of other young people from the North to work in the movement. He was one of forty-five whites and Negroes arrested during a protest march. While he was being searched at the jail by an investigator for the State Highway Patrol, the young man reportedly pushed the man. The officer promptly died of a heart attack. That was the official version of events. The sheriff charged Reuss on the spot with causing the man's death.

Friends of the young man, who was a student at Stanford University, told a different story. They said the officer began his search by ripping a civil rights button from Reuss's shirt. Then, they said, the young man removed a second button himself, handed it to the officer, and walked away. They said the officer went on to another person in the line, ripped a button from his shirt, then collapsed and died. The manslaughter charge was soon dismissed, and young Reuss resumed his civil rights activities.

The main goal of the activists was to register enough Negro voters to break the headlock that the white supremacists had on the state's government. Second-class citizenship was not an idle designation. The list of officially sanctioned disadvantages was a long one. If you were black, you could not even get your street paved without political muscle.

The immensity of the challenge was clear. The U.S. Civil Rights Commission held a hearing in Jackson early in 1965 and heard a stunning statistic. Only 6.7 percent of the eligible Negroes in the state were registered to vote.

Natchez, the home of those grand old antebellum mansions, broke into the news a few weeks after Michael Reuss's arrest in West Point. George Metcalfe, the local president of the NAACP, was sent to the hospital with two broken limbs and a damaged eye. Someone had planted a bomb in his car. That was the seventeenth act of violence against Negroes in Adams County in a matter of months. The black folks of Natchez were enraged.

Dr. King had to send his best diplomat, Andrew Young, to Natchez to remind the followers there that their only hope in the movement was nonviolence. He told them: "The white man of Western civilization has mastered the art of murder, and you can't compete with him on that basis."

Instead of taking up arms, the black leaders fell back on the petition. They sent a list of perfectly reasonable demands to the city authorities—hire Negro policemen, clamp down on the Ku Klux Klan, etc.—and the city predictably rejected all of them.

The next step was to announce street demonstrations. Governor Paul B. Johnson Jr. sent 650 National Guard troops to the town to "avert possible racial violence," and the Guardsmen patrolled the streets with drawn weapons. The demonstrations were called off. That left the black community in a familiar condition: angry and frustrated, alternating between a simmer and a boil.

White policemen across the South were, with a few exceptions, part of the political apparatus for maintaining white supremacy. Civil rights protesters knew they would probably be arrested in any of hundreds of small towns from Virginia to Texas. That was part of the nonviolent campaign: arrest, jail, rallies to denounce the police and their political leaders, then more marches, more arrests, more speeches, etc.

Sometime during 1965 I became aware of a new police tactic. Black victims might expect to be arrested. The first case was merely mentioned in passing as one of a long list of outrages made public at the Civil Rights Commission hearing in Jackson. An auto mechanic in McComb told the commission that a bomb had exploded in his yard one midnight in 1964. The police promptly arrested him. The motive for the bombing and possibly his arrest was that his wife had tried to register to vote.

Not to be outdone, Crawfordville, Georgia, came up with a truly

exotic solution to the outside agitator problem. A Ku Klux Klansman beat up a photographer for the Southern Christian Leadership Conference during a march. State Police officers took both men into custody. They found some firecrackers in the photographer's pocket. That put him afoul of a Georgia law that had been passed to regulate fireworks a few years earlier after several children had been injured by them. The Klansman was one of a trio who had been charged and tried for killing a black educator in 1964. They were acquitted, of course, by an all-white jury. The charge against him in the new assault was resisting arrest and interfering with the operation of a school.

The interesting part of the case came at the bail-bond hearing. The judiciary set the black man's at five hundred dollars and the white man's at one hundred dollars. The Kluxer made bail and went free in minutes. The other guy spent the night in jail. As it happened, a lawsuit was pending in federal court attacking the use of bail bonds to discriminate against African Americans. The Crawfordville case provided a timely example.

In Louisiana, a black man's home was firebombed, and the police arrested the victim. That happened in Ferriday, a few miles west of Natchez, Mississippi. Ferriday is the home of the singer Jerry Lee Lewis. I don't think he was in town when the bombing occurred.

The owner of the house was Robert Lewis Jr., president of the Ferriday Freedom Movement and, I assume, no kin to Jerry Lee. The police didn't want to talk about it to me, but a neighbor and friend of the victim told me that Lewis had rushed outside with his shotgun after the blast—he and his wife and five children were not hurt—and that the police charged him with aggravated battery when they arrived and saw him holding the gun.

One of the most curious atrocities in Alabama during the 1965 protests occurred in the western town of Greensboro. Whites made up less than 30 percent of the population but owned everything, including the government. The voter registration books in the spring of 1965 carried 4,824 whites and 236 Negroes. Black protests for voting rights brought the usual resistance. One day, 17 people were beaten so severely by the police that they had to be hospitalized.

At the height of the demonstrations there, an eighty-seven-year-old black man named Perry Small was found beaten unconscious. His

tongue had been cut out. The chief sheriff's deputy arrested two young Negroes and accused them of attacking the old man to silence him because, he said, Small had been heard criticizing civil rights activists. That was hotly disputed by a protest spokesman, who said the pair had nothing to do with the movement. Choosing which claim to believe depended heavily on one's race, and I have no doubt that Greensboro's grandchildren still adhere to the same standards of proof forty-five years later.

Greensboro became a case study of a Black Belt town where the rights movement never quite caught fire. There were demonstrations enough, along with retaliation that might have ignited a consuming anger—two churches burned, marchers beaten mercilessly by both the police and unofficial white supremacists, activist leaders jailed. At one point, the police arrested 435 people and tear-gassed 400 who had taken refuge in a church. Establishment whites sent covert messages to the black community that protesters would be remembered and retribution exacted.

The white minority seemed bewildered and angered. I sat in on a conversation with some white coffee drinkers at a café. One said, "I tell you what I think. I think they passed that voting rights bill with the idea of putting the niggers in charge down here." If he is still alive, I wonder what he thinks now. All across the South there are black sheriffs, police chiefs, mayors, state legislators, and even a few black members of Congress.

That same day, I talked to a businessman who told me that his wife had cleaned out their closets that week and removed all the unwanted clothes. In the past, he said, she would have given them to needy Negroes. Instead, she had burned them.

"The niggers are going to be in trouble around here when this is all over," he said, and I thought there was more pity than malice in his voice.

During another visit to Greensboro, I arrived late at an SCLC rally in a black church. The speaker was King's lieutenant Ralph Abernathy. All the seats inside were taken, and there was not even standing room. With several others, I had to stand outside an open window and take notes. The temperature outside was probably near 100 degrees. Inside, it must have been insufferable. We at the window could feel the heat

pushing out. Abernathy was exhorting the people to stop migrating north. Stay home and help with the movement, he said. Then, his peroration: "Do you know how cold it gets in Chicago and Detroit? You'll *freeze to death* if you go off up there!" The sweating crowd gave him a heartfelt "Amen!"

A few days after my trip to Greensboro, I was in the Mississippi Delta talking with a Harvard student, a pedigreed son of old Yankee stock. His name was Morton Peabody Prince Thomas. He had just been released from a hospital. His head was still bruised. Both eyes were black and swollen, and his ribs still hurt.

He was one of forty civil rights demonstrators arrested a few days earlier. After a night at the notorious Parchman penitentiary a few miles away, they had been returned to the Bolivar County jail in Cleveland. Most of the rest had been released on bond by Saturday night. Sometime during the evening, two white drunks had been thrown into the same cell with Thomas. They beat and kicked him for about fifteen minutes after learning that he was a civil rights worker. The jailer finally got him out, and a deputy took him to the hospital.

Morton Peabody Prince Thomas's story was a familiar one during those days: civil rights activists were jailed by the hundreds, and a fair number could count on being assaulted while they supposedly were being protected by their jailers. Only rarely were the assailants punished in court.

CHAPTER 17

The Story Changes

Writers habitually look for turning points. This or that battle that changed the direction of a war. A congressional victory for the forces of liberalism or conservatism. The University of Arkansas football team defeating its hated opponent the University of Texas, proving finally that the little guys have a chance. There was a turning point in the South's racial violence that we were slow to recognize. It was when the Klan finally overreached on one cold night in the winter of 1966 and murdered a Negro whom it should have left alone.

The victim was Vernon Dahmer, a prosperous farmer and businessman near Hattiesburg, Mississippi. He was very light-skinned, a detail that probably made a difference. A firebomb was thrown into his house while the family slept. The flames destroyed his house and nearby store. His ten-year-old daughter was seriously injured. The father ran to the porch and fired several gunshots at the fleeing car. He died of his injuries half a day later.

The Klansmen who murdered him must have been surprised at the reaction. Instead of open applause or quiet approval from their fellow white people, they found themselves denounced. The Hatticsburg Chamber of Commerce demanded that the killers be apprehended and punished. The local paper called the murder "a revolting cowardly crime." The three local banks collected a memorial fund for the Dahmer family.

Those white leaders chose to overlook the fact that the murdered man was not merely a respected black citizen. He was also active in the civil rights movement. He had been the president of the Forrest County branch of the NAACP. He had given shelter in his home to

Northern rights workers, the hated "outside agitators." But he himself was not seen as an agitator. He was a local man with solid standing in the community. White people dealt with him as an equal. Some probably had to stop and think to remember that he was "colored."

The FBI went after the killers and arrested them in the late spring of 1966. Their charismatic leader, Samuel Holloway Bowers Jr., went into hiding for a while, then turned himself in.

I risked my life for the story on the day he was arraigned in Hattiesburg. Jack Nelson and I learned only a few hours ahead of time that Bowers was going to appear in court. We jumped on a plane in Atlanta and flew to New Orleans. There we rented two cars—Avis's most powerful vehicles, a pair of Chryslers—and sped to Hattiesburg at eighty miles an hour. The route from New Orleans to Hattiesburg was not a mere farm-to-market road, but it was no interstate highway, either. Somehow we made it unscathed and arrived five minutes before Bowers was brought into the courtroom.

Punishing the Klansmen in a Mississippi court proved difficult, of course. Bowers was tried four times and never convicted. However, in 1970 he and several other members of the vicious White Knights of the Ku Klux Klan, his creation, were convicted in a federal court of violating the civil rights of the three rights workers in Neshoba County, the young men whose bodies were found in the dam of a farm pond outside Philadelphia. Bowers served six years for that. He left prison and became a Sunday-school teacher and quiet citizen for the next twenty-two years.

In 1998, with new leadership at the state level and with black voters making their voices heard from Tennessee to the Gulf of Mexico, Bowers was finally found guilty of the murder of Vernon Dahmer. He was sentenced to life in prison. He died there in 2006 at the age of eighty-two.

His organization was effectively put out of business by the Dahmer murder and its aftermath. But it must be acknowledged that Samuel Holloway Bowers Jr. made his mark on history. The FBI credited him and his White Knights with nine murders and three hundred beatings, burnings, and bombings.

Bowers was a shocking rebuttal of the old notion that the Klan was

a mob of white trash and common thugs. We didn't know it at the time, but he was from an affluent and educated family. One grandfather was a member of Congress for four terms. The other was a planter. Bowers himself was a small businessman. He seemed to be well read. He was also convinced that the nation's enemies—Communists and Negroes—were on the verge of taking over. He once ordered his followers to prepare for an invasion from the Gulf of Mexico.

■　■　■

All this craziness was momentarily swept away for me one day in August 1965 when I hurried to Arkansas to cover a horrendous accident. A Titan missile silo in the Ozark foothills had caught fire and killed fifty-three men doing repairs and maintenance. The atomic missile warhead had been removed. When we learned that, we understood how much worse it might have been.

Someone dropped a wrench, the wrench hit a piece of steel and struck a spark, and the spark ignited fumes. The words "blazing inferno," which appeared in most of the stories from the scene, seemed somehow inadequate as we all stood around thinking how it must have been for the men trapped in the bottom of the hole and along the sides as the oxygen was sucked out and the smoke and flames rushed in. When the silo cooled down enough to allow workers to bring the bodies out, they found some in the air ducts where they had crawled desperately looking for air.

The missile was 103 feet long. It sat there until the fire burned itself out. We learned later that it would not have launched itself because two ignition compounds, stored separately, had to be inserted to enable it to do so.

Only two men escaped. One of those got out by accident. He tried to follow seven other men on a ladder going down, but they were jammed on and moving so slowly that he decided, in his panic, to walk through the flames in the other direction. He made it to an access tunnel and on to safety. Both survivors went to a hospital for their burns. They told reporters that they heard screaming from a fellow somewhere below. "Help me!" he yelled. "Help me!" No one could.

Wretched as it sounds, I was relieved to get back to bigotry and meanness.

■ ■ ■

In August 1965, we recorded two events miles apart and notable in almost contradictory ways. First, President Johnson signed into law the Voting Rights Act, the culmination of the most powerful surge of nonviolent politics anywhere since the days of Mohandas Gandhi. Five days later, the nonviolent movement effectively came to an end. In the black neighborhood of Watts in Los Angeles, angry black people took to the streets. They trashed and burned buildings, attacked white people, and raised fears of a race war. They wrecked black neighborhoods, seemingly intent on some plan of redemption by self-destruction. Forty people died before it all ended. More than a thousand were injured and property worth about $40 million was destroyed.

"Watts ushered in a new era of black violence—the riot years," wrote Gene Roberts and Hank Klibanoff in *The Race Beat*.

The story changed permanently. Similar riots erupted in scores of cities, most in the North and Midwest. Roberts and other Southern reporters found themselves in these strange and unwelcoming places day after day. One of our number, the intrepid Karl Fleming of *Newsweek*, was clubbed senseless with a four-by-four piece of wood in Los Angeles. His skull, which he had risked in the meanest towns of the Deep South, was fractured in several places. He was astonished. When I heard about it, I remembered that day in Atlanta when angry young black men and women and school kids turned their hostility toward me and the other white reporters covering a riot in their neighborhood.

Large numbers of the SNCC members, even in the South, no longer spoke to us with friendliness if they spoke at all. Robert Moses, whom we had long respected and admired, announced that he would not speak to any white people, no matter how he felt about them personally, for the foreseeable future. It was a powerful political statement. In some SNCC offices, the more militant members began to carry guns. About that time, a split began to open in the organization over the Vietnam War. Many members started speaking against it publicly, saying there was no point in going to Asia to kill people of color who

had done them no harm when the U.S. government would not enforce equal rights for people of color in America.

The violence continued in one form or another from Texas to Virginia, and we covered it faithfully. I think we did a pretty good job. But the "riot years" and the accompanying hostility toward white reporters made the story harder to cover for slow-footed middle-aged guys like me. Most mainstream newspapers did not have enough black reporters, who might have been more welcome in black communities. The age of tokenism in hiring had proved to be a trap.

Roy, age five, firm in his opinions, and his sister Hattie. *Family photo.*

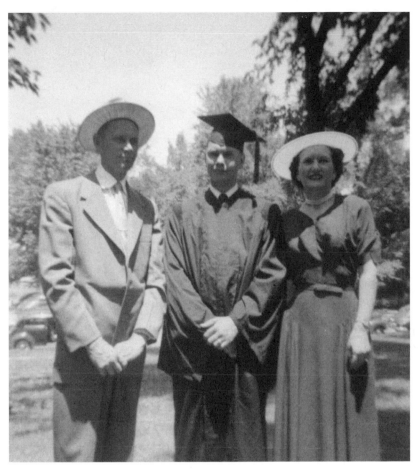

Roy and his parents, Roy and Ella Meredith Reed, on their son's graduation from the University of Missouri School of Journalism in 1951. *Family photo.*

Norma and Roy Reed and their children, Cindy and John, in the mid-1950s. *Family photo.*

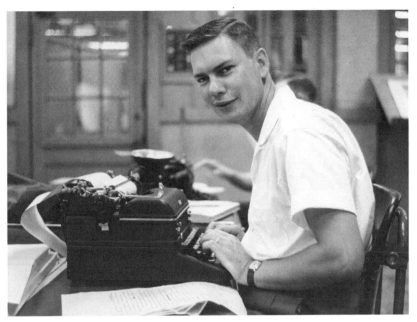

In the newsroom of the *Arkansas Gazette. Unknown photographer.*

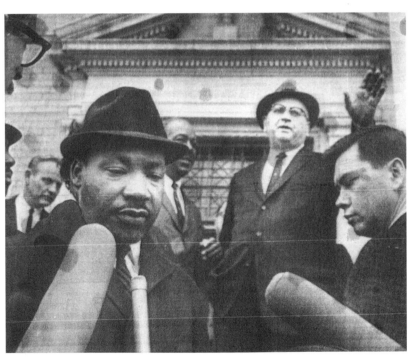

On my first day in Selma, I blundered into the picture when Martin Luther King was released from jail. The other man is public safety director Wilson Baker. *UPI photo.*

Caught asleep in the Oval Office. A smart-aleck friend's note said, "What I like is wide awake Washington newsmen." *UPI photo.*

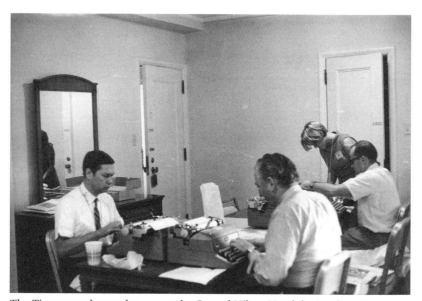

The *Times* rented several rooms at the Conrad Hilton Hotel during the 1968 Democratic convention in Chicago. While Mayor Richard Daley's cops were tear-gassing protesters and reporters across the street, Warren Weaver, John Herbers, Diane Henry, and I sat safely inside. New York Times *photo.*

I traveled with Hubert Humphrey when he was vice president and later when he ran for president. *White House photo.*

After her husband died, Mrs. Lady Bird Johnson invited several reporters who had covered the White House and the First Lady's activities to visit her in Texas. I was the only man in the group. *White House photo.*

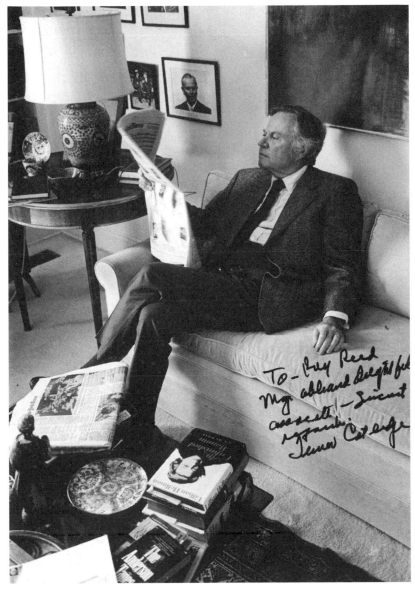

Turner Catledge, the *Times* executive editor, hired me, and when he retired to New Orleans, we shared an office. New York Times *photo.*

Times Talk, the paper's house organ, ran this photo of me and our daughter Cindy.
She had won a *Times* scholarship. *Photo by Chris Harris.*

President Clinton visited Springdale, Arkansas, before his hair turned white. The other couple were Gene and Joye Kelley of Rogers, whom I had written about when Gene was a delegate to the 1976 Democratic convention in New York. *White House photo.*

I offered a shoulder to this sleeping toddler in Lhasa when he got too heavy for his brother. I was there to write a chapter on Tibet for a National Geographic Society book in 1981. *Photo by John Holden.*

A chilly day with former Gov. Orval Faubus in Madison County, Arkansas. *Photo by Jan Faubus.*

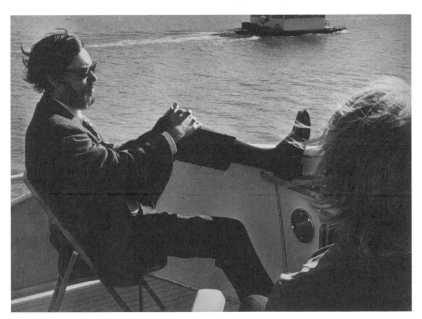

A dozen card-carrying Communists from Russia visited Greenville, Mississippi, and I took the occasion to write a profile of that unusual Southern town. To keep down political dissension, we all went for a boat ride on the Mississippi River. *Unknown photographer.*

CHAPTER 18

Reconstruction, Round Two

The elections of 1966 were revealing. Two main themes developed: the newly enfranchised black voters began to make their views felt, and the Republican Party, which had lain more or less dormant since the post–Civil War Reconstruction, started to come alive. The two themes were intertwined.

I developed an early affection for politicians without too much regard for their vices and virtues. It began in 1956 when I was assigned to cover North Little Rock at the *Gazette*. My reporting on a petty scandal at City Hall angered a veteran alderman, and he called me to his house one day and beat me about the head and ears as I sat in his living room. I had voted in a couple of presidential elections, but that was my first taste of politics at the personal level. You might say I got a taste of blood.

By the time I got to Selma, I had covered a number of elections in my home state and had become thoroughly engrossed. There were good guys and bad guys, issues that mattered and ones that didn't, backroom deals, behind-the-scenes puppet masters, and through it all the demanding work of criss-crossing the state by car and working into the night to try to make an election campaign fresh every morning for the readers, even when it had grown stale in my own head.

There was an intimation of political change in the Deep South as early as the winter of 1965. It took place in a ninety-mile radius around Jackson, the capital of Mississippi. That was the range of WJTV. The U.S. Civil Rights Commission had traveled to Jackson to hold hearings on racial atrocities. Surprisingly to some of us, WJTV chose to broadcast the hearings every day for five days.

The first witness was a frightened little black man who had been beaten nearly to death by a gang of white men for no apparent reason. Alfred Whitley was not a civil rights activist. He was just a middle-aged factory worker at Natchez. One day after work a year earlier, for no reason that he could explain, he was kidnapped by eight white men in masks and carried forty miles into the swamps. There they stripped off his clothes—it was February—stretched him on the ground, and beat him with bull whips until they were tired. They poured a bottle of castor oil down his throat and set him free.

He told the television viewers, "One of them said, 'Nigger, run!' and I began to run, and after a little way I fell down, and they shone their flashlights around in the dark, and then they emptied their guns at where they seen me last." They left him naked in the swamp.

Alfred Whitley's story was seen and heard as far east as Philadelphia, where three civil rights workers had been murdered in 1964, as far south as Natchez and McComb, where bombings and burnings had only recently subsided, and as far north as Belzoni, where the Reverend George W. Lee had been killed in 1955 for registering to vote.

The televised hearings coincided with a surprising development. A number of Mississippi's political and civic leaders had started rubbing their eyes and waking up. They had begun to see the damage that the Klan violence was doing to the business climate. Governor Paul B. Johnson, a segregationist, had suggested that Mississippians start respecting the law. Even the Jackson newspapers, notorious for their blatant white supremacy, covered the hearings with more than two columns a day. Dr. John A. Hannah, chairman of the commission, expressed optimism about the growing moderation of the state's leaders.

A scion of one of the state's most respected families took the occasion to speak out. Leroy P. Percy of Greenville, a cotton planter and banker, said Mississippians were tired of being led by the dead hand of the past. They wanted a change, he said.

Change came, slowly, but we saw a portent of it in a small electoral drama in Georgia that spring. A story that I filed from Atlanta on April 19, 1965, started this way: "The next Georgia legislature may include eight Negroes and a Grand Dragon of the Ku Klux Klan."

There were twenty-six black candidates in all, and at least six of them were said to have a better chance of election than the Dragon.

(He lost.) I reported another fact that was not well known outside the state. The state senate already had two black members, which put Georgia well ahead of the rest of the South in legislative integration. As it turned out, Georgia by the end of 1965 had ten black legislators—the second-largest number in the nation after Michigan.

A precious Southern custom was in its death throes in the late 1960s. Stump speaking, which required all candidates to show up on the same platform to be scrutinized (and hectored when the urge came on) by the voters at dozens of venues around a state, would disappear by the end of the decade.

Television got the blame, but I pointed out in one story from South Carolina that an absence of orators was also a factor. No one in the South Carolina election of 1966 could match the oratory of a Pitchfork Ben Tillman or a Cole Blease of the early twentieth century. Those men were not just racist demagogues; they were spellbinders who could hold an audience for hours. In modern times, only Fidel Castro could match them.

I filed a story about a stump speaking from Columbia and made the point that only one candidate was at all entertaining. He was Dero Cook, a convicted moonshiner. He ran for lieutenant governor on a platform advocating horse racing, dog racing, and open bars. The voters refused to take him seriously.

It puzzles me that no scholar has studied the connection between the decline of the Democratic Party in the South and the death of stump speaking. It is not true that no good stump speakers are left. Every state has one or two. If you could clone Dale Bumpers and plant half a dozen of him across the South, the Democrats would win the next election. They would whip the Republican Party the way Bumpers did it in Arkansas—with humor, ridicule, and cold, hard facts, all presented with the eloquence of a courtroom lawyer.

The years 1965 and 1966 illuminated three trends that would eventually change the South forever. First was the growing revival of "states' rights" as a vote-getter. For years to come, a promise to stop the encroachment of the hated federal government was considered a necessity in the electoral platforms of Southern white candidates. The government in Washington was presumed to be committed to taking away everything that was held dear in the South.

Second, those years saw a dramatic rise of the Republican Party as it capitalized on "states' rights" and stealthily curried favor with white supremacists.

I led a story from Columbia, South Carolina, with the observation that a Civil War general named States Rights Gist—yes, that was his name—was buried across the street from the capitol. He had got the name at his birth in 1831 when John C. Calhoun was turning "states' rights" into a household phrase in the South. The old doctrine had begun flowering again, I reported, and was achieving unnerving success from Virginia to Texas.

The Republican Party scored one of its early and prophetic victories in a special election in 1965. A segregationist congressman from South Carolina named Albert W. Watson, a putative Democrat patterned after scores of such around the South, very publicly supported Barry Goldwater, the Republican nominee for president, in 1964. The Democratic leadership in the House of Representatives stripped him of his seniority. He immediately switched parties and went home to run as a Republican. He won by a landslide. Senator Strom Thurmond of his state had already made the switch.

In Mississippi, Representative John Bell Williams, as conservative a Democrat as you could hope to find, was expected to jump parties that year. I covered his speech and reported, "He denounced the Democrats for 20 minutes but did not desert them."

Many other Southern Democrats got the Republican fever. In a few years, openly confessing Democrats were a minority in the region. Texas and Tennessee had a few, as did Kentucky and other Upper South states. Arkansas was the last real Democratic holdout. Bill Clinton stuck with the party right through his presidency and beyond. His friends Senators Bumpers and David Pryor, along with lesser-known officials like Representative Vic Snyder, all staunch Democrats, voted their consciences almost all the time and got away with it. But in 2010, the Republicans gained so many seats in Arkansas that it seemed probable that the party of Clinton, Pryor, Bumpers, and Sid McMath would soon join the Greenback, Bull Moose, and Know-Nothing parties in the yard sale of history. By the time Arkansas started to cave in, the rest of the South was already firmly Republican.

Along with Republicans, another class of voters provided the third

trend in the mid-1960s. African Americans had voted more or less freely in the Upper South for many years. But with the passage of the Voting Rights Act, they surged to the polls in the Deep South. They would be overwhelmed eventually by the sheer numbers of whites who switched to the Republican Party, but in dozens of districts they would become a powerful swing vote.

In a few years, Black Belt counties would be governed by black officials put into office by the newly enfranchised black-majority populations. In other places, black swing voters helped to elect white moderates over right-wing conservatives. I cannot document this, but I believe that much of the credit for the black voting surge should go not just to the civil rights movement but to the momentum that it created and that continued to swell and roll in black communities for years after the movement itself had disintegrated. Black citizens who had been awakened and coaxed out of their old slave-era fears went on marching. Now they marched to the polling places and marked their ballots.

The most vivid example I found was where the Voting Rights Act was born. My story from Selma on May 2, 1966, began this way:

> A year ago, Sheriff James G. Clark Jr. had little patience with the Negroes demonstrating for the right to vote. He simply locked them up.
>
> The Negroes registered anyway, thanks largely to the Voting Rights Act, and tomorrow they will be going to the polls by the thousands to try to vote him out office.

They did.

Even before he was beaten, Clark quietly acknowledged the changed landscape in Dallas County. He threw a barbecue and beer party and invited all the Negroes in the county. Only twenty-eight showed up, but his gesture had a significance beyond that. He wanted the world to know that he was not an ogre. The fact that he failed to sell that message did not obscure the fact that he had learned to read the new math of Deep South politics.

The new landscape changed almost too rapidly to keep up with. The Alabama Democratic Party scrapped its old ballot symbol, dating to 1904. It was a strutting rooster framed by two banners saying "White

Supremacy" and "For the Right." The new one replaced "White Supremacy" with just "Democrats." That made a lot of white folks mad. It made sense to black voters, though, and that was the whole idea. In the year since the Selma campaign, their voting registration numbers in Alabama had soared to 150,000.

For those who might have doubted the serious intent of the Voting Rights Act, they had only to divert their eyes to Mississippi. Twenty-five hours after President Johnson signed the act into law, his Justice Department sued that state to abolish its poll tax, one of the chief instruments of disfranchisement of black voters. The administration chose to act first in Mississippi because it had a smaller percentage of blacks registered to vote in 1964 than it had had in 1899, thanks partly to its use of the poll tax.

The Justice Department on the same day announced its intention to file similar lawsuits in Alabama, Texas, and Virginia, the only other states that still used the poll tax. The old tax had been quietly abandoned here and there over several years. In 1964, the voters of Arkansas scuttled the poll tax and adopted a modern voter registration system. The Faubus organization was skeptical of such reforms but sent mixed signals before the election. Word got out that one of the governor's main advisers favored voter registration. A local boss in an Arkansas River county told one of the campaigners for the voting machines that when he learned that the governor's man was for them, "I tell you what we did for you. We gave you an extra thousand votes and passed that son of a bitch." Thus did the governor prove that you can get right with God without making a to-do about it.

In 1964, the poll tax was outlawed for federal elections with the ratification of the Twenty-fourth Amendment, which made it unconstitutional to use the poll tax or any other tax as a requirement for voting.

The end of the poll tax turned out to be far less important than the dramatic increases in black voter registration. The young activists who ignited the voting rights campaigns practically ignored the poll tax. Their sights were set far higher. They wanted nothing less than complete equality at the ballot box and new millions of black voices heard in elections everywhere.

The Voting Rights Act provided federal examiners in the Justice

Department to fan out across the region to make sure that future elections were conducted without discrimination. States and localities could suffer financial penalties if they went astray.

Jefferson County, Mississippi, illustrated the challenge for black citizens. Only whites had voted there since Reconstruction: 1,500 whites and no blacks were registered as late as 1964. The NAACP went to work and registered between 700 and 800 black voters. But it was not until a federal examiner arrived and exerted his presence that black registration rose to more than 2,700—a comfortable majority and more than enough to elect a black mayor of Fayette, the county seat.

I interviewed the opposing white and black leaders there in 1965. Both were named Allen, as it happened—R. J. Allen, the white mayor of Fayette, and Ferd Allen, the local president of the NAACP. They seemed to like each other, in a way.

"I've tried to be good to our niggers every way that I know how," the mayor told me.

I asked Ferd Allen what he thought of the mayor. He said, "Mr. R. J. Allen? He seems to be a very nice fellow. He never has denied me anything." He paused and added, "'Course, he's a Southerner. You know?"

Mayor Allen's casual use of the word "nigger" in my story undoubtedly sent shudders of revulsion through our readers. The mayor, for his part, would have been hurt and puzzled by their revulsion. I have no doubt that he was a kind-hearted man who intended no insult. He had used that word all his life, as had his father and grandfathers. It would not have occurred to them that "nigger" was a substitute for an intellectual concept that placed a whole people on a lower level, that it was shorthand for "shiftless," "sorry," and "no-account," a belief that for generations had been so ingrained that it did not need to be articulated. If a black person was offended by the word, that meant he was uppity and had better watch out. The only thing worse than a shiftless black man was a successful one.

Mayor Allen was replaced soon by Charles Evers, the Mississippi secretary of the NAACP and the brother of Medgar Evers, the previous Mississippi leader of the NAACP, who had been assassinated in 1963.

Also in 1965, Charles Evers became a mover and shaker in a new biracial wing of the state Democratic Party. He worked with white

liberals like Hodding Carter III to wrest control of the party from the segregationists who had run it since the nineteenth century. They got it done, and black citizens became a working part of the state's political system—just in time to turn the system over to the Republicans for the next fifty years. But the Republicans never controlled the whole state. In numerous pockets, black Democrats held county and municipal offices. There was even a black congressman in one district.

Evers, a man with a sense of humor, demonstrated that his influence extended even to the Republican Party. When Representative Gerald Ford of Michigan was signed up to speak to a GOP fund-raiser in Natchez, Evers discovered that the event was to be racially segregated. He called attention to that, and Ford cancelled his speech. I can't imagine that Evers cared much what the Republicans did, but he enjoyed making mischief.

I took the occasion in my story to point out the Republicans' dilemma as they tried to extend their power around the South: would they turn their back on the party's Lincolnian tradition or blatantly court the white supremacists? They settled on a middle way. They abjured blatant racism and settled on a subtler form. It worked.

For a time, moderate Republicans were tolerated in places around the South. Governor Winthrop Rockefeller of Arkansas was openly pro-integration. He helped to open up elections to tens of thousands of black voters. In 1965 in Virginia, the Republicans nominated A. Linwood Holton, a Harvard man, for governor. He advocated equal rights for Negroes. He lost that race but won in 1969. However, he fell out of favor with a growing conservative majority. He ended up endorsing Democrats for office, including Barack Obama for president in 2008.

Another office-holder with a dilemma was George Wallace. His four-year term was running out, and he had to find a way to occupy his time until he could run for president again. He solved the problem by getting his wife, Lurleen, elected to take his place as governor. He ran the state government from the sidelines, making little attempt to conceal his involvement. It worked well enough until she got sick and died in 1968. By that time, her husband was well into his second presidential campaign. He had shaken up the Democratic primaries in 1964 by running well in some Northern states, enough to rattle the Democratic

establishment. He abandoned the Democrats in 1968 and ran at the head of the American Independent Party, a barely used, good-as-new outfit that he had found lying around waiting for a leader. This time he rattled both big parties. It began to appear that rattling his betters was his main goal in life.

Two states westward, Governor Orval Faubus faced a dilemma of his own. He had been in office twelve years, for six two-year terms. Should he risk humiliation by running again, knowing that the popular Republican Rockefeller was waiting to take him on again? Rockefeller had opposed him in 1964 and had got enough votes to scare Faubus. The governor later denied that he was still scared, but he chose to retire, anyway. George Fisher, the state's preeminent political cartoonist, captured the moment, the end of an era. The scene was a hillbilly polling station on primary election day in April 1966. One worker is saying to another, "Git on the phone quick, Ed! They left Orv's name off the ballit!"

Eight Democrats and two Republicans stepped forward to take his place. It was obvious that Rockefeller would be the Republican nominee, but the Democratic contenders had to walk a tightrope: how openly should they court the old Faubus supporters, especially in the courthouses and city halls, and how warmly should they go after the moderates and liberals? The winner was Jim Johnson, the noted segregationist. We in the press decided that his vote was a protest against the liberal policies of President Lyndon B. Johnson—no relation. Rockefeller defeated him in November.

That same year produced one of those strange-bedfellows stories that reporters love. In January, I traveled to Little Rock to report that Daisy Bates's husband, L. C. Bates, had quietly entered the Faubus administration by the back door. He had become an unpublicized adviser to the governor on the political interests of the black community. At Bates's request, Faubus had hired about one hundred Negroes for state agencies that received federal money.

That worked out well for both, so for the rest of Faubus's tenure he consulted Bates and a couple of his friends on blacks applying for state jobs. Faubus hired a sizable number, but he was careful not to take too much credit for them. Bates told me that he made sure the appointees were sound on civil rights. No "Toms" need apply, he said.

When I asked the governor about the arrangement, he said, "I've always been on a friendly basis with L.C." We both knew that was preposterous, so he said it with a grin.

I used this story to get in a dig at the self-righteous North on the question of school desegregation. I pointed out that since the turmoil of 1957, the schools of Little Rock had been desegregated as far as they could go without some new legal artifice. They had moved into the same awkward position of de facto segregation that had defined the Northern approach for years. It had long been policy in the North to assign pupils to their neighborhood schools, and if those neighborhoods happened to be all-white or all-black, and the schools ended up all-white or all-black, then those were the breaks. Little Rock would spend the rest of the twentieth century under federal court pressure to achieve something close to fair integration in spite of racially separate neighborhoods. By the turn of the twenty-first century, Little Rock was closer to that goal than most big cities in the North.

(Bedfellows stories have been a weakness of mine since Bob Douglas told me about a political rally he and a friend once attended in Little Rock. The speakers included a man and a woman who were known to be in a barely clandestine love affair. She spoke for one candidate, and her lover spoke for the opponent. The friend whispered to Bob, "Bedfellows make strange politics.")

For reporters, even-numbered years usually mean elections. The South got off to a rambunctious start in 1966 with a local election that became national news. The Vietnam War was becoming the country's most explosive issue. We were losing thousands of soldiers, and Vietnam was being torn apart. A young Georgia pacifist waded into the growing national protest almost inadvertently.

Julian Bond had made a name for himself as a spokesman for the Student Nonviolent Coordinating Committee. He had helped organize it. More than that, he had given it a handsome face that made him a minor star on television, and he had crafted its message in a way that only a talented writer could do. (He achieved some small fame as a poet, largely on the strength of a single couplet: "Look at that girl swing that thing. Everybody can't be Martin Luther King.")

I had known him for some time and liked his laid-back style. Few

of us would have called him energetic and hard-working, but he was eminently likable, and that helped to make him effective as the SNCC spokesman.

I had never thought of him as particularly ambitious. He was, but he hid it behind a quick wit and a mischievous grin. Some of his friends set in on him to run for public office. They saw him as a natural in a political role—smart, persuasive. Very reluctantly, from all accounts, he agreed to run for the Georgia House of Representatives. He won by a big majority.

Days before the legislature was to gather in Atlanta for its winter session, a reporter phoned Bond and asked what he thought about a statement that SNCC had issued condemning the U.S. involvement in Vietnam. He told the reporter he hadn't seen it. He asked the reporter to read the statement to him. Yeah, he said, I agree with that.

The fat was in the fire. He showed up for the first day of his term as a legislator and was met by an angry bunch of lawmakers—all white, of course—who said this man was disloyal and had no business in the Georgia House of Representatives.

Lawyers were hired. Federal courts were hauled in. The upshot was that young Mr. Bond missed his first year in the legislature. When the case was appealed to the Supreme Court, he was represented by Charles Morgan Jr., who ran the Southern chapter of the ACLU with vigor. Morgan had been run out of his hometown of Birmingham for speaking out against discrimination, and he was still mad. The Georgia legislature never had a chance. The Supreme Court installed Bond back in it, and he went on to serve twenty years in both houses, just to make the point that he was not going to be kept out of the place by a gang of rednecks.

The impassioned young men and women of SNCC scattered into various fields as they matured and as their movement matured and faded. Bond and his friend John Lewis competed for a seat in Congress in 1997. Lewis won and has been there ever since. Bond had some woman trouble in the 1980s, which was not surprising considering his Hollywood looks and charismatic style. He became active in the NAACP in later years, which might have upset people who were not aware of his establishment upbringing. His father, Horace Mann Bond,

was president of Atlanta University and a solid citizen of the city. Julian Bond became the NAACP's president in 1998 and held the job until his retirement in 2010.

■ ■ ■

By 1966, it had been twelve years since the Supreme Court had ordered an end to segregated schools, but many Southern districts were still resisting. Not brazenly but with a canny inertia, a deliberate doing of nothing. Most were integrating voluntarily with varying degrees of enthusiasm, but more than two hundred were doing so only under court orders—grudgingly, that is. The Johnson Justice Department intervened in the spring of 1966 to nudge those districts along. The case landed in the Fifth Circuit Court of Appeals in New Orleans, which in those days was populated by heroes like the great John Minor Wisdom.

The court laid down a set of guidelines to move desegregation forward uniformly across the South. The reaction was predictable.

Five Negroes registered at an all-white school in what was probably the most segregated patch of the old Confederacy, Plaquemines Parish, Louisiana—the wholly owned fiefdom of Leander Perez. White students refused to go to school, and private academies cropped up to receive them. That would happen in hundreds of districts in the years to come.

The Southern Governors Conference attacked the guidelines. Said they would force integration at an unhealthy pace.

Alabama, not surprisingly, edged to the forefront of the new resistance. Civil rights lawyers detected a pattern of foot-dragging in Governor Wallace's state. State officials said the only way they would integrate would be under a federal court order. That was arranged. I reported speculation that scores of school officials in the South were secretly hoping to get themselves under such court orders so that they could go back to their patrons and say, "Look, the feds are making us do it. We have no choice."

And thus the South continued to do the right thing, an inch at a time, and without large numbers of white people storming the streets making fools of themselves.

CHAPTER 19

Walking across Hell

James H. Meredith, who had integrated the University of Mississippi in 1962 at considerable cost in blood and temper, consumed three weeks of my time during the summer of 1966. I was not bored.

Meredith set out in Memphis intending to walk twelve miles south into his home state and on to Jackson to prove that he could do it. He might have intended to walk all the way to the Gulf Coast, but with Meredith you never knew what was in his mind. He dared anybody to stop him. A white man with a shotgun took him up on it and shot him down on the second day out. Didn't hurt him much, but he spent a couple of days in a Memphis hospital having pellets removed from his back. The assailant, Aubrey James Norvell, of a Memphis suburb, confessed and was sentenced to five years in prison. It was just as well that he confessed. Twenty or thirty people saw him do it, including police officers who did not lift a hand to stop him.

As the reader may recall, I was not one of those witnesses. I missed the shooting because I was with three or four thirsty reporters and photographers drinking soda pop in a country store a few hundred yards back down the road. We didn't know anything had happened until we saw people running down the highway. We all jumped in my rental car and sped to the scene.

From where I sit, I can see a Coca-Cola bottle embedded in glass on a bookshelf. A brass plaque on its wooden stand reads: QUESTION—"WHERE'S ROY REED?" CLAUDE SITTON, 6-6-66. Gene Roberts and Jack Nelson gave me the bottle at my going-away party when I moved to the Washington Bureau at the end of 1966. It took me a while to see the humor in it.

When the wires flashed the news of the Meredith shooting, my boss, Claude Sitton, the national editor, rushed to the wire-photo machine to scan the pictures coming in. (An AP photographer won a Pulitzer for his photo of Meredith lying on the pavement with his assailant visible in the bushes.) Claude was looking for me in the picture. "Where's Roy Reed!?" he demanded.

I didn't know I was in trouble. It took me about an hour to find a roadside phone and call Claude. During that lapse, the Associated Press had moved an erroneous story from Memphis saying Meredith had been killed. Claude's first question when he heard my voice was not where in the hell I had been but was Meredith alive or dead. I assured him that Meredith was alive. How did I know? Because when I got to him he was lying in the road talking and didn't seem to be seriously hurt.

"Hold on!" Claude said. He turned away to pass the information to his assistants. The *Times* radio station, WQXR, quickly broadcast the story that Meredith had not been killed. My bacon was saved. I won a publisher's award that month for my two-word report on the telephone: "He's alive."

Back at the scene, I was able to put together a decent enough story in time for our first edition. I was pumping a month's worth of adrenaline by suppertime. I have no idea where I stayed that night or whether I slept in a bed.

On the second day, I managed what I thought was a scoop. I made my way by stealth into Meredith's hospital room after a friendly nurse carried a note to him. He told me, among other things, that his main regret was not having a gun when he headed into Mississippi.

I noticed several other people in the room during the interview. I took them to be nurses and doctors. But one of them walked out with me and identified himself, a little hesitantly, as Bill Kovach of the *Nashville Tennessean*. When he had seen me leave the knot of reporters at the front door and head upstairs, he figured something was up, and he followed. Would I mind if he used what he had overheard from my interview? What could I say? We both got a story out of it, and Bill went on to high positions at several places including the *New York Times*. The cunning rascal retired as one of the most distinguished curators in the history of the Nieman Fellows program at Harvard.

Meredith flew home to New York after two days in the hospital.

Several civil rights leaders took up his march and carried it on to Jackson. There were notable detours.

One day Martin Luther King and other activists detoured to Philadelphia and marched to the courthouse, where they were blocked at the steps. King stood face to face with Cecil Price, a sheriff's deputy who had helped lynch three civil rights activists in 1964. Behind King were several hundred Negro and white civil rights protesters. Behind Price were a dozen lawmen with pistols on their belts.

Many years later, I was told of a few details about the 1964 lynching that had never been made public. They interested me because of an Arkansas connection. I interviewed Floyd Thomas of El Dorado, a retired FBI agent, for an oral history at the University of Arkansas. I learned that he had spent the summer of 1964 helping search for the bodies of the three murdered men. He told me about a tip by an old Indian from the Choctaw reservation. The man flagged down Thomas and another agent and told them where to find the burned car that had been used by the victims. It was not more than twenty feet from a busy highway, but hidden in a thicket.

Thomas and the other agent speculated that the men had burned to death and that the Klansmen who had killed them had removed the remains and scattered them in the woods. But they found no evidence of that, and the search for the bodies went on.

He said he had learned that the killings were accidental. His account went like this: the Klan's intention was to take the three men to the woods and give them a severe beating and turn them loose. But one of the Klansmen fired his pistol by mistake as he was using it to pistol-whip one of the victims, and the bullet killed one of the others. That left the Klansmen no alternative, as they saw it, except to kill all three.

After the dam holding the bodies had been located, Thomas was part of the crew that dug deep into it to find the corpses. The crew first inserted steel rods into the earth with an augur. When they withdrew the rods, they smelled the rotting flesh.

"A rotten human body smell is different than anything else. It can be a raccoon or anything else, but a human being body, it just smells different. At about three o'clock, we got down to the three bodies lying there. Two white people lying face down with their faces to the west,

and the black guy was on the right of them. He was lying face up with his head to the east and his face turned to the south. That's a Ku Klux Klan ritual burial situation."

Before the bodies were removed, the FBI called in local lawmen to witness the removal. Cecil Price was among them. He never showed any reaction, Thomas said—never acknowledging by word or expression that he knew anything about the lynching, even though, we learned later, he had been the deputy who had delivered the hapless victims into the hands of their murderers. At the dam, he grabbed a shovel and went to work with the FBI men, just doing what any good citizen would do.

I remarked to the old federal man that Price had served time in the pen for violating the activists' civil rights and somewhere along the line had got religion and repented. Thomas said, with what I took to be sarcasm, "Oh, all of them do."

On the day of the protest march in Philadelphia, two years after the killings, the protesters on the way to the courthouse had been terrorized by several white people in cars lurching toward them. A television cameraman was jerked out of the way of a pickup as it sped toward him.

I stood a few feet behind King at the courthouse. All the clichés applied: heavy air; tension you could cut with a knife. I remember thinking, *This is the day he will die.*

King understood that there was no time to linger and give a long speech. He just offered a short prayer, mentioning pointedly that some of the men who had killed Michael Schwerner, James Chaney, and Andrew Goodman were probably nearby. "I believe in my heart," King said, "that the murderers are somewhere around me at this moment." Price stood expressionless.

King went on, "I want them to know that we are not afraid. If they kill three of us, they will have to kill all of us."

And then this: "I am not afraid of any man. Whether he is in Mississippi or Michigan, whether he is in Birmingham or Boston. I am not afraid of any man."

Suddenly we heard a gunshot, then another, and another. People screamed and ran. I looked at Price and the other armed men. None of them had taken a gun out of a holster. I looked up toward a second-

story building, searching for a gunman. I saw no one. Then a more alert newsman solved the mystery. What we heard was not gunfire. Some fool, probably a Kluxer with what he regarded as a sense of humor, had thrown cherry bombs onto the pavement in the middle of the crowd.

King and his handlers left very quickly. He was hustled into a waiting car. The followers ran, pursued by yelling white men. The marchers were accompanied by a pickup truck in case of an emergency. Panic-stricken young people piled onto the pickup bed as it crept through the throng. A white girl tried to board but was caught by two or three local men. Friends on the pickup grabbed her arms and pulled as the white men held on to her feet. For a long time she was suspended above the ground, moving through the air in slow motion until her captors finally lost their grip and she was hauled across the tailgate and into the truck.

The local whites were not finished. They attacked the marchers with fists and clubs for several blocks, and young black men fought back. One white guy with a five-foot wooden club was separated from his group and soundly thrashed.

The marchers finally got to the black neighborhood. That evening a band of whites drove through and attacked the Philadelphia headquarters of the Freedom Democratic Party with gunfire. The black occupants fired back and shot one of the assailants in the head and neck with buckshot. He was not hurt seriously, more's the pity.

Half a dozen of us covered the gun battle by phone from a motel room in Yazoo City, about seventy-five miles away at the edge of the Mississippi Delta. Our designated man on the phone had called the headquarters and was talking to Ralph Featherstone, field secretary of SNCC, while the battle was going on. Featherstone at one point asked our man to hold the line while he went to a window and fired back at some men who were shooting at the house from a blue car at the curb. Our man relayed information to the rest of us as he got it and we made notes.

When the gunfire ended, we went to our own rooms, updated our stories, and phoned them to our papers, wire services, and TV networks. It was an inconvenient way to cover a story, but inconvenience was a job description for us at that time.

We had rented rooms in Yazoo City because we needed lodging near the next day's march. We did not seriously look for rooms in Philadelphia. Even if there had been vacancies, which was doubtful, none of us relished the idea of spending the night there. We had heard the stories from reporters like Claude Sitton and Karl Fleming about being accosted on the sidewalks by white thugs looking for outside agitators and visiting newsmen.

During the tumult and violence after the demonstrators had fled from the courthouse, several of us reporters melted into the angry white crowd. We resorted to the tactic of pretending to have nothing to do with it all. I chose to become a shoe salesman. I had noticed a shoe store nearby, and that seemed to offer a believable identity. I kept my hands in my pockets and my notebook out of sight and just watched and listened as I drifted along, keeping the action in view.

Many of us carried what we called the Claude Sitton memorial notebook. That was a standard stenographer's pad that had been cut off several inches from the bottom. The remainder fit nicely into a hip pocket. Claude had persuaded a supply store in Atlanta to devise the notebook some years earlier, and there had been a steady market for them.

The march resumed a day after the Philadelphia detour, and we fought heat, flies, and boredom. There were diversions. A cardboard box appeared on the back of a flatbed truck that had been rented by news organizations for the convenience of photographers and TV cameramen. The driver opened the box after it had sat there several days. A copperhead snake, understandably irritated at being cooped up so long, leapt out, scattering journalists as it hurried away.

The Meredith march ended with a noisy rally in Jackson. It had provided two weeks of news, but it had done more. First, it proved that Meredith had grown too optimistic living in New York. It still was not safe for a black man to assert himself boldly across the landscape of Mississippi. Second, the march launched a new rallying cry, one that proved to be a turning point in the civil rights movement.

It happened at Greenwood, one of the overnight stops. Stokely Carmichael took the platform in a bad mood. He had just been released from jail, one more time.

"This is the twenty-seventh time I have been arrested," he said. "I ain't going to jail no more. The only way we gonna stop them white

men from whupping us is to take over." Then he said it was time for the movement to drop its slogan of the past six years, "Freedom Now," and adopt a new and more demanding one: "Black Power!"

The crowd instantly took up the cry and made it ring through the church sanctuary: "Black Power!" The scene was broadcast on television screens across America that evening. The new slogan spread throughout the movement wherever younger black people gathered. It also threatened to divide the leadership for a time. Older leaders shrank from it and thought it was intentionally provocative to white people who might be sympathetic. But the young activists reveled in the consternation it caused.

I had a personal encounter with Black Power later that summer. I was at home in Atlanta one night when I got word that a riot had broken out on Boulevard Street a couple of miles south. The night before, in another neighborhood, a Negro youth had been killed and a white policeman wounded in an eruption of racial violence. I drove to the scene on Boulevard, parked on a side street, and walked toward the sound of the commotion. I could see a sizable crowd of what seemed to be young black men making its way down the street toward me. They were shouting, cursing, and smashing shop windows as they came.

I was standing in front of a row of stores with one or two other people when Andy Young joined us. We suddenly realized that while we talked, the mob—that's what it was—had come closer. It was no more than half a block away and moving steadily. Andy turned to a young black woman and asked, "Do you have a car?" She said she did. He said, "Put Mr. Reed in it and get him out of here." She and I walked fast to her car, and she drove me to mine. I moved it two or three blocks away where I could still see and hear.

I spoke to Jack Nelson later, and he told me he had been watching from another point on the street and had almost been trapped. He outran half a dozen guys down a side street and jumped into his car. Jim Giltmier, a white television reporter for WSB in Atlanta—an acquaintance of mine from Arkansas, where he had worked as a newspaper reporter—was covering the disturbance farther down Boulevard Street. Somebody hit him with a brick and knocked him unconscious. He was hospitalized for some time, and when he came out he wore a steel plate in his skull.

I remembered a conversation I'd had a day or two earlier with a SNCC activist named Willie Ricks. Emotions were running high in Atlanta's black neighborhoods. Just hours before I saw Willie, I had been jostled in a crowd of black youngsters in another part of town. A girl had spat on me.

I had known Willie for some time as an enthusiastic functionary in SNCC. He had worked in almost every state in the Deep South and had made a name as a reliable organizer and crowd warmer. He and I knew each other well enough to call each other by our first names. That did not mean we were friends. He was about fifteen years my junior, and I would have felt silly calling him Mr. Ricks. On his side, he was not about to demean himself by using a courtesy title on any white man during that era. No one was more firmly anti-establishmentarian than an angry black kid during the 1960s. Aside from that, all of us involved in the civil rights story on both sides had fallen into the first-name habit simply as a means of easing communication.

Willie had spotted me sitting in my car during the break in the action, and he got in and sat down. He seemed to need rest as much as I did. We chatted for a while, not about the weather but in a rather offhanded way about what had been happening in the streets. Then he started speaking philosophically. There was going to be a revolution in this country, he told me. In fact, it was already under way. It was going to become more widespread, and it was going to end in the deaths of a lot of white people. He turned toward me so that he could look into my eyes. He said, "I have to tell you that when the revolution gets here, if I ever see you in the sights of my gun, I'll pull the trigger." He said it in an even voice, matter-of-factly. I don't remember how I responded. I made no attempt to pass it off as a joke. Willie was serious.

My friend Andy Young went on to be a U.S. congressman and mayor of Atlanta. I lost track of Willie. I learned long after our encounter in Atlanta that Stokely Carmichael had been mistakenly credited with coining the slogan "Black Power" that night in Greenwood. Willie Ricks was the first to try out the new slogan. He had used it in front of a crowd in some little town where no national reporters were present. But other SNCC people were there. They saw the reaction that Willie got and knew that a new psychological warfare weapon had been discovered.

I Googled Willie a generation later and found some photos. He

apparently went on stirring up people on two or three continents after the glory days of the Southern movement. In one photo taken in 2009, he is wearing a colorful African robe. His hair and beard are white, and he is wearing specs. He looks like a cranky old grandfather.

Stokely Carmichael declared in Greenwood that he had been arrested twenty-seven times and he would not go to jail again. He was mistaken. Two months later, he landed in jail in Atlanta charged with inciting a riot. He refused to make bail.

Whether he incited a riot in Atlanta turned on a fine legal point. There was no doubt that he incited people. So did every other activist of any talent at all. But he and the others never told a crowd, "You all go out there and have a riot!" If the crowd got worked up because of his fiery rhetoric—well, that was not his problem.

Over the course of those few days in Atlanta—"The city too busy to hate"—we white reporters were left with no safe place to stop and catch our breath. Black neighborhoods, once our sanctuary, were now off limits. People occasionally asked me in later years whether covering the troubles in Northern Ireland was more dangerous than covering civil rights in the South. No, I had to tell them. In Northern Ireland, we just lay in bed and listened to the bombs exploding in pubs around town. Having to avoid the pubs was a small inconvenience, but we lived with it.

More important, the Atlanta troubles widened a gap between the nonviolent activists led by King and the Black Power advocates, who eventually coalesced into the Black Panther Party. Stokely Carmichael was its "prime minister." The Panthers spread across the nation while King and his followers expanded their influence into Northern cities, all beyond my purview. Stokely Carmichael eventually changed his name and moved to Africa. He died in 1998.

There was one more act of racial violence that I dealt with that fall before leaving it all behind for the peaceful precincts of Washington, D.C. In Wetumpka, Alabama, a black citizen named James Earl Motley, twenty-seven, was beaten to death by a sheriff's deputy. He had mouthed off to the deputy during an early-morning traffic stop. Motley was a passenger in the car and had refused to get into the sheriff's car. His body was removed from the local jail later in the morning. An autopsy performed that night found that he had died of "multiple

skull fractures." He had no known connection to the civil rights movement.

The local authorities refused to charge the deputy. When a federal prosecutor put the deputy on trial and charged him with depriving Motley of his civil rights, the jury acquitted him. Apparently, the jurors chose to believe the deputy's story that the man had not died of the blows administered by the deputy with his slapjack—blows that had left the back seat of Motley's friend's car covered with blood—but from injuries sustained when he fell against a fence post on the walk from the sheriff's car to the jail.

CHAPTER 20

Winding Down:
Beale to Bourbon

Beale and Bourbon, two of the most famous streets in the South, commanded my attention before I withdrew to Washington for a spell. The Memphis home of the blues and W. C. Handy, the street of "more living and more dying than any place in the world," had been rotting away since World War I. Instead of the blues, the few music halls left played mainly rock 'n' roll. I summed up the decline this way:

> Beale Street once boasted a bandit named River George, a three-story bawdy house run by a woman named Lou, a gambler so angered by an insult that he killed four men in one night, and a nightclub so lethal that a neighboring mortuary built a runway to its back door to expedite the handling of corpses.
>
> Beale Street crime, according to a recent report, now consists mainly of petty theft, youthful loitering, gang activities and small-time gambling.

So now, in 1966, the city fathers had set about cleaning up the old street and "sivilizing" it, as Huck Finn would have put it. The feds put up some money, of course, and in time Beale became a block-by-block museum where you could drink a bottle of beer while you read up on the glorious past.

Bourbon Street's problem was similar. Developers began to see money in the French Quarter, and they divined how to grab it: build skyscrapers! Well, not real skyscrapers, but multistory hotels with luxury suites and rooftop bars and restaurants that offered steaks and other food more congenial to the palates of up-river folks than crawfish and jambalaya.

The sazerac hit the fan when (1) the highway department proposed to build a freeway through the Quarter, and (2) the hotel builders discovered that the old-timers were right about building on sand and mud. The building will sink and fall. The water table was so high that a man with a shovel could reach water a few inches under the surface. One developer lurched into the news when he excavated a big hole next door to Pepe's Bar and the barroom wall cracked in several places.

Pepe's was the home of "the most flat-chested waitress in the French Quarter." It was also the Bourbon Street home of Judah P. Benjamin, the first attorney general and later secretary of state of the Confederate States of America. It mattered not that more of the population cared about the waitress than Secretary Benjamin. The preservationists jumped all over the developer, and he had to make some radical changes in his plans.

So did the highway department. The riled-up residents of the Quarter and their friends all over town finally beat back the planned expressway.

I sometimes wonder about another famous Southern street. When we lived in Atlanta in the mid-1960s, we used to treat ourselves to an evening at a little nightclub called the Wit's End. The highlight of every evening's performance was a song by a pair of singers entitled "They're Tearing Up Peachtree Again."

The song hit a chord in every breast. The city's street department apparently had a fixation about Peachtree Street. The engineers never got it repaired to their satisfaction. Every trip on Peachtree in those years was like running an obstacle course of barricades and fresh-dug holes. I paid a visit to the Wit's End many years later, after we had moved to another city, and was gratified to see that the song was still a hit, for the same reason.

There was one other story from the South that deserves a place in this memoir. Mississippi became the last "dry" state to catch up with the times during the summer of 1966. It goes without saying that Mississippi had never suffered unduly from Prohibition. I needed to buy a bottle of spirits occasionally to give to my host at a dinner party or to share with other traveling reporters. Everybody in Jackson knew the address of the best bootlegger. The front of the building looked like an ordinary house. You noticed from the front that the resident

seemed to have a lot of company. A steady stream of cars drove down a circular driveway that circled behind the house and, minutes later, emerged on the other side.

I took my place in line on those occasions and gave my order at a drive-up window in what might once have been a bedroom. The guy had any brand you wanted. The prices were lower than in any other state I covered. Mississippi for years had collected taxes on the illegal booze, so the state government was not losing revenue. But the hypocrisy grated on some nerves. My friend Bill Minor, the state's best reporter, who had been the *New York Times* Mississippi stringer for years, hated it. He was an expert martini maker, and after one or two he would wax indignant about the state's ludicrous liquor law. When legalization came to Jackson, he was the first customer in line at his favorite bar. He got a good story out of it for his newspaper, the *New Orleans Times-Picayune.*

Ending Prohibition called for some delicate political maneuvering. Governor Paul Johnson wanted the law changed, but he needed some event or circumstance to help get it done. Prohibition held the upper hand because of longevity; it had been in effect since 1908. A lot of church people liked it.

The governor addressed the legislature in February 1966 and demanded a change in the law, which he called "shameful, disgraceful, indecent and scandalous." A week later, the Hinds County sheriff raided the Jackson Country Club and hauled off all its liquor. The cream of Jackson society were there that night, and, as it happened, one of their guests was the governor. The raid was just what the reform campaign needed. In May, the legislature abolished Prohibition.

A more skeptical reporter might have wondered at the timing of that country club raid and whether the governor might have had a hand in it. Huey P. Long of Louisiana would have been capable of such trickery, and so would his brother Earl, as well as Governor Jim Folsom of Alabama and some others I could name. Governor Johnson seemed too sober and upright for such machinations. But who knows? He and the cabal who might have got it done are all dead now, and we will never know the truth.

Before I left the Southern beat, I spent the last day of 1966 at Fort Jackson, South Carolina. I went there to write about the travails of

Captain Howard Brett Levy, an army physician from Brooklyn, who was threatened with court-martial for speaking out against the Vietnam War. He had faced considerable hostility in and around the base. A typical confrontation began with an angry soldier or civilian demanding to know whether Captain Levy was a Communist. (He declared that he was not.) He had a handful of supportive friends, including his estranged wife, who stood up for him from as far away as New York. It was easy to understand the anger of fellow soldiers. Captain Levy had called Special Forces troops "liars and thieves and killers of peasants and murderers of women and children."

Levy had no use for the military or for anything in it, from the dress requirements to the demand that he learn to salute without keeping his left hand in his pocket. He was a civilian at heart and had been drafted because the army needed doctors. My old friend Charles Morgan of the ACLU was called in to defend Levy. His defense was heroic, but fruitless. Levy was sentenced to prison.

CHAPTER 21

The White House

Tom Wicker, the Washington bureau chief of the *Times*, arranged for me to transfer from Atlanta to Washington in early 1967 to be the number-two reporter on the White House beat. Max Frankel was in charge. He had been a distinguished foreign correspondent, and I was pleased to work with him. Our daughter Cindy was also pleased. We lived in the same neighborhood in Chevy Chase with the Frankels, and she picked up some nice change babysitting the Frankel children. Our son John was less pleased to be in Washington. He was mugged for the first time in his life on a downtown street.

We first lived in a rented house in Bethesda a few months before buying in Chevy Chase. An elderly neighbor made Norma feel at home. She invited Norma over several days a week for late-afternoon drinks. The neighbor made it clear that she was not a heavy drinker; she limited herself to one drink a day. Norma noticed that that was true. But she had a habit of "sweetening" her drink as it got low in the glass with a splash of gin, then another, then another.

I moved onto the White House beat at the nadir of President Johnson's popularity. He had enjoyed a series of triumphs immediately after succeeding the assassinated John F. Kennedy in 1963, but he had escalated American involvement in the increasingly unpopular war in Vietnam. By 1967, he was being denounced in the press and elsewhere every day. He had virtually stopped traveling outside Washington because everywhere he went he was greeted by hostile demonstrators. One chant in particular galled him: "Hey hey, LBJ, how many kids have you killed today?"

Max and I took turns standing watch in Austin or San Antonio

while the worried, exhausted president tried to rest at his ranch near Johnson City. Only rarely did we see him on those trips. His press secretary or one of his aides briefed us every day, always insisting on the accepted fiction that the president was working at the ranch. Piddling news releases about small matters were provided to give us an excuse to file copy every day. Most of our time, however, was spent on the tennis courts in Austin or in the cafes and cantinas along the river walk in San Antonio.

The reporters for the Associated Press and United Press International got special treatment because those wire services served thousands of newspaper and broadcast outlets around the world. Helen Thomas worked for Merriman Smith, the long-tenured White House correspondent for UPI, and did most of the agency's out-of-town traveling. Her rival at the AP was Doug Cornell. They scrambled like Olympic sprinters to beat each other by seconds in filing stories. But we began to notice that at the end of the day in Austin and San Antonio, Helen and Doug could be found in out-of-the-way places having drinks and dinner. When Doug retired in 1971, they got married. The marriage apparently thrived, even though Helen had made it clear that being a wife was not high on her list of priorities. Doug died in 1982.

Helen's ancestors were Lebanese. Her feelings toward Israel were frosty. She passed me at a lope one day headed for the White House press room after one of Johnson's news conferences. The president's message on the Middle East that day had annoyed her. As she moved past me, I heard her mutter, "Goddamned Zionist White House!" Some similar comment about the Jewish state, this time in a very public place, ended her long career many years later.

I was shocked when I started on the White House beat by another attitude that seemed to be widespread among the other reporters. Several of them were openly disdainful of the president. I suspect that at least a few of them let that disdain show in their copy, although I can't prove it at this late date. I do know that more than a few of them disliked this Texan and made no attempt to hide their feelings in the press room chatter.

There was a strong suspicion that he shaded the truth. That apparently annoyed those seasoned reporters. One would have thought

that they had never encountered an elected official who committed that sin.

I think they disliked Lyndon Johnson for another reason, one they would never have admitted to me. Lyndon talked funny. His voice grated on the cultivated ears of the Eastern press. He was from Texas, a state that has always aroused ill-tempered opinion from afar. I won't defend Texas; my own state sits next door to that bloated piece of geography.

I think the problem had partly to do with a bastard offspring of the alphabet. The letter *r* tells much of who we are in the diverse regions of the South. In the daintier parts of Mississippi, Alabama, and Georgia, and in cities like Charleston and Savannah, they treat the *r* as an uncouth sound, like belching. They glide past it so as not to leave a bad taste in their mouths. The sturdier parts of the South—the hills, the Southwest, Arkansas, Texas—use it the way they do in Ulster, where our Scotch-Irish ancestors came from and where they still treat the *r* with the respect it deserves. Lyndon's speech was a lineal descendant of the Ulsterman's, defined by a robust *r* and made sharper by an aggressive nasal drawl.

I once heard the Reverend Ian Paisley, a contemptible old bigot, preach a sermon denouncing Catholics in his Protestant church in Belfast. The only thing I liked about him was the way he growled his *r*'s. Lyndon growled his the same way, and a lot of snooty Yankee reporters didn't like it.

Johnson's detractors coined the term "credibility gap" to describe the distance between Johnson's public utterances and the facts. The "credibility gap" was used mostly in criticism of his Vietnam War policy, on which he could be exasperatingly unforthcoming. I didn't care for that policy, myself. But I was never seriously tempted to call the president a liar in public.

I tried to watch and learn from the older reporters. No one was older than Merriman Smith. Smitty had been covering presidents since Roosevelt and was credited with beating the rest of the press by several minutes on the news of that president's death at Warm Springs, Georgia. He hogged the only telephone in the house. When Kennedy was shot in Dallas, he grabbed the radio-telephone on the front seat of the wire-service car and hung on to it. Smith always took the front seat in the wire-service car and dared his Associated Press rival to challenge him.

In Dallas, Jack Bell, the AP man, flailed away from the rear seat at his enemy's head and back but never managed to grab the phone. Smith showed the welts on his back afterward. He won the Pulitzer Prize for his work that day. I understood from the beginning of my career that my fists and feet, not to mention my tongue, were too slow for wire-service work.

On one slow news day at the White House, Smith told some of us younger reporters about an episode with President Johnson a few nights earlier. Smith and his wife were entertaining ten guests for dinner when he was called to the phone. A nervous young UPI reporter apologized for bothering the man in his castle, but felt he ought to pass on a troubling series of phone calls. The first call had come from the West Coast, a second from the middle of the country, and a third from the East Coast. Each one claimed to have information that the president was dead. Could the White House reporter take a minute and check it out?

Smitty phoned the White House press office and got George Christian, the press secretary. He explained why he was calling. He told George he understood that this was just another silly rumor, but would he squelch it so he could get back to dinner? George said, "Hold on a minute, Smitty." The next voice Smith heard was the nasal drawl of the president of the United States. As it turned out, Johnson and Christian, his fellow Texan, were having a drink before calling it a day.

"How are you, Smitty?"

"I'm fine, thank you, Mr. President."

"What are you doing, Smitty?"

"I'm just getting ready to have dinner, Mr. President. We have some guests here."

"Smitty, how would you like to come over and watch a movie with me?"

"Well, that would be fine, Mr. President, but we have ten people here for dinner, and . . ."

"Bring them all with you. I'll have some cars there in ten minutes." And he hung up.

The cars came. Mr. and Mrs. Smith and their guests loaded up and rode to the White House. The movie was an old John Wayne western. The president watched from the back of the basement theater. Halfway

through, Smith noticed that Johnson had gone to sleep. The president woke up when it was over and said to Smith, "How did you like the movie, Smitty?" "It was fine, Mr. President." Turning to the projectionist, Johnson said, "Show it to them again." He got up and went to bed.

Covering the White House was often boring. We sat around the press room for hours waiting for morning and afternoon briefings by the press secretary or one of his assistants. People read newspapers and magazines. Some played cards. We tried to make ourselves useful by interviewing White House officials to flesh out issues of the day, but the resulting stories were generally more useful for the president in pushing his agenda than they were for our readers. Perhaps the best such story that I wrote in my year on the beat was a backgrounder on Marvin Watson, a strong silent Texan who was Johnson's gate-keeper. No one got to see the president without passing Watson's office. He was good at his job. Somehow, he agreed to an interview, but only after a lot of pushing. I'm not sure the story shed any light on the man except to reveal that Marvin Watson was secretive and doggedly loyal to his boss.

■ ■ ■

Part of my job on the White House beat was traveling with the first lady on her beautification tours. Most of the time I was the only man in the group of twenty-five or thirty reporters. All of them, including Mrs. Johnson, treated me like one of the girls.

We were on a plane going somewhere. Mrs. Johnson was napping in her sort-of bunk-bed beside the narrow aisle. I walked past, and she roused up and asked me to hand her a blanket. Just to make a little conversation, I said, "Are you cold?" She replied, a little tartly, "Sure I am!"

Years later, she was back on the LBJ Ranch. Her husband had died, and she was beginning to come to grips with life not just as a widow but as the most famous political widow in the world after Jacqueline Kennedy Onassis. At the urging of her old friend and press secretary Liz Carpenter, she invited a bunch of the reporters who had covered her in the White House to come down for a kind of reunion. The pretext was to promote her beautification program. When we got there, I was once again the only man. Once again, she treated me like one of the girls.

It was a pleasant event, tinged with reflections of her grief. She really did care for the rascal in spite of his philandering. And he, "true to you darling, in my fashion," cared for her. A woman reporter who had known the Johnsons since their Texas days once described Lyndon's habit. He would show up at an after-hours party on the pretext of needing to be there as Senate majority leader. He would stop inside the door, scan the room for the best-looking woman, head straight for her, and, more times than not, end up in her bed. But everyone understood that this was not even a one-night stand. My friend explained, "It was 'into bed, out of bed, and home to Lady Bird.'"

The president invited two reporters to the living quarters of the White House one day. Mrs. Johnson walked past and headed down the hall. Before she was out of earshot, the president told the fellows that there went the best sex—expressed with his customary crudeness—he had ever had.

Other reporters told about a day riding around the LBJ Ranch with him when they stopped to take a leak. One reporter, nodding toward Johnson's apparatus, of which he was proud, asked him, "Mr. President, aren't you afraid that a rattlesnake might bite that thing?" "Ah, hell," he replied, "it's half rattlesnake itself."

CHAPTER 22

The Viet Cong Has It In for Me

Protests against the war in Vietnam picked up early in 1967. A story of mine on January 31 told of a group of clergymen and laymen demonstrating in front of the White House to urge a reappraisal of American war policy. I thought the protest was remarkable for its restrained language.

A month later, LBJ reiterated in strong terms his refusal to stop the bombing of North Vietnam without some reciprocal reduction of military action by the North. That had been his stance; he saw no way out of Vietnam without appearing to accept defeat. In Texas terms, he would be tucking his tail between his legs and going home. Later that month, he flew to Guam to meet his advisers on the war. He wanted the country to see "forward movement" in the conflict at a time when millions saw only quagmire. I pointed out that he was willing to fly seven thousand miles to make that point. Max went with him.

As the war wore on, the president sought every opportunity to make the case for staying the course. He handed out at least two Medals of Honor, using the occasions to urge the country not to lose heart. He continued bombing North Vietnam. His generals and embassy people flew home regularly to back him up and to claim that the Americans and their South Vietnamese allies were gaining. They could see "light at the end of the tunnel," they said. He defended his political allies in the Saigon government even as one story after another revealed that those allies were a corrupt gang of thieves.

The protests at home gained volume, and the president found himself increasingly cut off from the public. He encountered angry and ever larger crowds of protests wherever he went, no matter what

the occasion of his trip. Finally, he confined himself more and more to the White House except for short drives in the capital.

During this time, I was assigned to follow Vice President Humphrey as he became the president's traveling salesman. I had a page 1 story from Doylestown, Pennsylvania, where Humphrey raised the alarm about the "Chinese Communist Peril," as the headline summed it up. The real threat to world peace, he said, was Asian Communism, "with its headquarters in Peking, China."

Days later, Humphrey was standing in for the president in South Vietnam with me and a horde of Washington reporters in tow. The reason for the trip was the inauguration of President Nguyen Van Thieu. Humphrey was met at the Saigon airport by Nguyen Cao Ky, the incoming vice president. Ky was regarded as a dashing scoundrel, a womanizer, openly corrupt, a swaggering air force officer who paraded around in his flight uniform and a lavender scarf. He fled to California after the fall of Saigon and bought a liquor store.

I wish I could have heard the conversation between Ky and Humphrey on the ride from the airport. Humphrey was one of the most genial and open politicians I ever knew, but he was also strait-laced to a fault. I once saw him backed against a wall in a dimly lit corridor of a Washington hotel by a brazen Texas blonde who seemed intent on gaining his virtue. He was blushing and grinning and stammering, and I'm dead certain that the blonde failed to score.

Humphrey and the traveling press corps made day trips to several military bases around South Vietnam. We were to be shown how much progress we and our South Vietnamese allies had made. The press group abounded with skeptics. We had read the stories by David Halberstam of the *Times* and other reporters who had chronicled the failures as well as the meager successes of the American mission. We knew we were being encouraged to file stories favorable to the military and to President Johnson's oversight of the war.

We returned each night to Saigon, where we were housed in the famous old Hotel Continental. Several American news companies had bureaus there. Working and living in the Continental had been a custom since the days of French colonialism. The hotel had a magnificent restaurant and the liveliest bar in town. Reporters, diplomats, free-lancers, spies, and men of varied and sometimes invisible nationalities

met there to socialize and ply their trades. It was a lot like Rick's Café in *Casablanca*. The open-air portico was a favorite place to sip a drink and watch the pretty Vietnamese girls putter past on their mopeds with white *ao dais* fluttering in the wind. Those long tunics, side-slit to the waist with two panels draped loose to catch the breeze, struck the visiting Western men as infinitely more feminine than the sober dress of American and European women.

R. W. "Johnny" Apple Jr., the *Times* Saigon bureau chief, was my unofficial host during this visit. He was a comer on the paper. In a few years, he would become one of the nation's best political reporters. I once heard him say that his Rolodex, which was the size of a round of Wisconsin cheese, had the name of at least one political source in every important county in the United States. He spent hours a day on the phone, and it paid off. It was Apple who first spotted the growing grassroots support for the unknown Georgian Jimmy Carter.

One night the new South Vietnamese president gave a dinner in the presidential palace honoring Humphrey and the U.S. diplomatic delegation. The press were all there, never shy about free food. I was there with Johnny and his wife, Edith Smith Apple, the U.S. vice-consul in Saigon. She was good company. She seemed to take a real interest in Johnny's colleagues. I had the impression that everyone liked her.

The banquet took place on the open-air first floor of the grand modern palace, which had been finished only about a year. Several hundred people milled around sipping drinks. Johnny and Edie, with me in tow, approached General William C. Westmoreland, the commander of the 535,000 U.S. troops in the country. The general stood making small talk with the three of us. At my urging, he talked about his native South Carolina, where I had spent a little time as a Southern correspondent. We were relaxed. The soft twilight was inviting; several people had drifted onto the lawn to look at the tropical flowers and soak up the contentment of the day.

Suddenly, the peaceful party was interrupted by an explosion. This was not the distant gunfire that every troubled city grows accustomed to. It was close.

"Incoming or outgoing?" Apple asked Westmoreland. The general cocked his head slightly, considered only briefly, and replied, "Outgoing." That was my introduction to the language of a city that

was subjected to regular mortar fire from the insurgent Viet Cong. If
the general had said the mortar round was incoming, that would have
signaled that we were under attack, and that the mortar troops were
starting to step in the shells. Spotters near the target would report by
phone to the men firing the mortars telling them how close their shell
had landed, and they would adjust the angle and range for the next,
and the next, until they had it right.

Guests on the lawn, those without benefit of the general's reassur-
ing words, began to rush toward the shelter of the porticoed building.
Then there was a second explosion, this one noticeably closer. The out-
side crowd moved in with more haste. Several seconds later, but before
Westmoreland could revise his estimate, a third shell exploded, this
one near enough to jar us. The crowd was on the verge of panic. The
general stood his ground, calm, seemingly paying no attention to the
ruckus and ignoring his bad call on the direction of the mortars.

That was the last explosion. We warily returned to our drinks. Only
later did I learn from Apple, who had left the party to go to the bureau,
that the mortars had been fired from a building half a mile away, that
the third shell had struck within feet of the fence surrounding the palace,
and that a fourth round had exploded prematurely in the room occupied
by the attackers and killed them all. That was the one meant to tippy-
toe into our party. It might have killed and wounded scores of people,
including perhaps the president of Vietnam, the vice president of the
United States, and the U.S. military commander, as well as Johnny Apple,
the estimable Edie Apple, and me.

The next morning at 4:00, I got up to go to the airport. It fell to
Edie to drive me across town to catch my official bus. Johnny stayed
in bed. Edie's car was stopped every half-mile or so by soldiers check-
ing for terrorists. She was one of the strongest people I had ever met,
a woman of immense character.

■　　■　　■

The Humphrey party made several one-day trips to U.S. bases around
South Vietnam before departing for Malaysia, where the vice president
conducted a quieter bit of diplomacy. The next stop was Indonesia.
Several of us, including Humphrey, went home from there with a

severe stomach disorder that laid us low for days. We thought we got it at a party. We had been warned not to drink the water and to confine ourselves to beer or some other beverage that had been sterilized. I'm pretty sure that Humphrey and I got our beer at that party from the same nice woman. She thought it would be inhospitable to have us drink out of bottles, so she poured the beer into glasses—which had been freshly washed and rinsed in the local water.

We made a side trip from Jakarta to Bali. The reporters were sent on a separate plane, and we noticed that several dozen cases of beer were stacked behind the cockpit. That was unremarkable until we noticed that the pilot and the copilot were guzzling beer. Their landing was a little awkward, but it turned out to be less harrowing than an event that evening. There was still another party, this time on the beautifully landscaped lawn of a grand hotel. Another reporter and I had made a fast trip downtown and bought sarongs to take home. We had noticed that the sarong was the dress of choice for large numbers of Balinese men as well as women. He and I boldly decided to wear ours to the party.

We had our first misgivings when we went outside and found that the guests were seated at tables only a few inches above the ground. We had to sit cross-legged on the grass as we ate. During the dinner, a dozen or two of the island's most beautiful girls went among us dancing to the music. They stopped every few feet and grabbed American men to join them. My friend and I breathed sighs of relief when the girls passed us by. We were pretty certain that if one of us had been tapped, his new sarong would have embarrassed him. There is an art to tying a sarong securely around the waist. We had not mastered it.

The party finally broke up, and the Americans headed for the hotel. Just as I got to the door, my sarong came loose and fell to my ankles. Luckily, I had kept my underwear on. That meant that I was slightly less embarrassed than I might have been. Even so, a large number of American women witnessed the event and called it to my attention all the way home across numerous oceans and continents.

■ ■ ■

In April, Johnson picked up a nice piece of moral support from the Most Reverend Robert E. Lucey, the seventy-five-year-old Roman

Catholic archbishop of San Antonio, an old friend from his Texas days. The president was in the congregation at a San Antonio church when the archbishop preached a sermon defending the U.S. intervention in Vietnam. He condemned "apathetic neutrality" as harmful to world peace. Johnson put a twenty-dollar bill in the collection plate.

The Vietnam War was Lyndon Johnson's undoing, and he deserved the criticism he got. Whether he deserved the contempt and even hatred that came from some quarters is another matter. I believe that Johnson thought he was doing the right thing. I believe that he agreed with his many advisers, including those on the left, who told him that it was imperative for America to intercede to stop the spread of Communism in Asia. His friend Humphrey, who spoke out against the growing influence of Communist China, spoke from his own experience in Minnesota politics. He had battled radical leftists there; he feared and distrusted them and their political kin around the globe. As a liberal Democrat, Humphrey saw the dark threat of authoritarianism at the end of the Communist rainbow. He understood Josef Stalin.

Johnson heard the same message from the foreign affairs experts in his cabinet and in his inner circle, many of whom were distinguished academics from the Ivy League. As for himself, when he remembered the poor Mexican Americans and the despised black minority in his native Texas, he could see no spiritual connection between his own liberal politics and the Communist Party of North Vietnam, which claimed to represent the interests of the poor and downtrodden in Southeast Asia.

In addition, he was haunted by the fear of failure in his presidency. He came to believe that he would be judged not simply for his domestic successes in civil rights and support for America's lowliest and neediest, but also for his management of the great military conflict he had inherited from John Kennedy. As a Southerner and a Texan, he had keenly felt the scorn that the Eastern elite made no effort to hide for him and his kind. A defeat in Vietnam would give those people even more reason to look down on him, he believed. He was a proud man and sensitive.

So it spun out of control, and he went home beaten and wounded to his core.

Meanwhile, he pressed his advantage on domestic issues. He

demonstrated his growing alignment with the civil rights movement by speaking at the Lincoln Memorial on February 12, Lincoln's birthday. While the Republicans satisfied themselves with a recitation of the Gettysburg Address by the Senate minority leader, Everett Dirksen of Illinois, in the comfort of the Senate chamber, the president stood in the chill and addressed several hundred men, women, and children at the base of the emancipator's statue. My story reminded readers that Johnson had come a long way since his days in Texas politics when he was considered at least a fringe member of the Southern bloc dedicated to preserving segregation.

On March 2, he found another venue of great symbolic value in which to deliver another ringing endorsement of equal rights and a reminder of his commitment to them. He showed up unannounced at Howard University across town from the White House to add his voice to the school's celebration of its one hundredth year. He noted that since 1957, the nation had added four important civil rights laws to the books. He did not have to point out to that audience that he had had a hand in all of them, either in the Senate as majority leader or as president.

The president was in one of his manic phases. He was all over town that day. He made a speech at the Office of Education. He announced that he was inviting all fifty governors to the White House in a couple of weeks. He held a series of receptions for members of Congress. He held his second unannounced news conference in a week. All that in addition to a series of private meetings in the Oval Office.

At the other end of the White House, Mrs. Johnson spoke to reporters to confirm that their younger daughter, Mrs. Patrick J. Nugent, was pregnant. This was the kind of day the president loved. Never mind that forty-eight hours later he might be huddling out of sight and snapping at his aides and anyone else who intruded.

Many of us remember that at the depth of the Greek tragedy that had become his life, he gave up the presidency—for which he had struggled and schemed all his life and for which he was probably better trained than almost any other president in our history—and announced that he would not run for reelection in 1968. But before that announcement, his party had already begun to try to resolve the tension that had made a debacle of the 1964 party convention in Chicago. The problem

was the South: how could the Democrats accommodate both the growing Negro vote and the old white conservatives who had dominated the party there—and kept an inordinate influence in it nationally—at the upcoming 1968 convention? A party committee tried to solve the dilemma with a package of rules that said to the world, "Listen. We hate it, but the South is finally going to have to join the Union."

My story about the committee pointed out that the eleven Southern states had almost three million Negro voters in 1967 and that that was almost twice as many as five years earlier.

■ ■ ■

Former chancellor Konrad Adenauer of West Germany died in April and thus gave Johnson an opportunity for one of his favorite social events—a funeral. He never saw a funeral he couldn't make time for. He and Adenauer had known each other for years, and the Johnsons had once entertained the old chancellor at the LBJ Ranch. Johnson had been severely chagrined when he got sick and had to miss the funeral of Sir Winston Churchill in 1965. He made up for that when Adenauer was buried. After a requiem mass in the old Cologne Cathedral, the body was placed on a boat and sent up the Rhine to a cemetery in his little old hometown of Rhondorf.

I drew the funeral assignment because Max Frankel did not want to go. He was much better qualified to write about Germany and European issues. He had covered foreign affairs for years. Not only that, he had been born in Germany. And that was the problem. He and his Jewish family had got out just ahead of the Nazis in 1938 when Max was eight years old. The memory was too raw.

Johnson was in no hurry to get home. While he was in Germany, he managed a lot of quiet diplomacy with every European of any reputation, from President Charles de Gaulle of France to Prime Minister Harold Wilson of Britain. He twisted the arm of the West German chancellor, Kurt Georg Kiesinger. The Germans were being hard to handle on a bunch of issues, including a treaty to halt the spread of nuclear weapons. Johnson and his crew were already having the usual trouble trying to negotiate with the Russians, and the Germans were complicating things by insisting that they be allowed to go ahead full

throttle with their own nuclear energy plans. If Johnson and Kiesinger made any progress, it was not apparent to us in the press. Johnson did persuade Kiesinger to come to the States for a visit sometime. Johnson knew that if he could get the stubborn German down to the ranch, on his home turf, he could probably wear him down. Feed him some barbecue, give him some whiskey. Things would work out.

I was fortunate in being paired with David Binder, the paper's correspondent for West Germany. He knew the language and the beat, and he wrote the stories from the funeral that bore on U.S.-European relations. He was also generous in guiding me with my own stories. And then, after hours, he introduced me to German nightlife. I have been to a lot of funerals, but for sheer spectacle, Dr. Adenauer's was my favorite.

■ ■ ■

Six weeks after Johnson and Senator Robert Kennedy had met privately to discuss the war, the White House was having to deal with the fallout. The meeting was being portrayed as not exactly friendly but less than a shouting match. The White House was reacting to a piece in *Time* magazine saying that Kennedy had called the president "an SOB." The magazine said that Johnson in turn had told Kennedy he never wanted to see him again. This eruption was the latest in a long-running feud that had started almost at once after Kennedy's brother had been assassinated in Johnson's home state. The feud would continue the rest of Kennedy's life until he was killed by a gunman in Los Angeles during his campaign to capture the Democratic nomination for president in 1968.

On June 13, 1967, I reported the appointment of the first African American to the Supreme Court. The page 1 headline said, "Marshall Named for High Court, Its First Negro." The accompanying photograph showed the president and Thurgood Marshall with their heads close together. Their faces were solemn. They looked a lot alike: hair combed straight back, strong chins, glasses, white shirts under strongly knotted ties. The only real difference was Marshall's mustache. The great civil rights lawyer could have passed for white if he had chosen.

He was being promoted from the position of solicitor general, but

that job was practically an afterthought in his career climb. My story pointed out that he was the best-known black lawyer of the twentieth century because of his legal battles against segregation. Little Rock was well acquainted with him. He had joined the Arkansas lawyer Wiley Branton in successfully opposing Governor Faubus's attempt to block the integration of Central High School.

Not many years earlier, Marshall's appointment would have been opposed and probably blocked by the Senate's resistant Southern bloc. I was gratified to write this sentence: "Non-Southern Senators applauded the appointment and Southerners accepted it, at least for the moment, in silence." The only Southern senator to speak out was Strom Thurmond of South Carolina. He opposed Marshall because he was a liberal. He did not mention his color.

Marshall got the job.

■ ■ ■

Covering the White House was intermittently interesting. Much of an ordinary day was spent sitting and waiting in the press room. The reporters were called into a briefing room in the morning and late afternoon for announcements by the press secretary. Bill Moyers had that job when I arrived on the beat but was already in the act of leaving. Within two weeks, he was replaced by another old Johnson friend from Texas, George Christian. The reporters liked Christian and sympathized with his challenge: having to stand before a room full of men and women who largely disliked and distrusted his boss and, twice a day, try to put the best face on every piece of news that came out of the place. We understood the rules. The press secretary was not to lie to us, but he was not obliged to tell us everything he knew. Every briefing was a game. Now and then, a reporter would be able to say, "Wait a minute, George. I thought you just said . . ." and George would show us his fanciest footwork and earn his salary for another day.

We all appreciated the occasional break in the routine, such as a trip out of town. One trip I remember was to Glassboro, New Jersey, to help cover a summit meeting between Johnson and Aleksei Kosygin, the premier of the Soviet Union. My job was to write color—material off to one side of the main story, which was written by Max. The *Times* would

usually have four or five reporters on a big story like that. Experts on all aspects of foreign policy would be flown up from Washington. The paper might have half a dozen stories a day until the big shot went home, then another two or three a day for the rest of the week while the experts and the analysts emptied their minds and notebooks.

The only remotely exciting detail in my story on June 26 was an account of how Kosygin's car and its motorcade got two miles ahead of the state troopers guarding the expressway. The troopers had to rush up the road at 120 miles an hour herding innocent drivers onto the shoulder and one or two into the ditch. The car I was in joined the rush.

One day Johnson jumped on a small jet in Texas and flew to St. Louis to meet with a group of Democratic governors. His spies had sent word that they had changed their tune and now, noting his recent rise in the polls, had decided that it would be politically advantageous to have him at the head of the ticket in 1968. Six months earlier, they had been grumbling about him. He was so carried away with the favorable shift that he let his taste for hyperbole get the best of him.

"Ours is the party—the first one in history—that has delivered 90 per cent of its platform," he said. "In doing that, we have given the country the greatest record of legislative accomplishments in 175 years." Some history teacher probably researched that claim and won tenure with his dissertation challenging his truthfulness.

It was only when I was doing research for a profile of the president's right-hand man, the secretive Marvin Watson, that I learned the reason for that miraculous turnaround among the governors. Watson had slipped out from Washington and spent the day in their midst, invisible to the press and public, a kind of Texas Pimpernel—"They seek him here, they seek him there." I was able to report that the statement the governors issued pledging their support in the next election was said to have been edited, if not actually ghost-written, by Watson.

There were harbingers of things not to come. The president, during a visit to Texas, forwarded to Congress a report on surface mining, pointing to its desecration of the environment and recommending that the feds step in and stop it where states refused to do so. As we know, the desecration has continued.

The next day the Johnsons drove to a little Catholic church at nearby Stonewall to see their first grandchild christened. The boy,

named Patrick Lyndon Nugent, was passed from one adult to another after the ceremony, prompting the president to observe, "This is unconstitutional. It's cruel and inhuman treatment."

Then they flew to Texarkana for the funeral of Mrs. Wright Patman, the widow of their old friend Representative Wright Patman, whom they had seen off not long before. They dropped in on Lady Bird's girlhood home at the tiny town of Karnack.

Thus did the lazy days of summer pass in 1967, and president and country were lulled into inattention. That came to an abrupt end when race riots erupted in several cities, first and most destructively in Detroit. Violence was so serious there that the president sent army troops to put it down. He established a commission to study race problems. It became known as the Kerner Commission for its first chairman, Governor Otto Kerner of Illinois. The commission took its work seriously, and its findings reverberated for years.

■　■　■

I discovered during the fall of 1967 that part of my job was to cover the White House dogs. There were six at the time, down two from the beginning of the Johnson administration. The departed were a pair of beagles, Him and Her, who had become famous when their owner lifted them by their ears to be photographed. That had touched off a public relations problem; some people did not buy the president's assertion that the beagles liked being hoisted by their ears. Her later died after swallowing gravel. Him ran under the wheels of a limousine.

A new dog came along by chance, a stray mongrel that Luci Johnson Nugent found at a service station in Texas. In no time, Yuki was sleeping on the president's bed and at his feet during Oval Office meetings. Mrs. Johnson had no use for Yuki. I once saw her overrule her husband and order "that dog" removed from a photo session.

■　■　■

I had not had a close call to my personal safety since leaving the Southern beat. My new complacency was shattered one summer night in Texas. The White House press was spending the weekend in San

Antonio while the president and first lady rested at the LBJ Ranch about fifty miles away. Some of my friends and I went out for the evening and after dinner got on a small barge carrying tourists up and down the San Antonio River. That stream is about the width of Hogeye Creek, across the road from my pasture. It is barely wide enough for two tourist barges to meet and pass.

Our barge was puttering along toward an outdoor theater. The stage was on one side and the audience on the other. The company that evening was performing *The Mikado*. We were all watching the scene on the stage and were paying no attention to the river ahead. Neither was our driver. When our boat was exactly centered between the stage and the audience, it collided head-on with a boat coming from the other direction. No one was hurt, and the opera continued without missing a beat. The audience loved it.

I spent a little time more or less alone with President Johnson, and in each case it was the result of some last-minute exigency. I would like to boast that I had a knack for persuading him to lend me his ear, but it never happened that way.

One day he was driven across the capital to make a speech, and somehow I ended up in his car. We were seated side by side. I knew that he used his hands a lot in dealing with people. I got the full hands-on treatment that day. During the entire ride, his right hand rested on my left knee, and he used it to help make his talking points. I don't remember the subject, but he was never without some issue that needed massaging. My knee was massaged along with his chosen issue that day. It was my impression that his right hand had a mind of its own, that it had been pressed into service so often and for so many years that it needed no coaching from his brain.

There was another such hands-on occasion at the end of a day trip to New Orleans. Johnson had spoken at an industrial plant, and we were preparing to leave for the airport. I made an unscheduled stop at the men's room and missed the press car. George Christian, the White House press secretary, saw me wandering around lost and hustled me aboard the president's helicopter. He thrust me into the last empty seat.

After I buckled the seat belt, I realized that I was opposite the president, inches away and knee to knee. In a seat just to my left sat the governor of Louisiana, John McKeithen. I learned later that the

governor had wangled a chance to spend ten minutes alone with the president so he could ask for some political favor. I also learned that the president knew what the governor was after and was happy for a chance to avoid talking to him. While McKeithen sat fuming, I was treated to ten minutes of uninterrupted small talk from the president of the United States—none of which I could hear over the noise of the chopper—accompanied by an uninterrupted knee massage.

■ ■ ■

There was no particular significance to the date, but on November 21, a day short of the anniversary of the assassination of his predecessor, Johnson signed into law one of the most visionary acts of the Great Society—the Air Quality Act of 1967. He chose to highlight the occasion by having the signing in the East Room. He began his remarks with a quotation from Dante's Inferno, introducing it as a weather report: "Dirty water and black snow pour from the dismal air to . . . the putrid slush that waits for them below." That would be the future for our own great cities if we failed to stop polluting the air, he said.

That law was the most ambitious to date of federal efforts to fight air pollution. It set aside millions of dollars to study the exact sources of the problem. Johnson had had to compromise to get the legislation through Congress over the resistance of industries that would have to spend money to clean up their emissions. Predictably, the old arm twister got more than he lost in the negotiations. Those same resisting industries and their paid help in Congress are still fighting two generations later. The contest, as usual, is between money and science, and at the moment, money is making a move. Air quality regulations are under attack.

Johnson took the occasion of signing the Air Quality Act to plug administration proposals for improving meat inspection and for getting rid of fabrics that were apt to burst into flame. While he was at it, he spoke up for a truth-in-lending bill. A bunch of congressmen were in the audience. Some were still nursing sore arms from the president's twisting.

CHAPTER 23

The Year I Lived with Hubert Humphrey

I filed seventy stories about Humphrey in 1968. Most of that coverage was after President Johnson announced on March 31 that he would not run for re-election. That announcement made Humphrey the favorite to be the Democratic nominee in the fall election.

I still call up a flush of anger at the *New York Times* when I remember the day that Johnson pulled out of the race. A large group of us reporters were traveling with Humphrey that day to Mexico City as he filled in, once more, for the president on a diplomatic mission. We noticed that Humphrey was uncharacteristically quiet on the plane flying down. I sat next to old Ralph McGill of the *Atlanta Constitution*, one of my heroes, and we remarked on the vice president's behavior. Ordinarily, he would be up and down the aisle chatting and joking with the reporters. Only later did we learn that he had stopped by the White House on the way to the airport and had been told by Johnson what he planned to do.

We all went to a party at the American embassy that evening. Humphrey stayed out of sight. Word went around that the president was getting ready to speak in Washington. We huddled around radios scattered through the lobby. I found myself knee to knee with old Senator Wayne Morse of Oregon, one of the most outspoken critics of the president's Vietnam policy. Morse and Johnson had been close friends in the Senate, and it clearly pained Morse to oppose him.

Johnson spoke only a few minutes, mainly recounting his efforts to bring a halt to the war. He said he had concluded that the best

chance for a peace treaty was for him to quit the presidency. "And so, I shall not seek, nor will I accept . . ."

Before he finished the sentence, I glanced toward Senator Morse. Tears were streaming down his face. I could only imagine the thundering of his emotions. I chose not to ask him. We exchanged a few perfunctory remarks, and I quickly left to find a phone.

I dictated a story about the embassy scene and the vice president's trip, including my very informed speculation that this would thrust Humphrey into contention for the presidency in the fall. My story was not published. I knew, of course, that the president's announcement would dominate our coverage that night. I also knew that the paper would have numerous sidebars. Mine should have been one of them. I never got a satisfactory answer as to why it was not. I'm still waiting— in case the editor who made that decision is still out there somewhere.

My second-day story on Humphrey's return to Washington was played prominently. A crowd of three hundred to four hundred people greeted him as he stepped off the plane, and it was obvious to them that their man would run for president. He spoke a few words and did nothing to discourage that idea. In the next twenty-four hours, he picked up endorsements from big labor and farm interests. The next day he got the steel workers' union, which was holding its convention in Pittsburgh. Before ten days had passed, former president Harry Truman had signed on as the honorary chairman of his campaign.

His main rivals for the nomination were Senator Eugene McCarthy of Minnesota and Senator Robert F. Kennedy of New York. There would be hard-fought primary contests, and the winner would not be determined until late in the season.

No other presidential campaign in our history was interrupted by the assassination of two huge public figures. First, on April 4, there was the killing of Martin Luther King in Memphis, and then, two months and a day later, on June 5, the killing of Robert Kennedy in Los Angeles. These were not merely disruptions; they were earthquakes. The whole country staggered and reeled. Riots broke out. Public officials were on the ropes trying to deal with the consequences. People stumbled from anger to grief to rage. Humphrey and McCarthy, the remaining candidates in the Democratic race, had the double challenge of handling their own emotions and making sure their public reactions were appropriate.

I was with Humphrey the day King was killed. He was scheduled to address a gathering of Democrats at a Washington hotel. As Humphrey and others waited on the speakers' platform, a hotel employee walked up and whispered to the master of ceremonies. The emcee had to tell the crowd, "We have just been told that Dr. Martin Luther King has been assassinated in Memphis, Tennessee." The whole hall was struck silent. Then there were gasps, and people started crying. The emcee, a man from Georgia, had the bad taste to try to continue the meeting. Humphrey got up and took the microphone and said, "People, we need to adjourn this meeting right now."

Humphrey flew to another engagement the next day, somewhere in the Midwest. On the way back, we got word that Washington was burning. We flew into National Airport about dark. As we approached, it indeed looked as if the whole city was on fire. The rioters actually had confined their destruction mainly to a black business section, some of it near the White House.

Philip Carter of *Newsweek* and I were seated next to each other. We were worried about our families. Smoke hit us in the face as we walked off the plane. We made our way to our homes, careful to drive around the troubled area, where some of our colleagues were on the street working the story.

Serious rioting broke out in virtually all of the big American cities by the next day. My assignment was Baltimore, an hour's drive from the District of Columbia. I spent the next two or three days covering that small part of the story, and dozens of other reporters fanned out to the other hot spots.

King's assassination and the aftermath would no doubt have been one of the biggest stories of the year in America, right alongside the presidential election, but it soon had to share that dubious glory with the murder of John Kennedy's closest friend, his brother Robert. People wondered whether our blessed country was being punished like some Old Testament tribe that had aroused God's wrath.

Humphrey and his press contingent were at the Air Force Academy in Colorado Springs the day Kennedy was killed. Humphrey was to speak at the academy the next morning. Late in the evening, word came of the Los Angeles murder. Humphrey was stunned and stricken. He liked Bobby Kennedy in spite of the younger man's attempt to defeat him for the nomination. He immediately returned to

Washington and canceled all his campaign engagements for the next several days.

I was assigned to help cover the Kennedy funeral. I met the funeral train from New York and followed the cortege to Arlington Cemetery. He was buried next to the brother who had been killed four and a half years earlier. Robert's widow and his sister-in-law Jackie Kennedy came and left flowers and tried to ignore the reporters, photographers, and anonymous mourners gathered round. Ethel Kennedy was pregnant with her eleventh child. All our stories mentioned that Rose Kennedy, the senator's mother, had come from Hyannis Port, Massachusetts, to be with his wife and children, but that his father, Joseph P. Kennedy, was too ill to make the trip.

President Johnson, ordinarily ready to attend any funeral of consequence, turned out for this one too. I figured he was there under duress. His feeling for the dead man was probably somewhere between contempt and outright hatred, and the feeling was mutual. St. Patrick's Cathedral in New York was packed with the famous and the important. Andy Williams sang "The Battle Hymn of the Republic." Four of the still-standing presidential candidates were there: Humphrey, Gene McCarthy, Richard Nixon, and Nelson Rockefeller.

■ ■ ■

During Humphrey's early campaign rallies, the band played Franklin Roosevelt's old campaign song, "Happy Days Are Here Again." That no longer was appropriate after the assassinations in the spring. But he knew he had to pull his followers out of the doldrums, and he did his best to set an upbeat tone as he resumed the campaign. Even though he was the presumed nominee, he understood that his troubles were not over.

He was no longer the flighty, talkative darling of the liberals, as he was in 1960 when handsome young John F. Kennedy beat him out for the nomination. Now he was the entrenched, middle-of-the road Democrat. That strengthened his hand, but it left him with an almost insoluble political problem: the Vietnam War. Would he align himself solidly with the man who had made him vice president? Or would he contrive to distance himself from LBJ and the war that the president owned and hated and couldn't turn loose?

Hubert Humphrey was a loving man. He cared for Lyndon Johnson in much the same way he cared for his wife and children. Disloyalty to Johnson was unthinkable. And yet, with hostility growing by the hour toward the endless war and the men responsible, he knew it would be reckless to claim co-ownership of the disaster. He tried to straddle the issue. It didn't work.

Humphrey's insiders began to wish they had never heard of Lyndon Johnson. They wanted him to disappear, at least during the campaign. They were terrified that the president might show up at the Chicago convention, flashing a spotlight of misery through association on poor Humphrey.

The vice president's public relations chief was a young Minnesotan named Norman Sherman. He had known and worshiped the older man since he was a student at the University of Minnesota. Humphrey looked on Norman as something like a son. One day during the convention, Sherman was giving his routine press briefing in a hotel hallway when one of the reporters, curious about the president's plans to visit the convention or not, asked Sherman, "What about Lyndon?" Sherman, whose wit often outran his judgment, shot back, "Lyndon who?"

The AP and UPI immediately put this exchange on the wires. Johnson kept the wire machines running in his ranch house all the time. He saw the story. Minutes later he was on the phone to Humphrey. I can't say how angry he was, but when we next saw Humphrey, he looked like a man who had just survived some natural disaster. Within half an hour of his spontaneous witticism, Sherman was without a job. The firing was painful for both men. Sherman was off the payroll for twenty-four hours, and then, as quietly as the thing could be managed, he was rehired.

Johnson never came to the convention.

Even without Johnson, it was a disaster. Protesters against the war clashed repeatedly with Mayor Richard Daley's policemen in a park across the street from the Conrad Hilton Hotel. The policemen beat dozens of them with batons, and the nation watched it all on television. When the demonstrators fled into the hotel lobby, the police used tear gas on them. For days, we got gas in our lungs and eyes when we walked through it. The whole lurid spectacle repulsed millions of voters. That no doubt helped to elect Richard Nixon in November.

CHAPTER 24

George Wallace Again

The *Times* shuffled its coverage after the convention. Max Frankel took over the main story of the Humphrey campaign. The editors assigned me to George Wallace, the volatile third-party candidate, who was running as the self-selected candidate of his new wholly owned American Independent Party.

I was familiar with his tactics from my days traveling Alabama, and I relished the chance to follow him around the country. The governor's announced aim was to get enough votes from the two main parties to throw the election into the House of Representatives. That would presumably make him a power broker, with the expectation that the Southern states might use their clout and his new influence to thwart federal efforts to desegregate schools and other institutions. That had been Strom Thurmond's hope in the 1948 election.

His "law and order" campaign worried both parties. Nixon, the Republican nominee, fretted that Wallace might attract enough conservative votes to make Humphrey president. He responded with a "Southern strategy," a not-too-subtle appeal to white racism that would come back to haunt him when he became president. Humphrey and his advisers worried that Wallace would drain off enough blue-collar voters in all parts of the country to weaken his party and put the Republican in the White House.

Thurmond's strategy of forcing the election into the House didn't work in 1948, but Wallace seemed to have a better chance. The nation was in turmoil because of the civil rights movement, the Vietnam War, a growing unrest among young people, and the assassinations of the Kennedy brothers and Martin Luther King. Wallace, still known in

Alabama as "the fighting little judge," was well positioned to exploit the discontent.

He aimed his message at Americans who were mad at somebody —the government, the faceless institutions, the Establishment, just about anyone in a position of authority. He appealed especially to restless young white men. Robert Kennedy had appealed to that group as well as to black voters. Wallace had amply demonstrated in Alabama that he had no use for black folks, and they returned the favor, but that still left a large voting bloc that was open to mischief.

He had been a boxer in his youth and still had the bearing of a little guy with a chip on his shoulder. "Pugnacious" was probably the adjective most used to describe him during his middle years. That was before a gunman nearly killed him during the next presidential campaign in 1972. He was a hard man to like. He always treated me with respect in our personal encounters, but I never warmed to him.

I did develop some sympathy for him the last time I interviewed him. That was after he had been shot and was confined to a wheelchair. He confirmed news reports that he had become a convert to racial integration. "I was wrong," he said, and I think he meant it. Whether he did or not, he got a majority of the black vote in his last campaign for governor.

His rallies in both the North and the South were disturbing to a lot of people, including us reporters. For one thing, he liked to point out members of the national press in the audience, apparently to invite the rowdies to take their anger out on us. No one did, beyond jibes and insults, but I think he wanted us to feel the threat. He probably would have stepped in and had his security forces stop any attack before it got too serious. But he might have enjoyed seeing one or two of his favorite enemies take a few punches.

More disturbing, though, was an air of threat and violence that he stirred among large numbers of his supporters. I sometimes feel a similar tightening in the air when I watch a hard black cloud march up the valley toward my house on the hill. In one story, an analytical article, I referred to the atmosphere in the rallies as "a spasm of mass passion." There were indeed occasional eruptions of minor violence at the rallies.

Richard Stout, an influential columnist for the *New Republic*, used stronger language. He had covered politics for more than forty years. He devoted one of his columns to the scene in Madison Square Garden

when twenty thousand loud supporters gathered to hear Wallace. Stout said nothing had prepared him for the spectacle he saw that night.

"There is menace in the blood shout of the crowds," he wrote. "You feel you have known this somewhere; never again will you read about Berlin in the 30's without remembering this wild confrontation here of two irrational forces." He called Wallace "the ablest demagogue of our time, with a voice of venom and a gut knowledge of the prejudices of the low-income class."

Some African Americans saw a connection with 1930s Berlin. One man watching a Wallace parade in Chicago carried a sign saying, IF YOU LIKED HITLER, YOU'LL LOVE WALLACE. Anti-Wallace protesters who showed up for his rallies picked up on the theme. "Sieg Heil," they shouted. He outmaneuvered them every time and turned the disruptions to his advantage.

"These anarchists are the kind of folks that people in this country are getting sick and tired of," he said repeatedly.

I never raised the specter of Berlin in my stories, and the editors would have cut it out if I had. But it was clear enough to readers, I suspect, when reporters described the tumultuous scenes in one city after another. In Milwaukee, for example, 5,000 excited white people outshouted 250 anti-Wallace protesters—most of them black—in the city auditorium. The police headed off what might have become a real battle that night. Before Wallace began talking, they blocked the door and refused to let in several thousand more white enthusiasts. That throng had to spend the evening outdoors—seething, I figured.

I had witnessed a reverse version of the Milwaukee event in 1963 when I was at Harvard University on a Nieman Fellowship. A student group invited Wallace to speak. Sanders Auditorium was packed, and not with the speaker's supporters. Wallace's traveling cohort were his only friends there that night. The students outdid themselves with acerbic questions and comments. But none were trained in the polemic arts, and he was. The kids fired a succession of sober, telling points. He responded in two ways: he either pretended not to hear them (he was partially deaf), or, like the Golden Gloves champ he had been in his youth, he just danced away from the thrusts and jabs. They never laid a glove on him.

Blue-collar workers were hot for Wallace from Ohio to New Jersey. A group of his supporters brought Confederate flags to his rally in

Newark. Outbreaks of violence became routine everywhere he went. Media people occasionally got caught in the crossfire. In Toledo, a heckler threw a stone and put a gash in an ABC technician's forehead. As for me, there was no shoving, no spit, not even any insults to amount to anything. Nobody laid a glove on me, thanks to my own artful dodging.

General LeMay's gaffe over using nuclear weapons in Vietnam was a problem for Wallace for some time. It took all his political skill to shift the talk back to race, the awful federal government, and the rest of his program. He was not averse to using fear, but, as I observed in a Sunday think piece, "His strategy, it seems, is to frighten the populace a little but not terrify it."

Aside from the daily story, there were always distractions on the Wallace campaign. He always had good country musicians to warm up the crowds. There was a band that always started with a foot-stomping version of "When the Saints Go Marching In." The musicians included two singers, pretty sisters from north Alabama, Mona and Lisa Taylor. They were as easy to like as their employer was not.

"Their main song, 'Are You From Dixie?' brought cheers of affirmation from 5,000 unlikely Southerners in Milwaukee Thursday night," I reported. Years later, Lisa became Wallace's third wife.

Then there was a night flight across the Rocky Mountains when all of us, Wallace and the entire press contingent, were well and truly threatened. The old prop-driven C-47, a tired leftover from World War II, sprang a leak and lost most of the oil from its right engine. My seatmate and I began to notice liquid splashing on our window. It didn't look like rain. I went to the cockpit and told the pilot, and he came back to take a look. He confirmed that it was oil. He was not disturbed. "It's okay," he said. "This plane is like an old hound dog. If it don't slobber some, it ain't feelin' good."

Word went around the cabin, and we all worked hard at being reassured. One of the reporters found out the next morning in California that the engine had lost over forty gallons of oil. If anybody wondered how close we had come to crashing on one of those snow-capped peaks, he repressed the question.

Wallace's use of the language was studied at length by the mostly Northern reporters. Not just the accent but also the way he used and misused words and phrases. One of his most vivid and effective images

was his description of those who mismanaged the federal government—
"pointy-headed bureaucrats." In that brief phrasing, he put in play not
only the overweening power of Big Government but also the presumed
stupidity of its people. Sometimes he added that the bureaucrats traveled
only on bicycles, clumsily, further justifying his contempt.

Another favorite phrase was "pseudo intellectuals." That was
aimed at the Ivy League and other centers of academic influence that
he blamed for the wrong-headed ideologies that had sent the nation
hurtling toward destruction. Unfortunately, he forgot to learn how to
pronounce the adjective; it came out SWAY-doh. The traveling
reporters nicknamed the lame old campaign plane "Pseudo II," and
we pronounced it the way he did.

In the election, he got almost ten million votes, carried five
Southern states, and came fairly close to throwing the election into the
House. Nixon defeated him in Tennessee and North Carolina by sta-
tistically insignificant margins. He carried my home state of Arkansas.
Political scientists scratched their heads for years over Arkansas's voters
of 1968. While favoring George Wallace, they also reelected Governor
Winthrop Rockefeller, a liberal Republican and a forthright integra-
tionist, and Senator J. William Fulbright, the international statesman
and a leading critic of the Vietnam War.

Wallace's yearning for the White House was unabated. But first,
he had to retrieve the governor's office. His wife Lurleen, whom he had
installed as governor after he was term-limited out, died of cancer in
May 1968 during his second campaign for president. He won a second
gubernatorial term in 1970.

He married again just before his inauguration, this time to a black-
haired beauty from a prominent political family. Cornelia Ellis Snively
was a niece of former Governor James Folsom, a populist and an inte-
grationist. He was six feet eight inches tall. They called him Big Jim. He
had been an early and unsuccessful champion of equal rights for blacks
when he was governor. He often made a spectacle of himself because, as
the saying went, he was bad to drink. He and several other dignitaries
were watching a demonstration by Pensacola's naval aviators one day
when he got off a memorable mot juste. One of the planes suddenly
tumbled off an aircraft carrier into the sea. The governor turned to his
companions and said, "Now if that ain't a show I'll kiss your ass."

Cornelia's mother, Ruby Folsom Austin, was about six feet tall.

They called her Big Ruby. When her daughter married Wallace, who was five feet seven inches tall, she told reporters, with undisguised disdain, "Why, he ain't titty high."

My introduction to Big Ruby was unforgettable. My friend Cecil Roberts, a liberal and a doyenne of the arts in Birmingham, drove me to Montgomery for Wallace's inauguration. She was a con artist who got along with her political opponents. She had sweet-talked Governor Wallace out of a lot of state money for her pet projects. We crashed a private party at Cornelia's mother's house. We arrived late, after most of the guests had left. Those remaining were well-oiled, as was the hostess. Cecil introduced me to her and left to chat with someone across the room.

I was astonished by the woman. She was tall, all right, but she was more than that. She was robust. She was built like a Viking warrior with her breasts thrust forward like weapons of war. I am not a little guy, but she looked down on me. If she had attacked, it would not have been a fair fight. She examined me the way a bobcat might assess a rabbit. I am pretty sure that what I saw in her eyes was alcohol-induced lust, but it might have been savage predation.

She began by ordering someone to bring me a drink. Then she backed me against the living room wall and pinned me between the twin peaks of her bosom so that I could not move in any direction. Somehow we carried on a conversation for fifteen or twenty minutes without changing position. I caught Cecil's eye across the room, and she grinned. I wanted to choke her.

Wallace was shot in Maryland a year or so later as he campaigned for president again. I was gone from the political beat by then. The reporters on the scene remarked on Cornelia's behavior during the chaos and panic. She draped her body across his as soon as he fell to the pavement. It was her protective instinct taking hold, the kind of thing her mother would have done.

I saw George Wallace for the last time in the summer of 1982. He was running for governor once again. He and Cornelia had divorced. He had married a third wife, the young singer Lisa Taylor, whom I remembered from the 1968 campaign. I got an immediate and surprising indication of how this last interview would go when I walked into his office and found him talking to Lisa on the phone. He told her I

was there and then he handed the phone to me so I could talk with her. She and I chatted leisurely about what we had been up to. I was stunned. The old Wallace would not have thought to offer me that small kindness.

I had never seen so dramatic a change in a personality. In the magazine article that I wrote, I spoke of a new mellowness, with only a few hints of the old venom. His change on the race issue had been reported widely, but I was skeptical. I asked whether he regretted the pain he had caused black people.

"Yes, and I was to blame for a lot of it." He lapsed into a moment of the old defensiveness, saying he had never harbored any personal animosity toward black people. He insisted that he had been sincere in his belief that school segregation was right, that he had not used the issue opportunistically. "Now, I believe that segregation is wrong. And I don't want it to come back. I see now that we couldn't live in a society like that. In those days, I thought segregation was best for both races. But a short time after that, I came to see that this society can't exist with a dual system."

I interviewed an array of whites and blacks. White liberals were still bitter toward him. A lot of blacks were forgiving and said they would vote for him. (Many did.) I ended the article with an anecdote. On my last day before heading home, a beat-up old car passed me on a narrow highway somewhere outside Montgomery and cut in front of me so sharply that I had to swerve toward the ditch. I was lathered in road rage. Redneck lout, I muttered, or something to that effect. The guy pulled into a driveway not a quarter of a mile farther, just proving that he could outrun me, I reckoned. I turned to look at the driver. I was astonished to see that it was a young black man. I jotted down the message on his bumper sticker. WALLACE FOR GOVERNOR, it said.

Personal happiness seemed to elude George Wallace, prancing along a step ahead of him everywhere he turned. He spent every day and night of his last twenty-seven years in pain from the assassin's bullets. He was divorced from both Cornelia and Lisa. But he dug in and survived, perhaps because, as he told me, he found some comfort from religion for the first time. He was seventy-nine when he died in 1998.

CHAPTER 25

Southern Strategy Redux

Richard Nixon became president, and my Washington assignment changed. As an experienced civil rights reporter, I was chosen to keep an eye on how the new administration handled that issue. Nixon had been one of the more liberal members of President Eisenhower's team. He was pro-integration. However, he trimmed his sails in the 1968 campaign to attract Southern conservatives. Once in office, he tried to have it both ways.

Lyndon Johnson performed one last service for black Americans before he left office. His proudest accomplishments had been with his domestic agenda, beginning when he was the Senate's majority leader. I have taken perhaps too much joy from the fact that the greatest gains on the race issue in a hundred years were the political work of a Southerner. Besides the landmark civil rights laws of the '50s and '60s, there was Medicare, which came to pass with the invaluable assistance of another Southerner, Representative Wilbur Mills of Arkansas, the capital's reigning genius on taxation.

Johnson was exceedingly proud of his civil rights record, and he feared with clear justification that reactionary members of Congress would try to dismantle it when he was gone. President-Elect Nixon had sent distressing signs that he would go along with their plan if he could do it quietly.

A week after Nixon was elected, Johnson flew to New York to address the annual meeting of the National Urban League. I covered the speech and described it as a warning to his successor. The car license plates in his home state used to say, DON'T MESS WITH TEXAS. Johnson felt that way about his civil rights accomplishments. The speech challenged Nixon to match Johnson's civil rights record.

To make sure there was no doubt what he meant, he listed the Civil Rights Act of 1964, the Voting Rights Act of 1965, and the Open Housing Act of 1968. All were made possible by organizations like the Urban League and their political allies and over the determined opposition of the segregationist Southerners who had dominated Congress for much of the twentieth century. Those same Southerners were still powerful, and they had put Nixon in office. Everybody in the audience knew that.

Nixon, a genius at hair-splitting, had left the impression during his campaign that he was sympathetic to white Southerners' resistance to school desegregation. He did so without ever saying that he would flout the 1964 civil rights law. Encouraged by Nixon's subtle statements, Southern Republicans advised school officials to go slow on desegregation and to work for Nixon's election in the hope that he would help them avoid compliance.

My new assignment—never described in so many words—was to watch for signs that Nixon was caving in to the segregationists. I caused a dustup with a series of stories suggesting that he was continuing his Southern strategy by stealth.

The first of those stories reported what the new administration was doing to placate white Southerners. The policy for some time had been to cut off federal funds for districts that dragged their feet on desegregation. Since foot-dragging was the main tool for resistance, now that the South had lost just about every federal court case on the issue, the policy had proved effective. Southerners loved to complain about the government's intrusion into their way of life, but they were more than willing to accept Washington's easy money. After a few districts were deprived of that money, the others began to see the logic of going along with the feds.

Nixon, however, felt an obligation to pacify his new Southern friends. His secretary of Health, Education, and Welfare, a fellow Californian and a loyal friend named Robert H. Finch, drew the dirty job. Finch by inclination was on the side of the integrationists. He was considered one of the more moderate members of the new administration. Within two weeks after his boss was inaugurated, Finch found himself on the hot seat. Yielding to Southern pressures, he announced that he would give five of the worst foot-draggers a sixty-day extension before taking away their free money.

The response was instantaneous. Roy Wilkins, executive director of the NAACP, expressed the outrage of millions. "The districts in question do not need another 60 days, since they have been dodging compliance with the law for more than 14 years," he said.

My second-day story described the compromise that had been forced on Finch. I found a source who told me that the secretary had had to beat down a White House aide who wanted to give the Southerners even more ground. Finch was a pretty good politician—he had had the good sense to reject Nixon's offer of the vice presidency at a time when a big cabinet post was a far better job—but he had never had to deal with Southern foot-draggers, who had been trained in the art since the end of the Civil War.

Two weeks later, he had a chance to redeem himself. Three more districts came up for review, and he cut them off without a penny. No money, no deadline extension.

Then he was handed a piece of lagniappe. Ruby Martin, who ran HEW's Office of Civil Rights, told me in an interview that she believed the South had pulled even with the North in desegregating its schools. She and others in the government agencies that dealt with such matters were ready to acknowledge that racial discrimination was not limited to white Southerners. Many black kids in the North were systematically discriminated against just as black kids were in the South. My story had two effects: it provided a satisfying bit of schadenfreude for Southerners, and it momentarily took a little of the heat off Finch.

A tone-deaf lawyer in his department got Finch in trouble again before the end of March, barely two months into the administration's tenure. The guy circulated a memo recommending that HEW relax the guidelines on desegregation to make them more palatable to conservative Southerners and that this should be done on the sly, without publicity. His boss had a better grasp of public relations and scuttled the plan as soon as it was leaked to the press—as any summer intern could have predicted it would be.

Ruby Martin retired, and Finch replaced her with a bright young Californian named Leon E. Panetta who, in the twenty-first century, would become head of the Central Intelligence Agency and then secretary of Defense. The new man's first act was to settle a dispute with a recalcitrant school district in Mississippi. The district caved in and

said, okay, if that's the way it has to be, we will go on and integrate. I thought I could hear a sigh of despair from Mississippi and an answering sigh of relief from Secretary Finch's office.

Two weeks later, HEW raised an iron fist against a school district in Michigan. It started formal procedures to cut federal funds if the district failed to desegregate, "underlining Mr. Finch's pledge to make school desegregation a national policy," I wrote.

■ ■ ■

Sometime during that summer, one of my stories annoyed President Nixon. I don't recall what it said except for a bluntly worded suggestion that the administration had begun repaying the segregationist South for its support in the election. Nixon told Finch to complain. Finch phoned Max Frankel, our bureau chief, and complained. Max asked me to explain my story. I did. He phoned Finch and said he stood by his reporter.

One of our conceits in the Washington bureau—not so privately held as to be totally invisible to outsiders—was that each of us was roughly the equivalent of a U.S. senator in our influence on public policy. I half-believed it was true the day I learned that something I had written had got under the skin of the president of the United States. I'm afraid I was a little puffed up about it.

The offending story might have been about a federal court hearing in Mississippi. The Justice Department had asked the court to give thirty-three Mississippi school districts more time to plan for desegregation. Finch wrote a letter supporting the delay.

I flew to Jackson to cover the hearing on the case, which was in the U.S. Court of Appeals for the Fifth Circuit, one of the stalwarts in enforcing school desegregation. It had ordered the thirty-three districts to fully desegregate when classes started in the fall, just a few days after the hearing. The development that caught my eye—and that I chose to put in the lead paragraph—was a rupture between the Civil Rights Division of the Justice Department and its legal ally of fifteen years standing, the NAACP Legal Defense Fund, Inc., known as the Inc. Fund.

After the Justice Department backed the thirty-three districts in asking for a delay, the Inc. Fund filed a motion asking that the govern-

ment be listed henceforth as a defendant instead of a plaintiff. That would have put the government lawyers in the distasteful position of herding with the diehard Southern segregationists.

The courtroom reeked of shame that day. A young Justice Department lawyer, Robert Moore, who had spent years working side by side with Inc. Fund lawyers, sat slumped across the back of an empty chair with his face buried in his hands while one of his superiors went through the motions of justifying the department's action. The other guy had flown in hurriedly to take Moore's place after Moore balked at performing a task he strongly disagreed with. Justifying the department's action required acrobatic contortions. Only days earlier, it had urged this same court to order the immediate desegregation of those same districts. Back in Washington, virtually all of the Civil Rights Division's lawyers at Justice had argued for immediate action, as they had done for years.

The Inc. Fund's lawyers looked very alone in the courtroom that day. The court's white bailiffs made no secret of their contempt for those outside agitators. When one of the New York lawyers only half-rose from his chair to address the judge, a bailiff pointed a finger at him and barked, "Stand up!"

The court denied the motion to make the government a defendant, but granted it a ninety-day delay. The Inc. Fund appealed to the Supreme Court. The Court needed only a week to consider and, on October 29, unanimously told the thirty-three school districts to desegregate "at once."

That decision was a turning point that was not widely appreciated at the time. It effectively put an end to the Court's policy of "all deliberate speed," an unfortunate phrase from its 1955 dictum on how desegregation should proceed. Those words had enabled half a generation of Southern officials to take their time. Ending "all deliberate speed" was an unintended consequence of the new administration's stalling tactics.

So the dismantling of school segregation moved forward. The Justice Department soon sued Georgia to force it to abolish its dual system. Instead of cutting off funds, which had proved effective but painful, Nixon and his advisers decided to take the fight back to the courts where it had begun. When a court ordered a district to get on with it, the district

could start receiving federal funds again. The administration's stated reasoning was that Negro children suffered most when federal money was cut off. That did seem to be the case. When white officials found that money was short, it was easy to find savings by firing Negro teachers and reducing services in Negro schools.

Nixon's further reasoning appeared to be that shifting the dirty job to the courts would concentrate the Southerners' anger on the judges rather than on him. Like the nimble-footed toreador that he was, he simply sidestepped the segregationists' wrath. That confirmed George Wallace's opinion that Nixon always stood "forthrightly on both sides" of any issue. Once a federal court ordered a district to get on with it, the administration did what it had to do. Justice Department lawyers began meeting with school boards all over the South to tell them that time had run out.

That awkward hearing in Jackson led to a shake-up in the Civil Rights Division. When it was over, James P. Turner, my old roommate back at the University of Missouri, ended up with a promotion to deputy assistant attorney general for civil rights. Initially, his main assignment was to expand the employment discrimination program. Over the next twenty-five years, he would be involved in a variety of discrimination issues, and on several occasions he served as acting assistant attorney general for civil rights. He's almost the only friend I have left from university days, and I treasure him. He is an unruly golfer, but a reliable friend.

All of Nixon's dodging and weaving gave the South another year to finish the job that the Supreme Court had assigned it in 1954—*fifteen years* before he took office. Nixon got credit for that one last delay, and he earned it. I wouldn't want that on my resume, but it takes all kinds.

Slowing down school desegregation was not his only favor to the never-enders. He tried, in vain, to appoint to the Supreme Court two Southerners with doubtful commitment to minority rights. He fulminated against "forced busing" to facilitate school desegregation. He tried to sabotage the 1965 Voting Rights Act. He cut welfare funds.

Kirkpatrick Sale in his book *Power Shift* expanded the list:

> He fired a series of upper-level bureaucrats who refused to go
> along with all his foot-dragging schemes, and shunted aside

Cabinet officials like Robert Finch and George Romney who displayed any nagging sense of responsibility toward American minorities. And he established an unblemished record for ignoring all reports of the U.S. Civil Rights Commission criticizing the Administration for its abysmal performance, fired its chairman when he tried to gain public support, and then refused to appoint another person in hopes that the whole thing might just go away.

Some thinkers looked back years later and decided that Richard Nixon was a liberal on race. They pointed to all the progress that was made while he was in office. Progress was made, but little thanks to him. Sitting in the Oval Office with shrugged shoulders and upraised palms saying, "What could I do?" is not the same as working for, twisting arms for, and finally signing your name as president to laws that truly changed the nation.

Lyndon Johnson acknowledged when he signed the Civil Rights Law of 1964 that he was handing the South over to the Republicans for the foreseeable future. Nixon was there to receive the gift. With his every gesture of sympathy toward the "Southern way of life," the white supremacists whooped and hollered and clapped their hands. And they voted Republican for the rest of their lives. Long before the end of the twentieth century, Democrats had become a despised minority almost everywhere south of the Mason-Dixon Line.

CHAPTER 26

Rescued in New Orleans

Gene Roberts, recently returned from Saigon to become national editor, asked me to open a bureau in New Orleans—the paper's first. I loved the city. I decided that it was time to live a more peaceful life. We left Washington and got to New Orleans late in the summer of 1969 just in time to welcome Hurricane Camille, which killed 259 people.

New Orleans received a glancing blow, enough to fill the city's eastern highway with houses and boats. I had to drive north about one hundred miles, then back south on another route to reach the main destruction at Gulfport, Biloxi, Pass Christian, and the smaller Gulf towns that caught the full force of the wind and water. Jon Nordheimer flew from the Atlanta bureau to Mobile and drove to the scene. He was not able to find a phone in time for the first edition, but he wrote some excellent follow-up stories during the next few days.

Our deadline in those days was normally about 7:00 p.m. Eastern Time. That could be stretched a little, but not much if we expected to get anything in the first edition. By the time I reached the coast, I had only an hour or so to interview people and make notes on what I saw. Then I had to speed back almost to Hattiesburg to find a working phone and dictate a story.

Driving was perilous. The highway was littered with trucks, cars, trees, and dead animals. Hundreds of large man o' war birds, which normally live their entire lives on the sea (don't ask me how), had been blown inland. Scores of the disoriented creatures were run over by cars as they waddled around in the roads.

My second-day story began, "Just what will a hurricane wind of 190 miles an hour do? It will snatch three large oceangoing ships from

their moorings and set them down on the beach, nosed together like three rowboats tied to a single chain." I guess it was a sign of my own discombobulation that I neglected the role of the twenty-foot waves in heaving those ships onto the beach.

There was a lot of talk afterward about how to make the coast safe from hurricanes. I pointed out in one snide piece that New Orleans had been talking about that for a couple of centuries. Thirty-six years later, after Katrina, they talked about it again. In 1969, as Camille bore down, I tried to get advice on preparing my own house. A hardware store owner told me, "Get yourself a bottle of good whiskey and sit back and relax."

His advice was not as cynical as it sounded. Hurricane parties had always been a tradition in New Orleans and the other coastal towns. I admit to partying a bit myself at the height of Hurricane Betsy in 1965. Four years later, I had to report on one such party in Pass Christian, Mississippi, after Camille. Two dozen friends had gathered for drinks in a waterfront apartment house. The police came and urged them to go inland. They refused. Only three survived.

Reporters like to say that if you find a good story, you need to tell it again every chance you get. As I write this, the Mississippi River is flooding towns and farms from Missouri to the Gulf. I used to cover those floods. Memories wash over me and I come up gasping for air, fighting the urge to drive to the river and start to work.

One of the luckiest breaks I had after I moved to New Orleans was meeting an experienced reporter who offered to protect my back when I had to be on the road. New Orleans was often in the news, and I didn't need to worry about missing a good story there while I was chasing elephants in Oklahoma or covering an election in South Carolina.

Norma and I were at a party soon after we settled in our new city. A woman introduced herself and asked whether the *Times* would be interested in signing her up as a stringer. Gene Roberts had recently instructed all the national correspondents to watch for women reporters who had interrupted their careers to raise their children and had begun to miss the reporting life. In five minutes, I learned that Fran Marcus had worked in several newsrooms from the Northeast to Louisiana, that her four children were old enough to take care of themselves, and that she was more than ready to resume her career. She

didn't need the money; her husband, Bernard, was a partner in the city's most prestigious law firm. She was on our stringer list before the week was out.

The byline of Frances Frank Marcus became a regular one in the *Times* for the next twenty-five years. Long after I departed for another bureau, she continued to file news and travel stories from New Orleans and elsewhere, including the islands of the Caribbean. She and I worked together for seven years, and our families became close. We rejoiced and sometimes wept over the comings and goings of our children.

I was working a feature story in northern Arkansas one day when the national desk found me and ordered me back to New Orleans as fast as I could get there. A ferry had collided with another boat on the Mississippi River a few miles upstream from the city. Scores of people were dead. When I reached the place in late afternoon, I found Fran already at work. She had interviewed everybody in sight and had the story practically finished. I had only to find a phone and call it in. Not only that, she had dragged her husband along to help. I think Bernie Marcus still holds the record for being the best-heeled assistant stringer ever to work for the *New York Times*.

■ ■ ■

The race story did not recur; it never stopped. On the evening of May 14, 1970, highway patrolmen in Jackson, Mississippi, shot to death two students and wounded nine others at Jackson State College, a black school.

That outbreak was touched off by uncontainable frustration and rage on both sides of the color line. White officers were weary from patrolling demonstrations and protests by people they didn't agree with and deep down did not like. The Jackson State students were fed up with years of abuse by white authorities in general. They started throwing rocks and bottles at white motorists. Trouble had been brewing for some time, and the National Guard had been called in briefly.

City policemen, who were not involved in the shooting except as bystanders, said that besides the rock-and-bottle throwing, they had heard sniper fire from the dorm. The students I interviewed said that wasn't true. A local television newsman happened to have a tape

recorder running when the violence started. I heard it. I caught the sound of students shouting, then the crash of a bottle, then a quick *bing-bing* that could have been two shots from a small-caliber weapon.

I don't know what a measured police response would have been, but consider how the forty highway patrolmen handled it: they waited two seconds after the gunshots from the dorm. Then, without warning, they started firing. What I heard on the tape was a loud and continuous roar of shotguns that lasted about thirty seconds. So many rounds of double-ought buckshot were spent that all the windows in one wall of the five-story dormitory were broken out. I saw pock marks in the bricks from the top floor to the bottom.

I pointed out in my story that double-ought buckshot would kill a deer at one hundred yards. I knew that because most of the men in my family were deer hunters.

Someone, probably my friend Bill Minor, the *Times-Picayune*'s reporter in Mississippi, reminded me of some pertinent history. Three years earlier, a riot by Jackson State students had brought the state's National Guard to the campus. The Guard had used buckshot. An African American delivery man with no connection to the riot except to be caught in the neighborhood was shot in the back and killed.

Just eleven days before the 1970 killings at Jackson State, members of the Ohio National Guard had shot and killed four students during an anti-war protest at Kent State University. The Jackson State violence would be buried and lost in the national memory in a few years. The Ohio incident, by contrast, is still remembered by millions of Americans. It is known in the history books as "the Kent State massacre."

The students at Kent State were unarmed, but the Guard's reaction was not unprovoked. For three days, student demonstrations had ended with the police clubbing people with batons and students responding with rocks and bottles. Two days before the killings, someone had set fire to the campus ROTC building, and a thousand people had stood cheering while it burned. The firemen were attacked and their hoses slashed.

The spirit of nonviolence was already in serious decline. Martin Luther King had been dead two years. Even before his murder, many black leaders were showing contempt for Gandhian tactics. In Europe, student demonstrations had turned violent by 1968. French young

people revived an old Paris custom of prying up paving stones and throwing them at the police. American students, deprived of that convenient source, came to the fray with their own rocks and bottles.

■ ■ ■

The elections of 1970 brought hope that the old politics of race was losing its grip on the mind of the South. I wrote as much in a story in 1971 and received what might have been a death threat for my pains. "Dear Sirs:" the typewritten post card said. "Your article in today's paper stating that 'Race' is no longer an issue is a DAMN LIE. If George Wallace is not elected in 1972, traitors like you will be taken care of in an appropriate manner. You have lied to the people long enough and there are millions of us who are prepared to remove your kind from society." The card was not signed. The writer had not read my story carefully. Of course, race was still an issue and would continue to be for the rest of my life.

School integration, for example, was still in the news, but in a new guise. The question of integrating or not integrating had been settled firmly, but the big issue well into the 1970s was busing. From Arkansas to Florida, cross-town busing of students to balance the racial makeups of schools failed to ignite as much anger as some of the hard-liners wanted. Orval Faubus used it to try to become governor of Arkansas again after a period of rest during which he shed his aging wife and acquired a newer model. He was whipped soundly by a moderate named Dale Bumpers, who simply refused to discuss busing or anything else controversial.

My last story on school desegregation was published in September 1976, and it got me in trouble with my mother. The story held up Central High in Little Rock as a model of reasonably successful integration. It mentioned that the school once known for racial violence was peaceful, while integration turbulence had moved to the North. My old paper in Little Rock reprinted the story. The local Chamber of Commerce promptly took credit for planting it in the *Times,* claiming that it had been placed there by its public relations firm.

Mike Trimble, an old friend from the *Gazette,* phoned me at my office in New Orleans to confirm that I had been working as a tool of

the Little Rock Chamber of Commerce. I responded with a little more indignation than I might have. "That's a goddamned lie," I said. He quoted me, and my mother read his story the next morning in the *Gazette*. She got on the phone and scolded me for my language. She was right, of course. A son ought to watch his language if it is likely to be read by his mother and her friends in the Piney Baptist Church.

■ ■ ■

In politics, signs of moderation flourished in the early 1970s. Florida rejected several conservative Republicans and chose as governor a moderate Democrat, Reuben Askew. In Georgia, Governor Lester Maddox could not succeed himself, and he was succeeded by Jimmy Carter, who would become a kind of national model of moderation.

There were similar indications elsewhere. My conclusion was that while race still mattered in Southern politics, it was no longer poisonous enough by itself to elect a candidate. I now believe, as I look back over forty years, that the big loser in 1970 was demagoguery. Faubus himself offered a foreshadowing of its terminal decline as early as 1956. He was opposed by Jim Johnson, a fire-eating segregationist. He told the voters in a calm, reassuring tone that he was no more of an integrationist than Johnson was, but that he didn't have to jump up and down and stomp on his hat to tell them that.

■ ■ ■

The hat-stompers no longer prospered, but they had the satisfaction of saying "I told you so." All-white private academies sprang up across the South for the children of determined segregationists. In 1970, I reported that seven hundred such academies had been established during the past five years. It appeared for a time that the white supremacists might prevail. The academies slowly faded away, and those remaining went to some pains to find handfuls of black students. But years later, you could still find segregated holdouts here and there, like those Japanese soldiers discovered in remote Pacific jungles in the 1950s, having still not got the word that the war was over.

For most segregationists, the war ended years ago. Haley Barbour,

the Republican governor of Mississippi, went on the air in 2011 to thank the Freedom Riders who had put their lives on the line fifty years earlier to desegregate the bus stations of his and the other Southern states.

White and black students in integrated public schools rubbed each other raw during those first years. In Bogalusa, a fight at an integrated high school lasted two hours and prompted the superintendent to close all the schools long enough for tempers to cool. Such incidents continued to make the news in many other places.

In my home state, the lifetime achievement award for alarums and excursions must go to the late Jim Johnson. He predicted that integration would lead to miscegenation—race-mixing, mongrelization of the races, he called it. He lived long enough to walk the aisles of modern Wal-Mart stores and see his nightmare come true. The latte-colored babies and toddlers with white mothers can be seen in almost every aisle. Even the term "miscegenation," once freighted with ominous portent, has become an object of fun and scorn.

The most serious violence during the fall of 1970 occurred in New Orleans between the police and an offshoot of the Black Panther Party. On September 14, the Panther group, which had been organizing adherents in and around a housing project named Desire (after the downtown street in the title of the Tennessee Williams play), uncovered two police informants in their midst. The pair were put on trial in a "people's court" consisting of about one hundred angry people who stood shouting their condemnation. The crowd found the men guilty and beat them with clubs and lead pipes.

Several hundred city and state policemen went after the Panthers the next morning. There was a fierce gun battle, and at least seventeen people were injured. One person was killed in a related incident later in the day. The police charged fourteen people with attempted murder.

I was there for the shoot-out. The Panthers sent word that no white reporters would be allowed in. Warren Brown, a young black man at the States-Item, was the only reporter permitted to walk freely in the area. He interviewed several people. The white reporters were limited to what the police told us and what we could see and hear. I watched from behind cars during the shooting.

Two months later, another tense confrontation ended without

violence. The police had gone back to evict the Panthers from an apartment building. Both sides again were heavily armed. The police chief negotiated with an intermediary and ended the siege after four hours, saying he wanted to prevent a blood-bath. Hundreds of young blacks had stationed themselves between the police and the Panthers. They probably would have been the first victims.

A week later, the police quietly captured twenty-five Panthers and their friends on their way out of town. The chief said they were in cars rented for them by the actress Jane Fonda. Twelve of them were held, unable to make bail, until their trial the following summer. A few days before the trial, a group of prisoners that included some Panthers captured two black sheriff's deputies and held them hostage for eight hours.

The twelve were charged with attempted murder. They were acquitted on a fine but significant legal point. The prosecution argued that the twelve had shown "intent to do war on lawful authority." That wasn't enough to convict. The judge had instructed the jury (ten black men and two white men) that to find the defendants guilty it must find that each had committed a criminal act or that one defendant by name had committed the act and had been aided by the others. The prosecution made no attempt to do that.

Aside from the acquittal, the trial was important for another reason: the judge was black. Israel M. Augustine Jr. was the first black criminal court judge in Louisiana since Reconstruction. He was a member of the city's black establishment and a friend of Martin Luther King.

William M. Kunstler, a famous white lawyer who had represented the Chicago Seven and other radicals, was on the Panthers' defense team. He had derided Augustine before the trial as "very much part of the white system." The judge responded, "Bill Kunstler doesn't know me very well. However I might feel, I'm a hell of a lot blacker than he will ever be."

■ ■ ■

I finished 1970 with a trip to the past—and an unexpected look at the future. Gene Roberts, who had come back from Vietnam to take over the national desk, provided the trip. He was always ahead of the crowd

in seeing national trends. As he once told his staff, it pays to zig while the others zag. I can picture him at his desk in the newsroom staring into space, saying nothing. He spent a lot of time staring into space and saying nothing. He could be so far inside his head that he might not hear a telephone or a conversation three feet away. He would sometimes forget whether he had eaten lunch.

On such a day in December, just before we slipped out of the turbulent 1960s into a new decade, he phoned me in New Orleans with a story idea so obvious that no other editor had thought of it. Fly to Chicago, he said, on a one-way ticket. Take the train home. Book a seat on the old *City of New Orleans*, which ran south through rural Illinois and Memphis, past Mississippi and Arkansas, and on to the city of its name. Find out who the other passengers are, where they are going, and why.

He knew the answer. Virtually all of my fellow passengers that December 19 were black people whose Southern families had moved years ago to Chicago, "the northernmost of the Southern outposts on the historic Illinois Central line," as I put it, and were heading south for Christmas. They would get off the train by the dozens in Memphis, Port Gibson, and other stations. They would share ham, collard greens, and muscadine wine with their parents, grandparents, grandchildren, cousins, aunts, uncles, nieces, and nephews. Some of the visitors had left Mississippi only a few years earlier. Others had left a generation or more before that. Old and young, all of them seemed to miss something they had left behind in that dark tumultuous homeland.

The *Times* always required a paragraph or two of background to explain why the story was important. Even a holiday feature story like this had to have it. Someone called that paragraph "the wisdom." Here was mine:

> This is the great trunk line that ties together the northern and southern extremities of the nation's middle. When thousands of Negroes began to migrate from the oppressive agriculture of the South after the Civil War, it was largely the Illinois Central that delivered them to the industrial North, out of the bondage of Mississippi into the Promised Land of Illinois.

About thirty-five years later, Isabel Wilkerson, who had been a *Times* reporter in Chicago, wrote a first-class book on black expatriates

who had left the inhospitable South and moved north. She noted at the end of her book that many had become disillusioned and had begun to return. Roberts, staring into space and saying nothing, saw that return coming in 1970. What he wanted from me was a broad hint of the return migration that was bound to happen, someday.

In 2011, the *Times* reported on the latest census figures. The 2010 population count showed a reversal of the twentieth century's Great Migration well under way. African Americans were leaving the urban centers of Illinois, Michigan, and New York and moving not to the old dens of poverty in the South but to well-to-do suburbs back there. Atlanta had replaced Chicago as home to the largest concentration of black Americans after New York.

The Reverend Ronald Peters, who had moved from Pittsburgh to Atlanta, explained the new allure of the South. He said it was refreshing to be part of a middle class that was no longer weighed down by the stigmas and stereotypes of the past—as it still was in the urban Northeast.

The *Times* story said, "There are now more than one million black residents of the South who were born in the Northeast, a tenfold increase since 1970." That back-migration had occurred since Gene Roberts sent me to Chicago to get on the *City of New Orleans* for a Christmas story to warm up the paper during the days of cold and damp.

The passengers I spoke to on that long, long day and night all those years ago had few good words for Chicago even then. A lot of them were already fed up and yearned to go back south. A woman named Susie Williams said she knew several who had done that.

"The North used to be the place to go," she said. "But now the South is going to be the North and the North is going to be the South." For the benefit of some historian not yet born in 1970, let it be recorded that Susie Williams of Mississippi-cum-Chicago said it first.

Twenty-eight-year-old Dewitt Howard was on his way home to take over the family's forty-acre farm south of Port Gibson. He had spent ten years in a Chicago factory threading laces in footballs. He said he had been robbed about fifteen times in the city. "I ain't never been robbed in Mississippi," he said. His memory may have been inflated by the beer and bourbon he had been drinking all day.

By 2:00 a.m., only a few passengers were left. Their heads pitched and rolled with the pitch and roll of the tracks. "The train was moving into New Orleans, past the raised tombs of the first cemeteries, past the first of the raised cottages and gingerbread porches." A porter who had been cranky with my man Howard during the afternoon had relaxed at last. He sat sweet-talking a comely matron. I pegged that as "the last evidence of holiday spirit on the City of New Orleans as it went home to Christmas."

■ ■ ■

The 1970s found me wandering far beyond the South for the first time. Most of my coverage out of New Orleans was in and about the old Confederacy, but not all. There was a trip to Miles City, Montana, in 1971 to record the end of passenger service there on the Burlington Northern line. I went to Berea College in Kentucky that fall because it had hired a bouegrass music expert, signaling a tentative acceptance of the hillbilly culture that it had been at some pains to put behind it for years. President Nixon that same year flew to Oklahoma to dedicate the $1.2 billion Arkansas River Navigation System, proclaiming the Tulsa suburb of Catoosa a "seaport." I wrote a news story, then a back-grounder explaining the significance of opening a new navigable waterway from Tulsa down the Arkansas River to the Mississippi and thence to New Orleans and the Gulf of Mexico.

When I was not roving beyond the South, the North was coming to me. Edward M. Kennedy, still a stripling in the Senate, flew to South Carolina to speak to the Jaycees. Letter writers to the local paper denounced the visit as an insult. The *News and Courier* pointed out that Senator Strom Thurmond, whose Carolinian credentials were beyond question, was on the same program. My story on Kennedy's speech noted that it contained forty-one typewritten lines of praise of John C. Calhoun, the state's permanent favorite son. Counting lines of type was the kind of thing expected of the nation's newspaper of record.

Vice President Spiro Agnew came down to Jackson and compared the tribulations of his boss to those of Abraham Lincoln. The event was a Republican Party fund-raiser. It drew 2,700 people at $100 a plate. In this case, we let the readers do their own math.

Hubert Humphrey was thinking of running for president again in 1972. He came to New Orleans in October 1971 to test the waters at Loyola University. Young voters would be vital, and he was still mending fences with them because of his reputation as a defender of the Vietnam War. He got a respectful reception. There had been a rumor that he could expect disruptions from some rowdies at next-door Tulane University. The disruption, as it turned out, was one guy who shouted a single word, which I described as "a familiar barnyard term that means 'nonsense.'"

The larger nation intruded in a bizarre criminal story during the summer of 1971. The New Orleans district attorney, Jim Garrison, was arrested by federal agents and charged with taking bribes to protect illegal pinball gambling. All our stories mentioned that Garrison was already notorious for his highly publicized contention that President John F. Kennedy had been assassinated not by Lee Harvey Oswald but by the CIA. Years later, Hollywood threw in with the nuts and made a movie, *JFK*, that tried to turn Garrison into a heroic visionary. Garrison was acquitted on the bribery charge in the '70s. He was defeated for reelection but won a seat on the Louisiana Court of Appeals. He died at age seventy, still apparently convinced that history had got the wrong man in Kennedy's assassination.

Aside from those external distractions, most of my reporting during the early '70s was on the South's still-dominant issue—race. Private white-only academies continued to spring up in black-majority districts. Integrated schools continued to grapple with student tensions ranging from self-segregation in classrooms to hallway brawls.

Even Arkansas, which had had little major racial trouble since 1957 in Little Rock, caught my attention in 1971. A notion was going around, mostly in the North, that race problems in the South had been solved. "The people of eastern Arkansas know better," I wrote. "During the last year, a 50-mile stretch of Arkansas's richest cotton and soybean country across the Mississippi River from Memphis has seen one black man shot to death by a white policeman, 10 blacks and whites injured by gunfire in three towns, numerous others beaten with clubs, tire tools and fists, and several buildings damaged by arson."

But I also found glimmers of change in unlikely places. Philadelphia, Mississippi, a perennial contender for the title of Meanest

Town in the South, turned itself around. My story began, "Those who used to come here with fear in their hearts [that included me] would not recognize the place today." For starters, the town's schools had abolished segregation thoroughly and with little friction.

An integrated law firm in New Orleans started training young black lawyers in how to represent the poor and still make a living.

And in politics, race lost a lot of its explosive power. It still mattered, but less and less each year. I wrote this lead sentence with confidence after a primary election in Mississippi: "Mississippi turned its back on the unbending segregationist politics of its past in yesterday's Democratic primary." That primary was held in the heat of August in 1971. Both candidates in a runoff were called moderates on the race issue, and neither man denied the accusation. The eventual winner in the general election was William L. Waller, a Jackson lawyer. He appointed a number of African Americans to state jobs. He will be remembered as the first local prosecuting attorney to try to send Byron De La Beckwith, Medgar Evers's murderer, to the penitentiary. It took many years and another trial to get the job done because white jurors in 1964 refused to do the right thing.

Governor Waller angered a lot of black folks by releasing from prison a Ku Klux Klansman who had been convicted of taking part in the murder of Vernon Dahmer, the black businessman and civil rights leader who was killed by the Klan near Hattiesburg in 1966. The man was assigned to a work-release program at a hospital. Even a few white leaders were critical of his release. The governor responded to the criticism by releasing a black murderer and by appointing a black man as assistant superintendent at Parchman Penitentiary. Waller's show of evenhandedness might have been more convincing if he had not also been remembered as a member of the Klansman's defense team at his trial.

Elsewhere, politics returned to its previous position as a summertime entertainment. Southern elections had always attracted colorful characters. There was an Arkansas man who filed for the Democratic gubernatorial nomination with no advance publicity and no prospects for winning. When a reporter phoned his home that evening to interview him, his wife answered. "Just a minute," she said, and turned to her husband. "This is the *Gazette*. Are you running for governor?"

Louisiana was especially interesting in 1971. My November 5 story reported that the ballot would contain seventeen Democrats, two Republicans, and one member of the American Party. "That number is considered excessive even in Louisiana," I wrote, "where only fishing and horse racing rival politics as a public diversion."

Two moderates won places in the runoff. One was Edwin W. Edwards, a bilingual Cajun who went on to win. He became known for his sporting nature. He flew to Las Vegas to play and gamble. When reporters questioned him about it, he said yes, he liked to gamble and could afford it, so what's the problem? He was almost as candid about his attentions to women. I once heard him proposition a woman reporter as a group of us walked down a capitol hallway in Baton Rouge. She turned him down.

Edwards served many years in the governor's office and then went to the penitentiary to spend his sunset years doing penance for public corruption. Lay aside his marital indiscretions (one bumper sticker reportedly said, VOTE AGAINST EDWARDS. THE WIFE YOU SAVE MAY BE YOUR OWN) and his legal indiscretions, and he deserves a better place in history. He was a true moderate on race. That counted for much in Louisiana and the rest of the Deep South during those years when we began to lose our fear and peek out from under the bed to see signs of light. Edwards's main opponent in a later election, after some of his official double-dealing had come to light, turned out to be David Duke, a Hitler admirer, a Nazi wannabe, and the founder of a new, more telegenic branch of the Ku Klux Klan. It was another bumper sticker that summed up the rational choice that year: VOTE FOR THE CROOK. IT'S IMPORTANT. A record voter turnout did just that. But Duke still got the support of a third of the state's electorate, including about eight out of ten young white men, according to Professor Lawrence N. Powell, a Tulane historian.

George Wallace joined the move toward moderation. He was inaugurated as governor for a second term and took the occasion to hint that he would run for president again the following year. He did. His inaugural speech eight years earlier had been a screed of defiance— "Segregation now, segregation tomorrow, segregation forever!" The word "segregation" did not appear in his second inaugural. Black and white students marched together in the parade afterward. Most of our

stories noted that he had sounded calmer in recent months, probably to prepare his audiences for a new and calmer presidential candidate in 1972. Who knows how far his new moderation might have taken him if Arthur Bremmer had not shot and crippled him sixteen months later in Maryland?

Speaking of quixotic presidential campaigns, I had the privilege of helping to cover a homegrown one. Representative Wilbur D. Mills of Arkansas, who was routinely identified in print as "the powerful chairman of the House Ways and Means Committee," floated his trial balloon in March 1971. By August, the nascent campaign had picked up enough energy to attract several thousand people to Little Rock for a rally to "persuade" Mills to run. Thirty-two of the most influential members of Congress showed up. The draft-me facade disappeared later, and he campaigned in earnest. I interviewed him a time or two and found to my surprise that he really did want to be president, even though at one point he had declared that it was a terrible job and that he would not wish it on his worst enemy.

Mills's career ended in a sex-and-alcohol scandal. He and a lover, Fanne Foxe, a nightclub stripper from Argentina, were stopped in his car by the District of Columbia parks police late one night in 1974. Ms. Foxe jumped from the car and ran into the Tidal Basin. The incident caused immense publicity and became known as one of the top sex scandals of the era. Mills resigned his committee chairmanship and confessed to being an alcoholic.

The ignoble end of his career was, like Edwin Edwards's, unfair to his legacy. He did much good for the United States. He was one of the most intelligent people ever elected to Congress. He knew more about taxes than any other human, and he tried to make sure that they applied fairly to rich and poor. He worked with President Johnson to enact Medicare and probably had more to do with its congressional approval than even the president. He served honorably in the Congress (he won a last term after his scandal, just to prove that the folks in Arkansas still understood him) and left a legacy that still serves the nation. He would have made a good president.

If a taste for liquor and women were a disqualifier, we could have shut down the White House generations ago. Americans understand that. I think of Jeff Davis, a popular governor of Arkansas at the turn

of the twentieth century. When one of his opponents publicly accused him of drinking whiskey, Jeff suggested that all the men who had never taken a drink should vote for his opponent and the rest should vote for him. He won in a landslide.

■　　■　　■

My reporting during the 1970s covered everything short of nuclear science. I became a farm reporter by virtue of owning and surreptitiously occupying a farmhouse with forty-five acres of rural land in the Ozark Mountains (often while Abe Rosenthal thought I was in my bureau in New Orleans). I wrote about cattle ranching in Colorado, organic farming in Maine and Vermont, cotton farming in Mississippi, and crawfish farming in Louisiana. I spent a little time with Scott and Helen Nearing, the back-to-the-land visionaries, on their lush little coastal farm in Maine. I visited E. B. White and his geese on that same coast but did not write about it because that was the covenant I made when I appeared unannounced in his front yard. I covered the great Mississippi River flood of 1973, including datelines that appear in this year's flood coverage. I wrote about steamboats, festivals, cranks, and celebrities. I wrote about the growing industrialization of the South and the rise of the Republican Party. On top of all that, I found time to cover state elections involving some of the best-known names in national politics, including old-timers like Senator John L. McClellan of Arkansas, who had already served thirty years. He won another six.

Two famous politicians died, and I recorded their funerals. Lyndon Johnson was buried in a family plot on his ranch. Winthrop Rockefeller was memorialized on top of Petit Jean Mountain in Arkansas, where he had come as a repentant playboy and had stayed to become one of the nation's exemplary office-holders.

After a decent period of mourning, Lady Bird Johnson invited me and a bunch of her favorite women reporters to the LBJ Ranch to write about her new life as a private citizen. I got a little mileage out of a cushion that she had inherited from her husband. The embroidered words said, THIS IS MY RANCH AND I DO AS I DAMN PLEASE.

A dozen friendly Russians visited Greenville, Mississippi, and gave me a chance to smart off about an invasion of Communists. It also

provided an opportunity to profile one of my favorite Southern towns, one right up there with New Orleans. For starters, the black citizens of Greenville were less oppressed than in other Mississippi jurisdictions. The white citizens were an interesting mix of conservative and liberal. Many of the latter were friends of the Carter family, which owned the local paper, the *Delta Democrat-Times*. Under the editorship of Hodding Carter Jr., who was known as "Big Hodding" by the time I arrived on the scene, the paper provided an umbrella of protection for Delta liberals, an endangered species by any standard, and for the more numerous population of political moderates. The paper had enraged almost all of the rest of Mississippi. The older Carter had long been a hero of mine. His son, Hodding III, became my friend and remains so.

My story on the visiting Russians took a detour to describe a loud, angry scene at Doe's Eat Place, the preeminent restaurant in Greenville. I caught two of my friends, Bern Keating and Clarke Reed, shouting at each other and pounding the table. Clarke, a businessman, was the head of the state Republican Party and a staunch conservative. Bern was a writer and a staunch liberal Democrat. A stranger might have drawn the wrong conclusion from the scene. The two were friends and next-door neighbors. They regularly shared drinks and garden vegetables. Greenville was that kind of town.

I dabbled in music reporting. My career was distinguished by an uncanny knack for missing the big up-and-coming stars. In Nashville, I blithely ignored a chance to write about Waylon Jennings a year before he became a national name. In Texas, I covered a country music festival and devoted many column inches to Roy Acuff without ever noticing a red-headed stranger named Willie Nelson. There is probably an adjective that describes the act of overlooking Willie and Waylon, the two best-known musicians of the Outlaws generation.

I believe that I am the only national reporter ever to have covered an elephant hunt in Oklahoma. The lead on my story said, "A pair of elephants has been lost here for a week and the people of Choctaw County are becoming a little defensive about it." The elephants, aged five and six, escaped from their circus and went exploring in the nearby woods and thickets. The circus had had to go on without them, leaving it to the sheriff and an inexperienced posse to find them. I interviewed

the embarrassed sheriff, who said, "They're just baby elephants, you know." He meant that they were shorter than the men hunting them and could easily hide in the thickets. The sheriff's friends kidded him so roughly that he was relieved when a convict escaped from the county prison farm and gave him something else to hunt. I never did find out what happened to the elephants. I like to think they may still be roaming the woods of eastern Oklahoma, middle-aged now, hanging out with the local sots and country singers.

About that same time, some guy made a public threat to assassinate President Nixon. He fled to the wilds of New Mexico, and I joined that search too. I think they found him, but he may be in cahoots with those lost elephants.

Off-the-wall feature stories were always welcome at the *Times*. I looked for them all over the map. I spotted a winner with the annual crawfish festival in the Cajun town of Breaux Bridge. (Note the spelling of "crawfish." Louisianians consider the crayfish a foreign animal. I pointed out that people in the North who had never eaten one should not be allowed to spell it. That was a dig at the *Times* stylebook.) I had just arrived and was checking out the booths on Main Street when a friendly stranger hailed me. It turned out to be Calvin Trillin. He was in town to write about the crawfish as food. I was there to write about Cajuns having fun. We both got what we came for.

Trillin was drinking something from a large water glass, and he recommended it as a good buy—Mateus Rose wine at seventy-five cents a glass, which made it an all-you-can-drink bargain. Both of us had been invited to dinner that evening at a Mrs. Champagne's. She was said to be the inventor of crawfish etouffe. I learned later that people all over the bayou country made the same claim, but that detracted nothing from the lady's hospitality. We were driven to her house in a sedan that carried the Crawfish Queen and her court, two other young beauties, along with the French consul-general. The three girls were obliged to sit on the laps of the three men. Trillin and I, full of cheap wine and bonhomie, rose to the occasion, but the poor Frenchman, a dainty little man, was mortified.

Dinner was a roaring success. Plenty of wine was served, not Mateus. I made a number of discreet notes during dinner, but to my certain knowledge Trillin did not even carry a notebook. Imagine my

surprise and awe when his piece appeared in the *New Yorker* two weeks later with meticulous detail on food and guests, all the names spelled correctly—French, Cajun, and American—all the quotations accurate, and every nuance of kitchen and atmosphere described with feeling and humor. The heroic drunks of *The Front Page* would have toasted him as one of their own.

■ ■ ■

I found such features easily in the South, maybe because Southerners need more ways to distract themselves from the heat and mosquitoes. Mardi Gras in New Orleans is too easy for a reporter after he has covered a couple, so one year I drove to Mamou in the Cajun country and did a piece on back-country Mardi Gras. The young blades dress up in ridiculous costumes and ride around the countryside on horseback and collect food for a giant gumbo. They call it "courir de Mardi Gras"—the running of Mardi Gras. I went alligator-hunting with another gang of young men with too much time on their hands. They didn't shoot the beasts; they looped heavy ropes around their snouts and shipped them to Arkansas, where there was a shortage.

The city of New Orleans made a political mistake and bulldozed the only hill in town, an ugly, erosion-cut little slope in Audubon Park that had been built by the WPA so the city's children would know what a hill looked like. Cutting it down caused such an outcry that the city had to build a new one. On a lazy summer day, I covered a steamboat race from the New Orleans levee. This was a race, I observed, between two of the slowest engine-driven vessels ever invented. Then the Oklahoma town of Inola decided that it needed a festival. Its neighbor Broken Arrow had Rooster Day. Inola came up with Hay Day and pronounced itself the hay capital of the world.

For pure nonsense, I never topped my very sober report from Charleston, South Carolina, on the town's biggest civic controversy of 1975. The City Council, in a fit of delicacy, had decreed that the horses that pulled tourists around in carriages had to wear diapers. The story got on the wires and went around the world. By the time I got there, I decided that my best approach was what we call a second-day lead. Referring to the embarrassed alderman who had sponsored the

ordinance, I wrote, "Joseph McGee wants the obituary writers to know that he does not wish to be remembered as the man who put diapers on the horses of Charleston."

Not all innocent features are trouble-free. I stirred up a hornet's nest with a story suggesting that the region's Southern belles were not very interested in the feminist movement that swept the nation during those years. I found myself denounced from Montgomery to the East Coast.

I revealed that Arkansas, long known as the most backward state, except for Mississippi, had become a hotbed of literature. I reported on a thriving writers' colony in Fayetteville, Arkansas's main university town. The story described the University of Arkansas's top-ranked creative writing program, which continues to send talented young writers out into the world.

One hot afternoon during the dog days of 1974, the national editor, Dave Jones, tracked me down in Hogeye, where I was hiding, and interrogated me. He needed stories. What's going on down there? he asked. I denied that anything was going on. He went on asking the question until I finally thought of something. Vacation Bible School, I said. What's that? he asked. I assumed that everybody knew what Vacation Bible School was, but it apparently was mainly a Southern phenomenon. Idle children just released from school for summer vacation were rounded up by the various churches in town and herded into classes to learn about the Bible.

I chose Charleston, Arkansas, more or less at random. I discovered that cleverly coordinated Bible classes could keep Charleston's children occupied for nearly a month, one week at a time, passing them from the Baptists to the Methodists to the Catholics, etc., until they were finally set free to face sloth and freedom on their own. I pointed out that thousands of Southern towns had this same arrangement. My New York editors were astonished and more pleased with the story than I thought becoming. It was just Vacation Bible School, for crying out loud.

■　■　■

A disproportionate amount of my coverage in those years concerned rural America. That meant paying attention to the special poverty that urban Americans never see: the men who cut and haul the pine pulp-

wood that makes paper; the low-paid, overworked women who cut up the parts and slice open the gizzards in chicken processing plants; displaced farm workers in the old plantation regions; the hunger for precious fertilizers in pristine swamps; and the primitive swamp rats who resist the corporate spoilers.

Even in rural fastnesses, I found unexpected treasures. There was a rodeo in western Arkansas for black cowboys. Pretty fair wine was being produced in northern Indiana, about as far as you can get from the mild wine coasts of California. College students filled with idealism fled to the woods to live like Thoreau. In Georgia, a spectacularly eroded patch of once-rich farmland—a "grand monument to carelessness"—had been turned into a tourist attraction called Providence Canyons State Park.

Of all the stories I wrote about American treasures, my favorite was about William Faulkner's town, Oxford, Mississippi. I settled on the conceit of dividing the story into three sections representing his famous Yoknapatawpha trilogy: *The Hamlet, The Town,* and *The Mansion.* I fetched up a lead inspired by a yarn I had heard from a friend at the *Arkansas Gazette* who had gone to Oxford to help cover Faulkner's death for *Time* magazine in 1962. Faulkner wrote at night at a stand-up desk. He drank while he wrote, and he shed clothes one garment at a time until sometimes he was drunk and naked when he finished the day's work. One night, my friend said, Faulkner ran out of whiskey while he worked. He had already shed his clothes. He put on a pajama top—just that—and walked several blocks to his bootlegger's. The sleepy bootlegger brought the author his usual bottle and handed it through the open door. Faulkner walked toward the sidewalk, then turned and went back. "Here," he said thrusting the bottle into the man's hands. "Put this in a sack. I can't be seen walking down the street carrying a bottle of whiskey."

My first task at Oxford was to find that bootlegger. I followed a tip and drove to a country store in a hamlet nearby. I approached the question as delicately as I could, and the owner handled it with the same discipline. Liquor had been legalized in Mississippi some years earlier, but who knew whether the statute of limitations still ran. Motee Daniels, his name was, reached behind a row of canned goods and pulled out a pint of whiskey. He held it out to me, and knowing what

was required, I took two hearty swallows and chased it with Coca-Cola. He did the same and chased it. We were then complicit in crime and ready to talk about William Faulkner without what you might call mental reservations.

Daniels liked Faulkner but had never read any of his books. "I thought he was a damn fool," he said and laughed to show that he knew he was mistaken. "He had a frame of mind that you could walk right up in his face and, hell, he wouldn't pay no attention." I was never able to get him to confirm the story of the author's half-clad trip to buy whiskey.

I wrote a similar profile of a village called Radwinter, not far from Cambridge University in England, a few years later. I turned up a cast of characters worthy of Dylan Thomas's *Under Milk Wood*. I found a World War I memorial in Radwinter that completely sobered me. A plaque in the Anglican church carried a list of names of all the young men of the village who had died in the Great War. Twenty-eight of them. In a village that never had more than seven or eight hundred residents over its several centuries, practically every man of military age was killed in that war.

A campaign began early in the twenty-first century to tear down a London statue of General Sir Douglas Haig, the commander who sent British soldiers to their deaths by the tens of thousands, wave after wave up from the trenches and into the fire of the German machine guns. The United Kingdom lost 885,138 men in the war. Haig was directly responsible for a large percentage of them. A later British prime minister, casting an eye back over the long animosity between England and Scotland, observed that Haig was the Scot responsible for killing the most Englishmen.

During that same period, I drove to another English village that boasted the longest-lived people in the country, according to a government report. The townspeople told me with a mixture of pride and embarrassment that they owed their long lives to the ancient practice of fertilizing their backyard gardens with human waste—night soil, they called it. I'd bet my farm that they are not allowed to do that anymore, now that Britain has more or less joined Europe with its modern legal constraints.

■　■　■

Old stories are hard to shake. Almost fifty years later, I still get the urge to drive to Alabama just to see the place and find out whether some of the bastards who caused so much trouble are still alive. Another story that fretted me for years after I covered it was Northern Ireland. Norma and I got on a train in Dublin one August day in 1985, six years after I had left the *Times,* and headed for Belfast to visit our son's Irish in-laws. We might have suspected that an omen was being cast as we waited to board and a commotion broke out in the station lobby. A couple of young robbers had been captured by some alert citizens and wrestled to the floor to wait for the police.

Our train crossed the border from the Republic of Ireland without incident. But minutes later, as we arrived in Newry, the first town in the North, we pulled to a stop. A train official went from car to car and told us to get off. We had waited outside several minutes when the guy came out of the train and told us to go back and get our luggage. He was agitated and a little impatient with us, as if we were supposed to be in on the gag. "We'll never find it if you don't get your luggage off," he said. We trudged back and got our bags.

"It" turned out to be incendiary bombs secreted in duffel bags. A thoughtful terrorist had phoned an advance notice of them. Suddenly a puff of smoke rose from one of the passenger cars. A minute later, a puff came from a second car, then from a third, then from the fourth and final car. Then came the flames. We stood on the tarmac dumbfounded and watched the whole train burn. The regulars on the trip noted that this train burning was the first in some time. It once was a regular occurrence on the coastal line, they said, but the hard feelings between the Catholics and the Protestants had slacked off a bit and the terrorists had pulled back. Something had caused a change of heart, evidently. Only later did we learn that our bombing was the fourth one on the Dublin-Belfast line that year. We finally arrived at our destination by bus, and our host, Una Byrne, John's mother-in-law, met us. She was mortified that her American guests had had to see that display of bad manners.

For Norma and me, the incident brought back memories of a bizarre encounter we had had with "the Troubles" years earlier when I was still spending a lot of time reporting from Ulster. I had become friendly with a man who had the improbable job of public relations

director for the Northern Ireland Tourist Board. He and I had shared a good many pleasant evenings over dinner and drinks during my frequent visits to cover the various outrages—pub bombings, knee-cappings, murders—of the 1970s. Ian Hill understood fully that his job was not only Sysyphean but also inherently ridiculous. Imagine some poor sod today trying to lure American tourists to downtown Baghdad. "Your money cheerfully refunded if you lose a limb!" In the 1970s, only fearless old American women looking for their ancestors' records and ardent British anglers coming to test the local rivers could be counted on to visit the lovely old towns and hills of Northern Ireland. So when I told Ian that I was thinking of bringing my wife for a holiday in the North, and writing a travel article about it, he immediately put me in touch with a string of the better hotels and restaurants from the glens of Antrim to the fine old resorts of Donegal. All of them needed the business.

Norma and I spent several days and nights drifting from one beauty spot to another. Our first day was in a town just across the border from the Republic. Ian had enticed a busload of Americans to risk their lives, as they believed, to cross the border and stay for lunch at our hotel before beating it back to safety in the Republic. We finished our holiday and flew home to London.

I dallied a few days before writing the travel piece. Then, on the morning I had set aside to stay home and write it, I retrieved the local papers from the doorstep and was greeted by screaming headlines about a new outbreak of bombings in Northern Ireland. The IRA had set off explosives in four of the five hotels we had stayed in, including the one where the busload of Americans had eaten lunch. There were no casualties, but the message was clear: don't bother to write that travel article for your newspaper. My travel editor got the message. I didn't have the heart to argue when he cancelled my story idea.

CHAPTER 27

Dixie Takes Washington without Firing a Shot

My last political reporting for the *Times,* not counting bits of exotica from the British Isles and occasional freelance stories after I left the paper, was during the 1976 elections. President Ford was being pursued by Ronald Reagan for the Republican nomination. The Democratic field included several famous men like Representative Morris Udall of Arizona, Senator Henry M. Jackson of Washington, and Governor George Wallace of Alabama. It also included Jimmy Carter, a Georgia peanut farmer who, in his beer-drinking brother Billy's words, was crazy enough to believe that he was going to be president of the United States.

It became obvious during the winter that Florida's primaries would make or break candidacies in both parties. The *Times* opened a two-man bureau in a chic Miami hotel. Douglas Robinson of the New York office came down to handle editing. I was to provide day-to-day reporting on the progress of the campaign as the candidates criss-crossed the state.

Doug and I spent a month there during February and March, and we took advantage of the hotel's swimming pool and the city's good Cuban restaurants. I got acquainted with one of my heroes from the paper, Anthony Lewis, who had set a standard for coverage of the Supreme Court that has never been surpassed. He had become a columnist.

We had converted a large suite into a working news bureau. Typewriters were set up around a long dining table. *Times* reporters

attached to the various candidates came in every day or so to write their stories. Lewis swept in one day to write his column. He took a machine at the end of the table and immediately started typing. He grinned as he began. The grin widened into a smile as he wrote, and before the column was finished he was bouncing in his chair. I had never seen such a celebration of the act of writing.

The suite was crowded on primary election day, March 9. All of us had filed lengthy background material to be set in type early. The only work left was to write a lead on each story. That was to be done as late as possible, before our first-edition deadline, as the early returns came in and as trends became evident. Johnny Apple, the paper's chief political reporter, paced the room in a nervous frenzy that got worse as the deadline grew closer. He was beginning to make a nuisance of himself. I decided to escape to a bedroom and take a nap. He had a small temper tantrum when he looked in and saw me asleep.

I wrote the lead story for page 1 and reported that Ford and the now-famous peanut farmer had won their primaries.

I covered a few political events during the summer. It became obvious in a few weeks that the nominees would be Ford and Carter. The paper assigned me to accompany a Democratic delegate to the convention in New York in July. I selected Gene Kelley of Rogers, Arkansas. He took along his wife Joye, whose name I misspelled the first day, and two of their five children. My stories commented extensively on the family's comparisons of New York City to Rogers, population thirteen thousand. A friendly cab driver confided that he himself would like someday to move to a small town somewhere. Where did he have in mind? "Miami," he said. The Kelleys tried to keep from laughing out loud.

With the prospect that a Southerner might win, the *Times* sent me back to New York to find some transplanted Southerners and tell the readers about these outlanders in their midst. I rounded up a representative bunch. The consensus was that they liked the big city well enough—some were getting rich; one young man was working for George Soros—but that all of them were homesick. And they still had trouble with the language even though some had become fluent in their adopted tongue.

Then Carter won, and the paper needed more. I did a magazine

piece on the continuing differences between North and South but emphasizing the inexorable Americanization of the lower states. I quoted my friend H. Brandt Ayers, who owned the newspaper in Anniston, Alabama, as saying that all Southerners should be admitted to the Carter White House without question, through the back door "like home folks." But Northerners should have to pass a test to get in. One of the questions was, "What is the average height of a grit tree?"

After I got him to sit down and be serious, I asked Brandy what it was that made Southerners different. "Scorn," he said. "Scorn, the one un-American experience. It explains why we behave, good and bad, the way we do. . . . Scorn is the one experience that is applied to every-body in the whole vast region. We were formed in some fundamental way by the most awful un-American experience imaginable. America never knew that. America never thought to scorn the Midwest or the Far West. Only one people for 100 years have looked out over the bar-ricades and [indignation colliding here with metaphor] opened the doors very tentatively and defensively, and what comes through it? Sarcasm! Words so cheaply spoken, but they have an effect crushing to the spirit. So what they get in return is a chorus of 'Dixie.'"

CHAPTER 28

London

I phoned Dave Jones, the national editor, during the fall of 1976 and told him I was travel-weary and needed a break. Maybe I could move to New York for a year or two and work on the copy desk. He took the suggestion to Abe Rosenthal, the executive editor, who made a suggestion of his own: how about the London bureau? Has anybody ever turned down an assignment to London? Remember what Samuel Johnson said. The man who is tired of London is tired of life.

We flew there early in 1977. When I first learned that I would make the transfer, the London bureau chief was Bob Semple, an old friend from my Washington days. But before the move took place, Semple was transferred to New York to become foreign editor. He was replaced by Johnny Apple. I didn't know what to expect.

Apple's father ran a chain of grocery stores in Ohio. Johnny was expelled from Princeton and finally graduated from Columbia University in 1961. He spent two years at the *Wall Street Journal* and NBC News, then got a job at the *New York Times*. People who dealt with him back then described him as overconfident, abrasive, and seemingly immune to insult. One day in the city room he walked up to David Halberstam, a Pulitzer Prize winner, and told him he had heard good things about him at a social gathering the night before. "Fuck off, kid," said Halberstam, without looking up. Apple showed no sign that he felt the reproof.

The assumption seemed to be that Apple had a thick skin. I doubt that. A good reporter—and he was good—has to be sensitive. When I knew him, he came across sometimes as blustery, but I never took that to mean that he felt no pain. He had to be aware of his reputation for arrogance.

He was assigned to the Albany bureau soon after the *Times* hired him. The thinking was that the kid had talent but needed seasoning. He was thrown with a group of topnotch reporters from papers all over the state. His reputation as a pain in the neck grew as fast as his reporting skill. The Albany veterans habitually gathered in the same bar at the end of each workday. After a few weeks, they realized that they were spending too much drinking time talking about the boy from Ohio. They laid down a rule that anyone mentioning Apple had to put a quarter into a kitty for buying drinks. Doug Robinson, already an old Albany hand for the *Times,* walked in after one grueling day and threw a five-dollar bill on the table. "I've got some things I want to say about Apple," he said.

I now have some things I want to say about Apple. He has been dead for several years, time enough for an assessment. For the most part, even his numerous detractors admitted that he was an excellent reporter. He would become one of the celebrated political reporters of his time, and along the way he would make a reputation as a bon vivant, a gourmand, a world traveler, and a master of the corporate expense account.

I heard stories of his occasional big-footing, taking over stories being worked by the reporters under his jurisdiction. But when I first met him, in Saigon, I found him frankly charming. His boyish out-spokenness would have been hard for a new acquaintance to fault. Besides, he had by then acquired a wife who already was known among the Asian press corps as brave, smart, and entirely admirable.

Soon after we both arrived in London, Johnny and I made a deal. We acknowledged over lunch one day that both of us were known in the New York newsroom as prima donnas and that we had to take care not to fall out over some professional or territorial matter.

We kept that pact. He never got in my way in anything that mattered. We agreed that British politics was his story. Northern Ireland, where the Catholic-Protestant conflict was in full swing, was mine. We understood that I would travel the British Isles for features and background stories that appealed to me. He did the same. The only time we came close to a difficulty was when I discovered that one of the paper's New York reporters had poached a story that I had been expecting to do, a feature on the popular new novelist Margaret

Drabble. I always suspected that Apple knew that the guy had slipped over from New York to do the story and never mentioned it to me.

Johnny and Edie had been divorced some years earlier, and he was enjoying the bachelor life in London. He came to the bureau one Monday morning and announced to one and all—men and women, reporters, clerks, the whole staff—that he had bedded a baroness over the weekend. I don't remember having any further personal conversation with him. A few months later, I left the paper and went home to Arkansas to teach journalism. I suppose that one factor in my decision might have been that I no longer cared for Johnny's company. He was very far down in my list of discontents, however.

He eventually married another woman, and they lived a sumptuous life of fine food and grand style, traveling among the elite of several continents. Now and then I saw his byline on a story from some exotic foreign village with a four-star restaurant. He and his new wife traveled ceaselessly, he adding girth with each new continent. I could not repress in my mind the words of Fitzgerald: "They were careless people, Tom and Daisy . . . " He died in 2006 at the age of seventy-one, full of acclaim and foie gras.

■　　■　　■

Norma and I rented a house in the Vale of Health in Hampstead a few miles north of central London. The Vale was an encroachment on Hampstead Heath. Much of it had been a marsh full of mosquitoes for centuries. But it had the advantage of lying a few hundred feet higher than downtown London, and that made it attractive in the eighteenth century. In the early days, it was known as Hatches Bottom. A smart land dealer drained the swamp and changed the name to the Vale of Health, and Londoners started building there. It celebrated its bicentennial while we lived there. We joined the celebration and invited the neighbors to tour our garden, one of the largest—if least trimmed—in the neighborhood. We also threw a Fourth of July party in that garden to celebrate our own beginnings, which predated the Vale's by a few years. On both occasions the neighbors all turned out, no hard feelings on either side.

The several dozen houses in the Vale had names; ours was Fig Tree

House because the garden had a fig tree, which had been nurtured and protected as a kind of endangered species. Fig Tree House sat in the center of the neighborhood, and as we ate breakfast we could watch the neighbors walking to Hampstead High Street or the Tube stop. The house had four stories and so many rooms that we never occupied more than half of them. Ours was the third *Times* family to live there.

The neighbors included a number of famous people, including the actor Alan Bates. He was married to the beautiful actress Victoria Ward—the mother of his twin sons—and was believed by the local gossips to be the lover of two neighbors, a pair of beautiful sisters. Much later, it became public knowledge that Bates also had a succession of male lovers. That crossed the line into extravagance, in my estimation. A friend of ours, Louis Heren, the deputy editor of the London *Times,* lived next door to the actor. He was acquainted with all the women in the Bates drama and liked them. He was indignant that the actor might prefer this or that "fancy boy" to all those beauties.

I never met Alan Bates. Neither did I meet Alfred Brendel, the famous pianist, who lived across the street from us. I heard him practicing regularly and occasionally caught a glimpse when he went outside. I did, however, have dealings with his beautiful wife. Our house had a large garage, and she rented space in it for her car. She paid me fifteen pounds a month. She still owes me a month's rent.

Christopher Trevor-Roberts lived across the street on the other side of us. He had tutored Queen Elizabeth's children. He was Welsh, and because of that, I suppose, he had the best singing voice in the Vale. He led parties of carolers around the neighborhood during the Christmas holidays. I can't sing a lick, but I always went along. The parties afterward were merry.

Several houses bore blue plaques certifying that famous people had lived there. There was one on the D. H. Lawrence house and another on Leigh Hunt's, although there was some anxiety about the provenance of the latter. It was established, though, that the poet moved to the Vale after he got out of prison for libeling the Prince Regent. It was said that his visitors included Byron, Shelley, and Coleridge as well as various political progressives. John Keats lived near the Vale, and his blue plaque was genuine. Across the way in Highgate Cemetery was the tomb of Karl Marx, visible from a distance because

of the oversized bust at the top and often made more so by the red paint dumped on it by people with strong opinions.

Mr. and Mrs. Brunker lived across the street from us. They told stories of German bombers during World War II dropping their surplus bombs on the Heath before heading back across the Channel. Mrs. Brunker was standing at her kitchen sink the day a bomb blew up Jack Straw's Castle, an ancient watering hole, at the top of the hill. Shards of shrapnel and splinters from the pub came through her window.

We were dismayed some years after we returned home to learn that Fig Tree House had been bought by a real estate company that turned the place into three houses, adding two new ones in the garden. Norma and I went to see for ourselves the last time we were in London. We got as far as the gate and couldn't bear to look further. I think they cut down the fig tree.

Louis lived about fifty yards from us in Fleet House, so named because a spring in his garden was one of the sources of the Fleet River. The Fleet flowed to the Thames and arrived there in a more direct route than I ever did. I never seemed to find the same route twice on the several occasions when I drove to work instead of riding the Tube. I got there by simply driving downhill, unable to remember the correct turns, until I made it downtown. Our office was a few steps from Fleet Street, the most famous newspaper street in the world, the home of many of the country's big dailies.

I was introduced to Louis by a family of American neighbors, Bobby and Alex de Joia. They had moved from New York during the communist scare of the midcentury, not because they were Reds but because they were offended by our national hallucinations that saw a traitor under every bed. They became good friends and remained so until they died.

Louis Heren was denied promotion to chief editor of the fabled old London *Times* almost certainly because he was the wrong class. He was brought up poor in the city's East End. He described his origins as half-Irish, half-Jewish, and half-Basque. The *Times* would not want a man of Louis's caste and egalitarian tastes calling the shots for that noble paper, where the Tory Party found its Scriptures every day.

Louis and I stayed in touch periodically until he died in 1995. He once came to visit in Hogeye and left me with two secrets. He was a

devoted martini drinker, a taste he had acquired during a long tenure in Washington as his paper's chief American correspondent. (He had also spent several harrowing years in India, among other challenging foreign assignments, and was on a train during the violent separation of India and Pakistan. The train was attacked, and a lot of people were killed. He was in first class and apparently spared because of his nationality.)

Louis showed me how to begin mixing the martini by rinsing the olives in water to remove the salt. That was not a concern over sodium intake; he reckoned that the salt distorted the taste of the gin. His other secret was the gin. He had been a devotee of Beefeaters for years. Then one day his paper had as a lunch guest the chairman of the Beefeaters company. Louis stayed behind to thank him for many years of happy drinking. The man confided that he should switch from Beefeaters to the house brand of the big grocery chain, Sainsbury's. It's our gin, he said. We just slap the Sainsbury label on before we ship it. It's about half the price of Beefeaters. On our next trip to London, I stocked up on all the Sainsbury's gin that I could get through customs.

When Louis died, his children arranged a reception at his house in the Vale. Bobby de Joia gave us a report. The children knew that plenty of food and wine would be necessary. Before they could go to the store and stock up, Louis's monthly order from the Wine Society happened to be delivered—not a few bottles but three cases of the society's best.

■ ■ ■

Bob Semple passed on a story to me when he left London. He had wanted to go to the English coal country and visit the town of Wigan. George Orwell wrote a famous book, *The Road to Wigan Pier*, describing his own extended visit there. I can still see in my mind the filthy wet towel that was the only one his landlady provided for all her boarders. And I still see the black spots permanently imprinted on the miners' spines from the years of bumping the low ceilings of the mine shafts as they walked half-crouching to their place of work each day. My own story was considerably less dramatic because the government had forced the owners to improve conditions for the miners. As a

result, Wigan was a pleasant little town. The most interesting thing I came away with was the old joke about the town's name. Wigan was miles from the sea. In past times, talk of spending your annual vacation on the beach at Wigan and hanging out on the "pier" was considered the height of humor in England.

■ ■ ■

I spent much of my time in Northern Ireland covering the Troubles—the bombings and assassinations—and the political upheaval that accompanied them. But other stories claimed my attention as well. I flew to the Canary Islands in March 1977 to help cover the worst airplane disaster in history. Two airliners collided on a runway at Tenerife and killed 583 people. I have a picture glued to the ceiling of my memory: 583 rigid, blackened corpses stacked like firewood in the hangar.

Racism became a political problem, and I found that it could be as bad in Britain as in the States. I spent time covering the Reverend Ian Paisley, Northern Ireland's leading anti-Catholic politician, and found him to be as fine a demagogue as the ones I had known in the American South.

There were features, both light and heavy. A London shop made me a pair of bespoke shoes. I visited a shop in the Cotswolds where I could have bought a bespoke suit of armor but didn't. I compared the sedate decorum of the U.S. Congress with the raucous barracking inflicted on opposing speakers in the British Parliament. I wrote about periodic outbreaks of nationalism in Scotland and Wales and about the incomprehensible native language of the Welsh, which seems to be made up entirely of consonants. I wrote a feature about the weavers who make Harris tweed and came home with enough to make several jackets.

President Carter flew over and visited the little town of Washington in County Durham, in far northern England, where the local English is a challenge to the American ear. I tried to interview some men in a bar and found that I couldn't understand what they were saying. They couldn't understand me, either. A bilingual chap came over from a table and interpreted for us. The president was a big hit. As one of the men in the bar put it, "'E's an okay bloke."

I flew to Assen in the Netherlands to cover a train hijacking by a group of militants. I did some light carousing there with Arthur Ochs Sulzberger Jr., the son of the publisher of the *New York Times* and himself the publisher-in-training, although he denied that he was interested in the job. He was working as a reporter for the Associated Press. He beat me on a story or two, and I decided that he was a good reporter and an okay bloke. We spent about a month there before the difficulty was settled by a military attack on the militants. Among other things, I discovered that the average Dutch person speaks better English than most Americans and a hell of a lot better than the Englishmen in County Durham.

I was entertained by a change at Debrett's Peerage Ltd., the ancient and sober company that recorded the lineages of Britain's titled families. The outfit was about to go broke. It ended up in the hands of an international group of investors who promptly hired as its top executive— gasp!—an American. His qualifications included a hyphenated name, several years' residence in London, and a well-practiced upper-crust English accent. Harold Brooks-Baker rescued Debrett's and turned it into a money-maker by publishing such outlandish books as *The English Gentleman*, by Douglas Sutherland, a Scottish gentleman with a sense of humor.

I summed up the book's message this way: "A gentleman does not drive a Rolls-Royce unless it is very old and smells of dogs; does not own more than two suits, one for funerals and one for visiting London; stuffs his handkerchief in his sleeve, not his breast pocket; shows toleration for his children and affection for his dogs; speaks to the engineer before a train trip because of an old belief that he owns the railroad." The book was followed by others of that ilk, as they say in Scotland. Brooks-Baker caused hard feelings in the aristocracy of Virginia by publishing a genealogy of President Carter suggesting that he might be a blue blood of the Old Dominion instead of a lowly peanut farmer from Georgia.

Norma and I flew up to the Shetland Islands for a look around, and I filed a couple of stories, one on a shortage of Shetland ponies and the other on a political movement that threatened to tie the islands closer to the Scottish mainland, against the wishes of a lot of Shetlanders. "The attachment to Scotland has always been fragile," I wrote, "a little like that

of southern Alabama to the United States." One gent took us to a high point on his sheep-grazed land and waved with pride at the treeless landscape. Norma asked whether he missed trees. Not at all, he said. Shetlanders were opposed to them. Why, she asked. Because trees obstruct the view, and we want to see what the neighbors are up to.

I took an interest in another island nation under threat. Lundy sits in the Bristol Channel midway between Devon and Wales. It had once been a self-sufficient stronghold that paid no British taxes and boasted a band of pirates who plundered the sea-lanes for miles around. Time had overtaken the place by the time I got there—once again with Norma, who remembers having to wade ashore from a boat because a gale was blowing too hard to risk docking. We found that Lundy's twenty-six inhabitants had become irretrievably British, more or less against their will, and were fully reliant on their neighbor for food and everything else. They had even consented to pay British taxes, which seemed fair since they relied on the British armed forces to protect them from roving filibusters who might be watching for a chance to attack.

A thoroughly odd sex scandal that could occur only in Britain popped up during my last year there. Jeremy Thorpe, an MP and a former leader of the Liberal Party, was charged with conspiring to murder a male model with whom he was accused of having an affair. He was acquitted in 1979, but along the way the story degenerated into a tabloid's delight, complete with a hit man cornering the model on a Devon moor, changing his mind, shooting the man's Great Dane instead in order to collect his fee, and hundreds of thousands of printed words to raise the eyebrows of the reading public. Every day for weeks as I rode the Tube home I saw the headlines in the neatly folded *Daily Mirror* reporting that day's latest in large black headlines.

It was not exactly a sex scandal, but my story on the divorce of Princess Margaret and Lord Snowdon noted that she and her friend Roderick Llewellyn, seventeen years her junior, had been the object of excited speculation in the London gossip columns for two years. If we had had the advantage of later revelations about the convoluted sex life of Alan Bates, we would have learned that the princess, according to a book on the actor's life, had unsuccessfully joined the line for his affections. You can read about it in Donald Spoto's biography *Otherwise Engaged: The Life of Alan Bates*. My story pointed out that

Margaret's was the first dissolution of a marriage in the immediate royal family since Henry VIII's to Anne of Cleves was annulled in 1540.

■ ■ ■

At the end of 1978, when we were ready to come home, there were Englishmen still alive who were disappointed that they had not been allowed to fight the French instead of the Germans in the last two wars. The antagonism was centuries old and mutual. I tumbled to this during the summer when I went to Dover to report that the town was gratified that one more attempt to tie England to the continent, a half-built tunnel, had failed and had been abandoned. The lead on my story quoted a crusty old man who said, "Every nation has its natural enemy. Ours is France." An old *Gazette* friend, Richard Allin, had returned from a trip to England some years earlier with a tale about a man on a city payroll whose job was to go up the hill every morning and look across the English Channel to see whether the French were coming to attack. Allin thought the town was Dover. I ended the story with that information, saying it could not be verified.

In a few weeks, here came a note from a reader in New York with a yellowing clipping enclosed. The clipping was a column from the *Guardian* by Michael Frayn, who would later become a famous playwright. It established that the town was not Dover but Winchelsea, down the coast a few miles. Frayn's column started like this: "Every now and then they find some forgotten island in the Pacific inhabited by Japanese soldiers who have still not heard that the Second World War has ended. This, I now discover, is nothing. I have just found a place in Sussex where they are still paying a man to look out for the coming of the French invasion fleet."

I laid the clipping aside until late December, when I drove to Winchelsea and filed what would be my last story before leaving the *Times.* Sure enough, there had until recently been such a fellow on the town payroll, or so he claimed. He was a retired truck driver, now dead a few years, who apparently saw a chance to earn tips from the tourists. The town indeed had employed a person for several centuries to climb the hill every morning to watch for a French invasion fleet. The city government well into the twentieth century authorized a salary of a

little over two dollars a year for the position. It was true that four or five centuries earlier the French and the English had taken turns sacking each other's coastal towns, and Winchelsea was at the heart of the plundering. But peace had broken out, and the sea itself had receded two miles and was barely visible from the town. I found an old guy in a pub who still did not trust the French. Keeping a lookout was not a bad idea, he said.

This was my kind of story. I cannot think of a better way to finish a reporting career.

One last memory from 1978. I had been called to Washington in the early 1970s to write an advance obituary on Hubert Humphrey. It was long and wordy, as befitting the voluble Humphrey. I got up one morning in London and learned that Humphrey had died. The obit appeared under my byline January 1, 1978, all five columns of it. I remembered a day in 1968 when he had just begun his campaign for the presidency. As he walked into a Washington hotel ballroom, the band struck up "Happy Days Are Here Again," which I think was Humphrey's favorite song.

> Happy Days are here again,
> The skies above are clear again,
> So let's sing a song of cheer again,
> Happy Days are here again.

CHAPTER 29

Is There Life after the New York Times?

You may not have noticed much of Roy in this book that calls itself a memoir. That's because reporters are seldom as interesting as the people and events they write about. Furthermore, I have deliberately avoided lurid confessions, philosophical musings, and cosmic speculations. It's not that I have a lot to hide, but some things are none of your business. I don't have much use for the New York school of tell-all autobiographers.

As it happens, I am quite ordinary: husband, father, mediocre golfer, inattentive citizen. I have never parachuted from an airplane. I have never climbed a peak higher than West Mountain in Hot Springs National Park. I have seldom been in danger of dying in an accident, although there was that unnerving night when George Wallace's campaign plane, hired on the cheap, dribbled most of its engine oil onto the Rocky Mountains, and a night in Germany when the speeding car I was riding in seemed certain to break free of the highway and fly off the mountain, and a road in Tibet—more on that in a moment.

I have never been shot at or seriously assaulted if you don't count some pushing and shoving during riots and an ear-boxing by an angry alderman early in my career. I remember a shoot-out between the Black Panthers and the police in New Orleans when some of the reporters thought the Panthers had expanded their line of fire to include us. If so, their aim was lousy.

My family are also soothingly ordinary, excepting grandchildren, who are all above average. A few moments in our family history stand

out. There was the diving catch by our son John, age nine, and his throw to first for the out on a ballfield in Atlanta. And the day that Norma became a hero to our daughter Cindy during a heated confrontation with a school principal in New Orleans over a charge of playing hooky.

I have chosen to skip lightly over the sixteen and a half years that I taught journalism at the University of Arkansas. I am also passing over the years since 1995 when I retired to write freelance articles and books and entertain a small herd of cattle. All of it has been rewarding. I have never been bored. I enjoyed teaching, even though I never felt at home in the classroom. The university was extraordinarily generous in giving me the time to write without pretending that it was scholarly research.

During my summer vacation of 1981, I spent six weeks on the most glamorous trip of my life. I went to Tibet to do a chapter of a *National Geographic* book, *Journey into China*. I got the assignment from an old *Arkansas Gazette* friend, Kenneth Danforth. After working for *Time* magazine all over the world, he had settled into a major editorial job in the book division at the *Geographic*.

Researching and interviewing required two interpreters: (1) English to Chinese and (2) Chinese to Tibetan. The first step was handled by a bright young Minnesotan named John Holden. His Chinese was flawless, best I could tell, and he was also helpful in putting people at ease when we talked to them. The Chinese government provided the second interpreter and a driver. The driver was a fearless little Chinese guy who saved our lives once and risked them all over again another time.

We were riding up the side of a mountain on a shelf road. We were on the abyss side with no guardrails and no shoulder. Suddenly, coming straight at us, was a truck hogging both lanes of the road. Our driver instantly swung sharply to the right, inches from the edge. We could look down about a thousand feet, or maybe five miles, who knows? I saw the driver of the truck as he hurtled past. He had a maniacal grin on his face.

A day or so later, we had to stop the vehicle and wait half an hour for water from a monsoon downpour to drain off the road. It was rolling furiously down the slope blocking the road for about a hundred

yards. When it was still three or four feet deep, our driver tired of waiting and plunged in. I am not a praying man, but I was hoping that the gods of the Buddhists and the Muslims in our car might be looking down on us.

I spent some time with Tibetan monks and came away with the dangerous knowledge that more than a few of them were anti-Chinese activists. Some months later, the government staged one of its periodic crackdowns, and among the targets, I believe, were men who had been friendly to me.

I met Tenzing Norgay, the mountaineer who climbed Mount Everest with Edmund Hillary, in a village near the Nepal border. When he found out that we were nearing the end of our journey, he suggested a route that would save us days of needless backtracking and a lot of expense. Just walk across the border over there, he said, naming a spot nearby, and hike on down to Katmandu. It's only about forty miles, he said, and you have to cross only one glacier. As for the national border—well, no one pays that any mind, he assured us. The locals cross back and forth all the time. We thanked him kindly, stuck with our car, and took the long way back.

Our numerous Chinese handlers were already antsy about our motives. We had been poking around in Tibetan politics too much to suit them. I don't know what *their* motive was, but on our last evening in Lhasa our hosts got John and me so drunk that we had to be carried into our guesthouse and dumped on our beds. We were sick for forty-eight hours.

■ ■ ■

Regarding my career as a landowner, I have owned a farm at Hogeye for thirty-six years but am still considered a newcomer. Never mind that I have achieved senior status and am now the second-oldest person in the community, ranking just behind a retired English teacher who stays healthy by working in moderation, eating well, and drinking premium whiskey. In spite of many years in the country, I am not at home as a farmer.

The truth is, I have never been at home anywhere except in the newsroom. That is my natural habitat. I once wrote that I had become

reasonably settled except for one thing: I didn't have a place to be buried. I have a modest proposal for my heirs. Cremate my remains and ask some friendly editor to find a place for my urn in his or her newsroom. I don't ask for so lofty a resting place as the copy desk or the wire editor's office. Just park me on the back of some untidy reporter's desk. And if people use my urn as an ashtray, what can I say? I do have one request. I would like for the urn to be inscribed with these words in thirty-six-point Cheltenham Bold type: BEWARE OF FALSE TITLES.

Most reporters love their work. That is not based on scientific evidence; I have run no survey. I know it is true because I have known few reporters who were not happy in their work. They grumble and grouse and curse their editors, but they are happy with it all, maybe because they are happiest when they are angry.

They are happy but not necessarily secure. Virtually all reporters worry about being fired because anxiety is embedded in their makeup. That keeps them on their toes, keeps them running every day to avoid the anger and scorn of the editor, who they believe to be an unfeeling brute, although few are. I went through a period of thinking that the *Times* executive editor, Abe Rosenthal, was a brute. I noticed, though, that a lot of people considered him a superb editor. He was relentless in pushing reporters to get the story. I once asked Gene Roberts, who was then working under Abe as national editor, how to explain Abe's success. Is he cool under fire? I asked. "No," Gene said. "He's hot under fire. That's what makes him good."

Some reporters who profess to be unhappy are faking it, pretending to be morose or cynical because they think that is expected of the mythical hard-bitten reporter. Far from being cynical, reporters generally prefer to believe what they are told. If they don't, sources dry up and stop telling them anything. More important, their curiosity dries up if they stop believing. All it takes to cure a dangerous gullibility is being stung a few times; then the youngster learns the wisdom of the adage, "If your mother says she loves you, check it out." Those who become truly cynical and unhappy seldom make good reporters. They may do a serviceable job on the police beat, where cynicism can be a defense against madness, but they lack the deeper innocence that impels the better reporter to keep learning and climbing. I adhere to

Turner Catledge's definition of a good reporter: one who has insatiable curiosity and an irresistible urge to tell.

The urge to tell gets short shrift in the journalism textbooks and the conventional wisdom. Old Joe Wirges of the *Arkansas Gazette*, the best police reporter I ever knew, kept his insatiable curiosity all of his long life, but he could not write a lick. He simply was not interested in that skill. I suspect he thought that good writing was unmanly. Maybe he was right. I have always thought of myself as manly enough, but I admit that I have taken a large and unearned pride in my words. Occasionally, in my younger days, I thought of myself in the most secret, closely held part of myself as a poet. I outgrew that conceit, and I am a better man for it.

Nevertheless, there is no denying the satisfaction of seeing your byline on a well-written story. If the story is on the front page, the satisfaction is doubled. That means that large numbers of people have seen it and read it and maybe have nodded or smiled over some appealing turn of phrase. Jim Bailey, my favorite sportswriter, is always worth reading. Every news story or column of his has at least one sentence that makes me want to say, "Listen to this, Norma." I have no interest in boxing stories unless they are written by Jim. Years ago, he covered a match in Little Rock and noticed that the eventual winner had trouble keeping his trunks on. They were too large and kept sliding down, meaning, Jim said, that he had to fight one-handed, the other hand being required to hold up his trunks. When the boxer was awarded a winner's belt afterward, Jim noted that nobody ever needed one more.

Friendly readers sometimes send reporters flattering letters that we called "mash notes." That only encourages us, and in the wake of a few mash notes our prose may turn a vivid purple. The only corrective for purpling is a stern note from the editor or an unsubtle rewriting of two or three of our stories. "This is a good story, Roy," one of my editors used to tell me on the phone, "but I think the lead needs a little work." Or maybe he would say the paper had a space problem that day and I needed to trim my story. I would pout and grumble, then rewrite it, and in every case I improved the story by cutting it, even when it meant depriving unborn generations of whole paragraphs of my best prose.

Reporters work long hours and forget to put in for overtime. They

get caught up in the story and keep going past the point of good sense. Sometimes exhaustion can stop the most determined reporter in his tracks. I phoned Claude Sitton late one Friday night and whined that I had run out of steam and would finish the weekender I was laboring over the next morning. He needed it that night. Claude said, in his most winning south Georgia accent, "Ah, Roy, just get a cup of strong black coffee and go back to work." I did. Claude had been there as a reporter. What he was really saying was, "I'll tell you when you're tired."

But there is no doubt that reporters go to extraordinary lengths to avoid what society considers sensible work. They put themselves in harm's way. The greatest war correspondents scoff at danger but secretly yearn for it. I never covered a war unless you consider it war to be shoved around and called vile names by enraged segregationists. Covering terrorist bombings in Belfast was not especially dangerous. I listened to the nightly explosions from the safety of the tenth floor of the Europa Hotel. They bombed the ground floor one night, but I slept through it.

In the worst of violence at home or abroad, I never felt anything more troubling than a heightened anxiety. I knew that luck and ordinary caution would keep me safe. Still, sticking with a job that might have crippled or hurt me made no sense from the point of view of saner citizens. None of us did it for the pay. Compared to the wages of those daredevil Mohawk Indians who used to walk the steel beams on skyscrapers three hundred feet in the air, the average reporter's pay was pitiable and justly so.

Aside from occasional danger, good reporters routinely abuse their bodies, their minds, and their families. We accept the low pay as a fair trade-off for being allowed to do something we love. Most of us can't explain very clearly why we do it. I think it may be because we cannot imagine anything else we would rather do. Remember *The Front Page:* Hildy Johnson summons all his strength and walks away after a great scoop that has just landed in his lap. He does take a few minutes to write and turn in the story, but then he resigns from the paper so that he can keep his promise to marry the woman he adores. His editor, Walter Burns, saves poor Hildy from this lapse by a piece of callous trickery and keeps him on the job.

Early one morning, I heard a reporter being interviewed on

National Public Radio. Charles Bowden talked about his book *Murder City: Ciudad Juarez and the Global Economy's New Killing Fields.* He described the daily reality of the city across the river from El Paso: 50 percent unemployment, 100,000 manufacturing jobs lost, the only remaining jobs paying slave wages, over 2,000 murders a year because of the drug trade, a survey finding that 40 percent of the young men of the city aspired to be contract killers for the drug cartel—chilling, terrifying facts. The interviewer asked him why he kept going there, putting his own life in danger with every trip. His answer moved me deeply.

"There have to be witnesses," he said. ". . . Somebody has to write this down."

■ ■ ■

For the most part, the *Times* got its money's worth out of me. Some of the editors didn't think so, but that's the way editors think. One of the toughest jobs for an editor is persuading reporters to produce and to do so voluminously. Some of us are not naturally productive. When I finally left the paper, it was not because I couldn't keep up. I could, but at great expense to my slow-moving instincts. Abe Rosenthal once dispatched one of his underlings to London to chew me out for not writing enough. We had an unpleasant discussion over lunch and he went home unsatisfied.

Even the hardiest reporter finally wears out. I have known only two or three who kept their energy, restlessness, anger, or whatever sustained the essential reporting spirit until retirement age. Most drift off into public relations, teaching, or some other form of sloth.

A few go into book-writing. Of those, a blessedly small handful make the mistake of thinking they can write fiction; most stick to what they know, nonfiction, dealing in facts. It takes a very odd reporter to detach himself from facts sufficiently to make up a story from scratch. The primal urge of the old reporter would be to pick up the phone and check it out before putting anything on paper. The novelist can't do that except for the detail here and there to keep from looking like a fool. He has to spin the facts right out of his noggin.

When I read the novels of Charles Portis and realize that all of that

detail—conversations, plot twists, dangers, escapes—all of it came entirely from his imagination, I think back to the young fellow in the *Gazette* newsroom recording the ordinary crimes, misdemeanors, civic club luncheons—the daily bread of the newspaper—and all the while some part of his mind must have been wandering off into the head of a crotchety, one-eyed old lawman who would be deciding whether to shoot the bastards now or hang them later. One day, I think, the quarrel between the two parts of his mind became too much, and he left the London bureau of the *New York Herald-Tribune*, the best newspaper job in the world, and set off to spend the rest of his life just making it up.

Aside from the wear on the imagination, innocence, and sense of decency, reserve strengths that keep the reporter going to exhaustion, other burdens become heavier by the year. In my case, travel became unbearable. I think most people like to travel. As Nellie Forbush of Little Rock put it in *South Pacific*, we like to get away and see different places and people, even when we don't always like what we see. It's called broadening if we need an excuse to satisfy our inner Presbyterian.

Toward the end of my reporting career, airplanes and airline terminals became almost painfully abhorrent. The food, the noise, the unhappy children screaming in frustration, the unhappy parents straining to stay calm, the loud and incessant public address announcements, the snail movement of queues for the ticket counter and the baggage check-in. On the planes, there were the uncleaned toilets, the bad food, the bad coffee, the slob in the next seat, the noisy bore in the seat behind, the lout in the seat ahead who lowered his seat-back onto your lap. Those were mild problems compared to earlier years when I always found myself seated next to a chain smoker. The government finally stopped the smoking, thus alienating hordes of 1960s free-enterprisers who opposed any form of regulation. The only nuisance lacking in the old days but with us now, thanks to progress, is the egotist three rows ahead who wants all of us to listen to his cell phone conversation while we're sitting on the tarmac.

I'm not the only air traveler who has had problems. I was walking through the Atlanta airport one day when I heard this message on the public address system: "Will the party who left a gold wedding band at Gate Twenty-three please return and claim same?" I still wonder what happened. Did a forgotten carry-on bag lead to a divorce?

For the reporter whose job requires travel, the youthful love affair with the exotic eventually wears thin. The end of the affair for me came early one morning in a hotel room. I woke up and didn't know where I was. I lay there thinking for some time. Then I got out of bed and found the hotel stationery and learned that I was in a hotel in Ireland.

I flew home to London and began to plan the breakup. I eased out of it over a few months, but immediately wrote the letters that would bring me home to Arkansas. In the meantime, I guarded against a repeat of the Ireland experience by traveling with two or three familiar books to plant at my bedside in case I forgot not only where I was but who.

This is how it felt, set down in a homecoming essay, when Norma and I flew off to Arkansas:

> We left Heathrow Airport two hours late because of the fog, and were lucky at that. Behind us were travelers who had been in the terminal all night: Hindu women in saris, tending children; haggard Scots drinking whiskey. When we reached the Atlantic, the two of us drank a private toast with airline champagne. First, to England—thanks and goodbye. Then to each other, and an end to wandering. Seth and Clarrissa Timmons met us at the Fayetteville Airport. They took us to Hogeye, and we declared ourselves at home.

That was more than thirty years ago.

Someone asks me now and then whether I miss the reporting life. Of course I do. I read a story that is not covered to my satisfaction. Some editor fails to see a story possibility right under his nose. Something happens on one of my old beats, and I feel the urge to fly to it and start to work. Even on slow news days, I occasionally feel the itch to cover something, somewhere. I could head to Mississippi, which has always been news-prone. Something happens there every day. I could parachute in blindfolded and know that I would find a story wherever I landed.

My intention in this book was to call up a golden time in my life and in the life of the press. However, I don't want to leave the impression that all my recollections are benign. Not all of my days with the *Times* were happy. There were plenty of aggravations: meddlesome editing, bad decisions on stories, lots of minor irritations. For example,

there was the day Abe Rosenthal, the executive editor, insulted me to my face in the newsroom. He called me a mush-mouth. In his defense, he did not intend it as a personal insult. He had a low opinion of Southerners generally, and I was near at hand.

Abe: I admired him greatly even when I wanted to throttle him. How could I not admire him? He was a working-class kid from Canada who moved south and conquered America. Any Southern hillbilly could appreciate that accomplishment. A bunch of us national correspondents were having drinks one evening at his penthouse soon after he had been promoted to executive editor. He had joined three or four of us on the roof, and as we stood soaking up the view, he swept his arm across the skyline and exclaimed, "Mine! All mine!" I loved the gesture. It summed up the entire man. Before the evening was over, I'm sure he did something else that made me want to slug him.

I must wind up this story before I get mad all over again. But since this may be my last chance, there are a couple of things I want to get off my chest. I've dealt with a lot of editors, and most have been smart men and women. But even the best occasionally suffer lapses in judgment. I recall being asked to write an article for *Esquire* magazine in the early 1980s. Mine was to be one of several about the one hundred most promising young American couples. The idea was to get ahead of the curve in predicting who would become famous and influential. My assignment was to profile Bill and Hillary Clinton, who at that time occupied the governor's mansion in Little Rock. I interviewed them extensively, and they were pleased to have their young reputations expanded in a national publication. Just before publication, the editors learned that the expected advertising for that issue had fallen short. Several of the articles had to be left out. I have often wondered about the subsequent career path of the *Esquire* editor who decided to leave out Bill and Hillary.

I've already told about being scooped on Margaret Drabble by a *Times* guy from New York. I'm thinking now of another incident. Sometime during the early 1970s, I produced a well-researched, well-written story from New Orleans about the writer Walker Percy. I read all his books and spent some time with him at his home in Covington, north of Lake Pontchartrain. My story emphasized an interesting theme in his writing, the cultural divide between the Americans north

of the lake and the Creoles south of it. I quoted from a letter to the editor he had written about the state's politicians in Baton Rouge. He said they were plundering the state with Catholic gaiety and Protestant efficiency.

The paper never printed my story. I never knew why. I suspect it was simply laid aside until it finally disappeared. Some years later, the *Times* dispatched another reporter to do a similar story on him, and it was good. But what the hell?

I made one more attempt to report on a well-known author. During my last months in London, I went to some trouble to do a story on Shaun Herron, the author of *The MacDonnell*, *The Whore Mother*, and a bunch of other excellent novels, several of them dealing with his native Northern Ireland. He had moved to the Republic of Ireland partly to get away from the violence and aggravation in the North. He had recently published another book.

I flew to Dublin, rented a car, and drove one of Europe's most perilous highways to Cork, then went on south several miles to the coast where he lived. He and his wife served lunch, and we spent a thoroughly pleasant afternoon. Once again, I filed a story. Once again, it was never printed. I'm still sore about it.

INDEX

ROY REED was a reporter from 1956 to 1978, after which he taught journalism at the University of Arkansas for sixteen years. He is the author of two books: *Looking for Hogeye* and *Faubus: The Life and Times of an American Prodigal,* and he is the editor of *Looking Back at the Arkansas Gazette: An Oral History.*